BEYOND CHILD POVERTY:
THE SOCIAL EXCLUSION OF CHILDREN

BEYOND CHILD POVERTY:
THE SOCIAL EXCLUSION OF CHILDREN

EDITED BY

ALFRED J. KAHN AND SHEILA B. KAMERMAN

THE INSTITUTE FOR CHILD AND FAMILY POLICY
AT COLUMBIA UNIVERSITY

Table of Contents

Tables, Figures, and Exhibits

PREFACE

How deeply, carefully, or specifically do Americans want to look at our disadvantaged children? Here we consider a useful concept in such examinations, which has become popular in Europe: social exclusion.

Clearly, those engaged in the policy debate are not satisfied with what we now do. Our 1996 welfare reform chose "dependency" as its main target (we would monitor how much caseloads fell). As we write, there are those who want to adopt poverty reduction as the primary TANF target in the reauthorization legislature. But there is also comprehensive legislation in Congress, initiated by the liberal Children's Defense Fund, which would "leave no child behind." President George W. Bush has borrowed the very same phrase, but for a more conservative package. What does all this mean? Is the United States ready for "social exclusion," or some other summing-up of disadvantage that goes beyond poverty?

The Columbia University Institute for Child and Family Policy convened a conference on May 3–4, 2001 at the University, on "Social Exclusion and Children." It was designed to help reframe the current child poverty debate, and to stimulate a new and broader discussion of child well-being. The conference focused on U.S. child and family policy issues, but drew on the European concept of social exclusion as a new, different, and perhaps more valid way of framing the issues. The meeting included much discussion of European developments; but the primary focus was on the United States—the possible policy, program, and research implications of the use of the social exclusion concept.

The meeting involved policymakers, public administrators, policy scholars, practitioners, community leaders, communications researchers, advocates, and other opinion leaders (see Appendix). It was designed to make the social exclusion concept more visible in U.S. child development research, and child and family policy, discussions. It began with two papers by European policy scholars on the social exclusion concept, the rationale for its development, and how it has been implemented in one or another country. These were followed by a paper on social exclusion and children at risk; a panel session with presenters from the UK, Canada, and France, discussing the concept as it relates to their own countries; a paper on the central issue of whether "poverty" or "social exclusion" adds more to the policy-political-public debates about improving child well-being; and a paper on childhood social indicators and the issue of measuring social exclusion among children in the United States. Each presentation was followed by comments by U.S. policy scholars and/or practitioners who raised questions and launched the general discussion. The conference ended with pre-sentations by a diverse panel whose members reacted to the whole discussion, with both panelists and participants suggesting next steps.

Several of the authors edited and revised their papers in reaction to the conference experience. In offering these papers and a report, the Institute for Child and Family Policy expresses its appreciation to the Ford Foundation, the conference funder, and particularly to a supportive program officer, Helen Neuborne. We thank paper authors, panelists, discussants, chairs, and all participants for creative and lively contributions to what we define as a significant debate.

We also want to acknowledge the outstanding work of our manuscript editor/book designer, Penelope Franklin.

Sheila B. Kamerman
Professor and Director, Institute for Child and Family Policy

Alfred J. Kahn
Professor Emeritus

Social Exclusion: A Better Way to Think about Childhood Deprivation?[1]

Alfred J. Kahn and Sheila B. Kamerman

"Social exclusion" is a multidimensional concept, involving economic, social, political, cultural, and other aspects of disadvantage and deprivation (Lenoir 1974; Room 1995; Magrab 1998; Klasen 1998). It is often described as the process by which individuals and groups are wholly or partly closed out from participation in their societies because of low income as well as constricted access to employment, social benefits and services, and other aspects of cultural and community life. A key component is the framing of the issue as social and community exclusion, rather than individual and personal culpability. While some policy scholars use the term interchangeably with income poverty—or income poverty and unemployment—it is increasingly distinguished from financial poverty and focused instead on the idea of restricted access to civil, political, and social rights and opportunities. Social exclusion is particularly devastating for children, because if they encounter it when very young, it deprives them of the experiences—including access to health care and preschool education—that they need for a good start in life (Bradbury and Jantii 1999).

Since it was first developed in France in the mid-1970s (Lenoir 1974), the concept of social exclusion has been increasingly used in the international social policy literature—in studies carried out by the UNICEF Innocenti Research Centre in Italy; reports of the European Union (Commission of the European Communities, 1994; Eurostat 2000, 2001); and recently in the work of the Organization for Economic Co-operation and Development (OECD), both through the Centre for Educational Research and Innovation (CERI) and at a high-level ministerial conference held in London on October 9–10, 2000. Social exclusion is a concept that goes beyond the limitations of income poverty as a measure of economic well-being, to include several additional social, political, and cultural dimensions. It could reframe the discussion of child and family well-being, from an emphasis primarily on the individual or personal responsibility of parents to that of societal—or social and community—responsibility.

Poverty and social exclusion do not arise from any single cause. Rather, various restrictions of civil, political, and social rights and opportunities combine to trap particular groups in situations of severe disadvantage. Although income and financial assets are still considered key elements in achieving positive outcomes for children, the concept of social exclusion is not primarily concerned with those elements (nor even with disability) but with the broader range of capabilities people enjoy or fail to enjoy. In this sense, the concept is closely linked to the "capabilites" approach developed by the Nobel Laureate economist, Amartya Sen (1992), which calls for efforts to ensure that people have equal access to basic capacities, including integration into the community, participation in community and public life, self-respect, and human rights. In short, in addition to the capacity to lead a long and healthy life, people should be educated and have the resources necessary for a decent standard of living.

There are several compelling reasons to explore an alternative concept of assessing child well-being. The first is a fast-growing dissatisfaction with the limitations of the conventional measure of income poverty used in the United States. A second reason is that the "poverty" framework has apparent limits in rallying the public will required to mount policies that can lift families out of poverty.

Earlier efforts in the United States to go beyond the limitations of a strictly financial measure have employed the concept of the "underclass" (Jencks and Peterson 1991; Jencks 1992; Katz 1993). This concept stresses individual involvement in a series of pathologies and, in the view of some scholars, smacks of Social Darwinism. In contrast, although "social exclusion" pays attention to some of the same problems, it also reflects concern with racism and discrimination as possible causes, as well as a concern that socially excluded children will pose a threat to the future well-being of society if they grow up with little stake in the existing order.

Social Exclusion: Concept and Rationale

Phipps and Curtis (2001) point out that "almost everyone who writes a paper about social exclusion begins from the idea that it is hard to explain what social exclusion is!" But the key point, as noted by Atkinson (1998) and referred to by Phipps and Curtis, is that social exclusion is something that *happens to* an individual, rather than something that he or she chooses.

Throughout the social exclusion conference, it seemed clear that the European idea of "social exclusion" does not offer Americans a well-defined concept for acceptance or rejection. In her contribution to the volume Chiara Saraceno, as both a rigorous sociologist and a high-level participant in government policymaking, points out that in European international organizations, especially the European Union (EU), "social exclusion" has become a paradigm for focusing on dysfunction; it is seen as an improvement over "underclass" or "marginalized." Clearly, as noted already, European scholars and policymakers have adopted it as an effort to go beyond "poverty" or, perhaps, to incorporate poverty approaches such as that of Peter Townsend (1962), who sees in poverty not only the lack of resources but also an inability—because of such a lack—to participate in one's own society. We might prefer Adam Smith's (1776) poverty definition: Poverty is to be without "whatever the custom of the country renders it indecent for a credible person, even of the lowest order, to be without." But an important duality persists. Does one not need to differentiate between (as Saraceno states it) "poverty and material deprivation... reviewed in the light of social rights thinking" and "social disintegration, marginality, un-belonging, and uprootedness"? The social exclusion analysis seems to touch on both, but both are not always addressed in discussion. The discussion seeks to recognize causation at the "macro" level, for example, unemployment or migration, as well as at the "micro" level, for example, personal experiences leading to lack of opportunity.

Saraceno reports that the concept is popular in Europe, despite lack of agreement as to what social exclusion is or how it is caused. She also notes Amartya Sen's caution against an overemphasis on either poverty or social exclusion, since "neither the offering of resources nor the granting of rights is sufficient to avoid social exclusion if the specific capabilities and functioning of the individuals are not addressed."

Saraceno sums up her understanding of the patterns of discourse in an a discussion of three traditions—the French "solidarity"; the Anglo-American liberal interest in exclusion mechanisms and the involvement of actors in their rights; and the economic analysis of inequality and economic exploitation. Each tradition generates its own correctives. The EU discussion is not definitive, in part, because it fluctuates among these approaches.

Saraceno concludes that "community membership without individual rights may be as . . . exclusionary as access to social rights without access to community membership." For her, social exclusion is more developed as discourse than as concept. She illustrates this with regard to unemployment (how context shapes differential consequences) and time (poverty as a dynamic phenomenon; there are "temporarily," "repeatedly," and "longterm" or "persistently" poor people—with diverse consequences for exclusion). Saraceno concludes by noting that efforts to cope with theoretical and methodological issues when using the social exclusion concept (or metaphor) are replete with risks. Perhaps, she suggests, social exclusion is more a social policy concept than a theoretical and research one. It is "a means for a society to assess its performance and its risks with regard to social cohesion and individuals' well-being."

During the discussion, Janet Gornick noted that, for many Europeans, the essence of social exclusion relates to economic and social rights, whereas U.S. culture and politics tend to reject the notion of positive rights—which is thought to imply a right to have needs met by the state. Thus, we reject most international covenants. We in the United States do, however, recognize the other dimension—belongingness vs disconnection from social institutions—but we seem to set the bar very low.

Gornick introduces yet another issue: the link between the exclusion of women (as childcare workers, as teachers, or as single mothers) and the exclusion of children. She would agree with Saraceno that we should consider the effects on children of the "deeply gendered nature of child caregiving."

In her chapter, Gornick stresses that "fundamental elements of exclusion—the relativity, the external causation, the long time horizon—are at odds with aspects of American political culture."

Despite the lack of agreement regarding a "social exclusion" definition, it seemed clear at the conference that participants were seeking a way to move beyond the poverty concept. A measure of income poverty by itself (even if it were a better measure than that currently used in the U.S.) would not be adequate. Nor were many satisfied with a construct that focused on bringing income up to the poverty threshold, rather than to some concept of a decent standard of living or well-being.

The initial consensus was that social exclusion would not be a satisfactory organizing concept if used merely as a variant on poverty and material deprivation, although it could be a useful supplement to the existing measure. There was dissatisfaction, as well, with viewing "social exclusion" as a counterpart to the concept of the "underclass." There was agreement that it was closely linked to the construct of "social rights" and that Americans were not yet comfortable with this concept, although it recurred at several points and in the final session. There was disagreement over whether one could develop measures of social exclusion as such, or only in relation to particular domains (e.g., health, education, employment, housing, social protection)—or whether measures of "child well-being," as a positive construct, might not be preferable.

John Micklewright, from his perspective as a leading UK policy scholar with much international experience, offers here a view of the concern with social exclusion in international bodies (especially the EU) and in the UK, and of the effort to introduce social indicators into the discussion. He does not dispute Saraceno's account of the social exclusion concept. He quotes a UK definition of social exclusion from the government's Social Exclusion Unit: "a short-hand term for what *can happen* (emphasis added) when people or areas suffer from a combination of linked problems such as unemployment, poor skills, low incomes, poor housing, high crime environment, bad health and family breakdown." "*Can*" happen does not always mean "*does*" happen, and the fate that "can happen" is not actually described, so what we are left with is a description of examples of circumstances that may lead to exclusion, rather than a definition of exclusion itself. Yet the fate described clearly, in some sense, means "shut out from society."

So Micklewright, too, argues that exclusion is a concept defying clear definition and measurement, making it a difficult policy target. He documents this well, deferring to the EU's task force reports and data. The data are in many ways useful and used (note the Blair administration's explicit goal of eliminating child poverty in twenty years) but is the "exclusion" concept, Micklewright asks, essential to these uses? Indeed, some still argue for a poverty focus, while others respond that this concept creates sensitivity to a broader agenda.

If we wish to highlight children, Micklewright would emphasize what Atkinson (1998) lists as the core elements in any discussion of social exclusion:

- relativity—the proper contrast population (we need data on consumption and living standards and the proper contrast place [e.g., locality, nation, region]);

- agency—we must ask: who is doing the excluding? (where children are concerned, the key actors are parents and the society); and

- dynamics—a concern with future prospects and the impact of the experience on children's development.

Micklewright emphasizes the question of *who* excludes children—parents, schools, employers, and governments—and *how*. He notes that parents have enormous influence on their children's well-being, and perhaps their own lack of skills and resources contributes to exclusion of their children. Schools can exclude through expulsion or by failing to achieve adequate standards. Employers may exclude by barring youth from labor markets. Governments, both local and national, can exclude by providing inadequate public services (e.g., health, education, housing) and interventions.

He suggests that many questions are raised in the United States as to the usefulness of the concept. In a final section, however, Micklewright argues that perhaps the introduction of social exclusion into the U.S. debate could usefully stress "disadvantage" and attract policymakers who will not tackle "poverty." Our poverty measurements are shamefully inadequate, but U.S. panel studies and work on well-being indicators are much envied by scholars in other countries. Moreover, there are signs of potential progress on state level indicators and of using the "welfare to work" research platform.

Micklewright offers several conclusions, but his first builds on Saraceno: "Don't look to exclusion as a *substitute* for poverty" (emphasis in the original). If it has value added, it is as a *complement* or *supplement,* and that is how it is used most of the time in Europe. One must be prepared for the fact that the concept may mean all things to all people. We need to explore what a particular focus on *child* social exclusion means in the United States. Do Americans want a more inclusive society, where children are concerned? Do parents who are "included" (employed?) rear children who demonstrate more positive outcomes? And, finally, he says, we must reflect on the past—would the concept have helped in the War on Poverty or in the welfare reform debate?

The questions remain, however: Are Americans willing to relinquish their adherence to an absolute measure of income poverty, for a far more relative measure such as social exclusion, when they have not been willing to accept the relative measure of income poverty that is used in almost all the other advanced industrialized countries? If Americans are not prepared to confront the continuing problem of child poverty, will they be interested in a concept that goes beyond income poverty or a concept that goes beyond negative behavioral indicators? Does the United States have the political will to confront the notions of inequality and injustice inherent in definitions of social exclusion?

Peter Evans brings the special perspective of his various OECD studies of children at risk, children with disabilities, and disadvantaged children to the discussion of social exclusion. He stresses the importance of cross-national comparability. He adopts Sen's "capabilities" approach: "social exclusion" defined as a lack of the capabilities to participate in and be recognized by society, on a basis of equality and equal opportunity.

Evans' UK illustration of constructive projects, and his chart of childhood risk factors, are of special interest. The precursors of adult social exclusion are found in childhood. The OECD is trying to gather international comparisons of children at risk and the policy/program responses to these risks. Three categories of children at risk are identified:

- those who are disabled;
- those with learning difficulties for no apparent reason; and
- those with learning difficulties because of disadvantage.

Evans cites the "rights" in the UN Convention on the Rights of the Child and questions recognizing the special rights of physically and mentally disabled children while not acknowledging similar rights for those disadvantaged by birth, background, or circumstance. Why, he asks, should all children not enjoy the same rights? His approach is not a utilitarian one of maximizing wealth or consumption by creating human capital, but rather an approach that would maximize the potential of each child, whether or not it promoted economic growth, development, or global competition. Evans observes that it seems to be accepted that children will be disadvantaged as a result of disability. On the other hand, it does not seem to be accepted that children will be disadvantaged as a result of being born into a poor family.

The discussion continued in the conference sessions. It was noted that we cannot reach consensus on a definition of social exclusion within our own very diverse country, let alone with other countries. We agree that social exclusion has many dimensions; within each dimension there is a choice about equality of opportunity versus equality of outcomes. If social exclusion is multidimensional, however, are the dimensions connected with an "and" or with an "or"? This makes a substantial difference. If the connection is with an "or," and one is excluded because one has no job, or a low income, or has not finished high school, then one is always socially excluded in some manner. If the connection is with an "and"—if one must have both this and that, in other words, multiple barrier or risk factors—then we end up with a small group that may not be very useful for social policy discussion. It was argued that in the real world, the "ands" are inevitable and the "ors" cluster and overlap, as in earlier discussions regarding multiproblem families. Families may come to public attention because of one factor, but others emerge over time.

Another special population, it was said, is welfare recipients. The question was asked: To what extent was U.S. welfare reform designed for social inclusion, or reduction of exclusion? It was pointed out that the reform was not necessarily directed at moving children out of income poverty, but rather at some of the social correlates of poverty and welfare dependency. There was the assumption that, even if income didn't improve, children would be better off if their mothers were in the paid labor force. Does this mean we in the U.S. are ready to pay attention to social exclusion? Perhaps more important, how does maternal employment relate to child social inclusion? Welfare reform studies of impacts on children show that school-aged children whose mothers have paid jobs are more likely to be involved in social activities. But what about preschool-aged children? (Moreover, there is some evidence that older children, who may not be well-supervised while their mothers work, may have a greater tendency towards delinquent activity.)

Seventy years ago, women were socially excluded if they had to work and couldn't personally take care of their children. Today, poor mothers are told that inclusion is achieved by having a job, rather than staying at home. Is paid work essential for identity, legitimacy, and social inclusion? Why is caring work not viewed as productive work, or as facilitating social inclusion?

Three Country Cases: Social Exclusion and Children in the UK, Canada, and France

According to John Hills, referring to a report from the UK government's Social Exclusion Unit, "social exclusion is a short-hand label for what can happen when individuals or areas suffer from a concentration of linked problems such as unemployment, poor skills, low income, poor housing, high crime, bad health, and family breakdown." This is more than income poverty and joblessness and includes, in particular, being cut off from the social and economic life of one's community.

An advantage of the concept of social exclusion is its consistency with the multidimensional nature of child well-being. The UK has focused on the high rate of child poverty and the large increase in it that occurred between the early 1970s and the late 1990s. (Unemployment rates [as of the conference date] are high, and currently 15 percent of children live in households where all the adults are unemployed.) As mentioned above, in many ways "social exclusion" has been a code word for "poverty," thus allowing policymakers to address poverty without having to use the word. The UK has embraced the concept, and by doing so seems to have moved to a multidimensional approach and a much more comprehensive policy menu.

Most important, the UK has made a huge commitment to eliminating child poverty, with the Blair administration announcing that child poverty (income below 60% of the median) would be reduced by 25 percent within five years and completely eliminated within twenty years. The new initiatives are multidimensional, comprehensive, and include a variety of strategies. They include: the Working Families Tax Credit; an increase in Income Support (social assistance) benefits for families with children under age 11; an increase in the maternity allowance (a cash benefit for new mothers); an increase in the universal child benefit; an increase in the child tax credit; the offering of baby bonds (modest funds allocated at birth and available for a child's use later in life); a national child-care strategy; a national minimum wage; an early intervention program called Sure Start; a program for early school leavers called Connexions; the implementation of Education Action Zones; and the development of the aforementioned Social Exclusion Unit within the government, which focuses on youth problems such as teenage pregnancy and homelessness. The UK is following a work-based policy that is in harmony with public consensus and political will. While "social exclusion" is not a substitute for "poverty," the social exclusion framework may help researchers and policymakers to examine linkages, child-to-adult trajectories, and long-run effects.

Christa Freiler noted that social exclusion and inclusion are not yet widely used in Canadian social policy discussions, except in discrete ways. For example, social inclusion is a goal within the disability movement, particularly with respect to children. Addressing child and family poverty has become a priority for government. Nevertheless, one in five children is living in poverty, an increase of 43 percent since 1989, when the government promised to end child poverty by the year 2000. There is a growing concern about child development and early childhood learning, and a renewed interest in such universal programs as child allowances.

Currently in Canada, she said, the concept of social inclusion is being advanced by the Laidlaw Foundation as a future vision for achievement, stressing such elements as equal opportunities, belonging, power and participation, and reducing social and economic inequalities, The key questions are, again: exclusion from *what* and *why* and inclusion into *what* and *how*. The question of *into what?* is being answered by the Foundation, with the recommendation of a universal approach to bringing people into the larger society.

Jeanne Fagnani spoke about the roles of government and family in France and how French social institutions complement family roles. The focus of her remarks was on social exclusion and the low-income family in France. Her argument is that, in France, being a child in a poor family does not necessarily lead to being socially excluded. Families take many forms, and poor families are the beneficiaries of generous social policies. France has one of the best records in the EU with regard to child poverty, (after the

Scandinavian countries and Belgium). Infant mortality rates in France are among the lowest in the world, thanks to the child health program begun right after World War II. The proportion of children living in income poverty in France has remained stable over the last two decades.

Fagnani also said that there is strong public support for child and family policy in France, with particular emphasis on in-kind benefits over cash benefits. The French early childhood education and care policies are particularly generous, and important in preventing social exclusion of children. Numerous studies have shown that it is very beneficial for all children, particularly those from poor and/or immigrant families, to attend preschool—which, in France, includes all children aged 3–5 and almost half of all 2-year-olds, regardless of parents' income or employment situation. The National Ministry of Education encourages participation of children in early childhood education programs because such participation reinforces learning, provides for social, emotional, and physical development, compensates for deficits at home, and enhances cognitive development The integrated settings of both the *crèche* (nursery) and the *école maternelle* (preschool) are publicly funded and widely supported, and viewed positively by the society.

Fagnani went on to explain that in France, children are considered to be a public good. The government is seen as having a duty to protect and provide for all children. There is a sense of reciprocity; families receive benefits (e.g., family allowances, housing subsidies, health care), and in exchange, parents must comply with the full responsibility of raising children.

Efforts at Measurement

Two of the U.S. author teams rose to the challenge of going beyond poverty with measurable concepts of social exclusion. Robert Haveman and Andrew Bershadker begin by explaining their dissatisfaction with the concept of social exclusion. They point out that if it is defined as a process that prevents people from full participation in society, it begs a number of questions: What is "society": is it the person's immediate community, some form of the majority—or something else entirely? What is "exclusion"? If a person has many work-related contacts but lacks personal ones (he/she lives alone, shops alone, "bowls alone") is that person "socially excluded"? Is the relevant measure the quantity of contacts, the quality of contacts, or some combination? What dimensions of inclusion (labor market, consumption, recreation) determine whether a person is included or excluded? If a person is receiving public assistance, are she and her children included or excluded? How do we account for the subjective aspects of social exclusion given the differences in individuals' perceptions of their status? What measures are available to assess social exclusion, and what data are available?

Going beyond the limitations of the concept of social exclusion, they present a sophisticated critique of resource-based concepts of poverty and (clearly influenced by Sen) offer an alternative concept of poverty that rests on individual capabilities of the adults in the family—"self-reliant poverty." Their measure identifies those families lacking the ability to generate a minimum need level of income from their efforts; individuals living in such families are called "self-reliant poor." In addition to formalizing the concept and highlighting its assumptions, they apply this new measure to the U.S. population of children under 6 years of age and examine trends in self-reliant poverty for those children, and for various demographic sub-groups, for the period 1975–97. They also compare the trends and population of the young self-reliant poor population to the population of children who are officially (income) poor.

They find that the prevalence of self-reliant poverty has grown more rapidly than has official poverty; there are some unexpected "intertemporal patterns of self-reliant poverty" for various population groups. They conclude with a comparison of self-reliant and official poverty as indicators of social exclusion. For family structure, race, and connection to the public support system (EU dimensions), the self-reliant poverty measure is a superior indicator of social exclusion. The measures are equally effective on educational dimensions.

According to the authors, while the measurement of income poverty is a difficult and daunting task, the measurement of social exclusion poverty confronts even more difficulties. The concept of "self-reliant poverty" reflects social exclusion better than a measure of income poverty. While both the official and self-reliant children's poverty rates increased over the period 1975–97, self-reliant child poverty grew more rapidly. The highest self-reliant child poverty rates are concentrated among the population groups that are generally recognized as among the nation's most vulnerable: blacks, Hispanics, single-mother families with children, and those with low levels of education. Over most of these years, the concentration of children in these groups who were poor by the self-reliant criterion exceeded their concentration in official poverty. If these characteristics are also measures of "social exclusion," the population of children in self-reliant poverty seem to be more outside the society's mainstream than the population of children in income poverty.

Considering the possible adoption of a social exclusion framework in the United States, Lawrence Aber, Elizabeth Gershoff, and Jeanne Brooks-Gunn explore alternative definitions of social exclusion of children drawn from the European literature. They note that the large gap in the research agenda, as laid out thus far, has to do with the need to link the concept of social exclusion to existing measures of child well-being, or to new measures yet to be developed. They point out that the concept is really only relevant to countries with robust economies—countries that have already confronted and addressed the problem of income poverty and successfully eliminated child poverty, or achieved low rates of it. This is not yet the case in the United States, but they feel the potential is there.

Aber and his colleagues point out that the way we label or frame a problem does have significant implications; calling a problem "social exclusion" may make a difference. They admit that, generally speaking, social exclusion of children is largely associated with social exclusion of their parents. Obviously, we cannot fully separate the two, especially with regard to very young children. However, we know that where adolescents are concerned, individual characteristics and abilities help shape experiences of inclusion/exclusion; and the experience of social exclusion can have a significant impact on young children's development. In addition, there are risk factors linked to social exclusion that are not social exclusion itself and are separate from measures of child well-being—such as minority racial and ethnic status. The authors emphasize the need to capture the multidimensional aspects of social exclusion and the values that are implicit in such a construct, in order to provide new insights into causes and solutions and new strategies for development of effective policy interventions.

The Aber group identifies eight relevant domains (basic living; family economic participation; housing; health; education; public space; social participation; and the subjective experience of social exclusion). They suggest possible measures of each (rather than a generic category of social exclusion), identify the major available U.S. data sources (*Kids Count Data Book 2001; America's Children: Key National Indicators of Well-Being, 2000; Trends in the Well-Being of Children and Youth*), European data sources (Eurostat and the European Community Household Panel [ECHP]), and dimensions for which they found no identifiable data sources. They note the need for different types of indicators: necessary indicators; normative indicators; and desirable indicators. They introduce a research agenda involving the potential uses of available indicators and further indicator development. They conclude by pointing out that we must direct attention to exclusion "from what" as well as exclusion "by what" (and *who* is excluded, by *whom*). We must determine the forces, processes, institutions, and groups that are causing or leading children to be socially excluded.

In response, Maria Cancian noted the importance of identifying how social exclusion differs from poverty, the advantages and disadvantages of each concept, and what measures could be used to assess the extent to which the objectives are achieved. The official poverty measure has as its advantages:

- Some agreement on definition (this is key)
- Relative ease and agreement with regard to measurement

• Identification of a problem that can be directly addressed by policy (e.g., reducing poverty by means of cash transfers)

Its disadvantages include:

• Some problems with regard to how it is measured

• Substantial variation in the consequences of poverty for different individuals and groups

• The existence of deprivation among the non-poor, not only the poor

• A "blaming the victim" focus

The advantages of the social exclusion concept include the development of a strategy that could grow from a reframing of the problem; a potentially more sympathetic response; and possibly improved analyses of causes and solutions. Social exclusion creates a context for a more comprehensive and multidisciplinary perspective that may lead to improved policies.

The discussion that ensued raised a variety of questions: How would one understand exclusion? The study of social indicators is a revived, major, cross-national enterprise, and is seen as basic and preliminary—and perhaps as deferring the demand for conceptual consensus. The list of indicators offered suggests where the cross-national discussion is now focused.

• Income Distribution

• (Income) Poverty (pre- and post-transfer)

• Jobless Household

• Regional Cohesion

• Early School Leavers (school drop-outs) not employed or in training

• Long-term Unemployment

The current indicators work now also covers: health care; housing; access to caring services; training, education, and conditions of work (Duffy 1998; Mejer 2000; Mejer and Linden 2000), and now reports a number of non-monetary indicators such as the percentage of households that cannot afford:

• to eat meat/chicken/fish every second day;

• to keep home adequately warm;

• to buy new rather than second-hand clothes;

- (in the case of those aged 16 and over) to participate in social, cultural and political activities;

or whose members are so excluded as to be unable to talk to neighbors.

A British report (UK 2001) on preventing social exclusion identified a series of negative indicators (terms used to reflect usage in the United States) in addition to low income:

- workless households
- teen out-of-wedlock pregnancy
- drug use among youth
- high rates of adult illiteracy
- school dropouts
- homelessness

We note that these seem very close to the earlier U.S listing of the characteristics of the "underclass." However, John Hills uses a broader definition of social exclusion: he sees the term not only as a shorthand label for a concentration of linked problems, but as a term that describes the state of being cut off from the social and economic life of a community. In the United States and elsewhere in the world, racial discrimination and immigrant status could be added as well.

Inevitably all the issues raised with regard to the concept of social exclusion become obvious as one seeks measures at the national, state, community, group, family, and individual levels. At least one cited framework links absence of social rights to the particular distribution of patterns of belonging.

Ultimately, the question seems to be whether indicators of child well-being are any different than indicators of social exclusion, and to what extent the social exclusion concept extends beyond material deprivation. The European participants at the conference noted how far ahead the United States is in the development and use of childhood social indicators, raising this question even more pointedly by asking: What does adding "social exclusion" do to go beyond what can be found in *America's Children?*

Conclusion

One goal of the conference was to explore the implications of the social exclusion concept for data and research. If there was consensus on the meaning of the concept, we could then move towards identifying relevant measures. As a result, the basic question addressed repeatedly during the conference was: What is "social exclusion?" There was agreement that social exclusion implies more than lack of income, and thus signifies something more than income poverty; and that it is a multidimensional concept that affects adults, and thus parents (and their children) and can lead to negative outcomes and trajectories for children. Although it is possible to compensate the children of socially excluded parents, many children are affected negatively when their parents are socially excluded, and some are affected directly when they themselves experience social exclusion. In short, as noted by Irwin Garfinkel, the concept of social exclusion seems to have two important aspects:

1. Material inequality. For those very far from the norm in material resources, the ability to participate in society is compromised. The concept of income poverty clearly addresses this problem, and social exclusion adds nothing to it.

2. Participation (including such things as employment, voting, and social activities) This is where the concept of social exclusion seems to go beyond inadequate resources and poverty, but the problems of measurement become more complex. How does this relate to children, and what needs to be done so that children will not be left behind?

With some basic agreement on this conceptualization, a question that received a great deal of attention was: How can the social exclusion of children be measured? What are the values that should be included in measuring social exclusion? It was agreed that not only is social exclusion different than poverty—and that a measure of poverty would not be equal to a measure of social exclusion—but that social exclusion is also different from child well-being. Instead, social exclusion should be viewed as supplementary to income poverty and complementary to lack of child well-being. Some participants remained convinced that even if we were to agree on a definition of social exclusion, we are not ready to measure it—primarily because there is no consensus on whether it is or could be an overall, integrated construct, or a series of discrete domain measures.

Another question that received a good deal of attention was: Is there more value in having a multidimensional construct, like the UN Human Development Index or the UN Human Poverty Index, or a series of one-dimensional measures that can track the situation/condition of children separately, as, for example, in the eight domains suggested by Aber and colleagues (e.g., basic living, family economic participation, health, education, housing, public spaces, social participation, subjective experience of exclusion)? Some argued that indicators in these multiple domains would lead to a clearer focus on the most effective policy interventions, while others were convinced that these are already too many domains, and the multiple indicators in each domain are even more of a problem.

Just as Saraceno held that social exclusion is a concept but not a scientific construct, others argued that it is also a political and philosophical tool, permitting closer examination of values, but not readily turned into a quantifiable measure or measures. Also, it is not a substitute for other values, such as equality of opportunity, safety, or reducing poverty. Certain issues that were raised earlier in the discussion emerged again in the final summation. For example, the "and/or question," that is, to be identified as socially excluded must an individual suffer from all the negative indicators or just one? Frequency, intensity, duration, cut-off points, and optimal levels all must be addressed. For at least a few of those present, the fact that this concept originated in Europe was enough to label it as probably politically unacceptable in the United States.

Periodically, participants brought the discussion back to children. "How does all this relate to children?" was another repeated question. The answer is not clear. If parents are socially excluded, are outcomes for children always negative? There is some evidence that when former welfare-recipient mothers are working in paid employment (achieving social inclusion) and obtaining higher income, this leads to positive outcomes for school-aged children; but negative outcomes have emerged for adolescents, and the consequences are unknown for infants and toddlers (Morris, Duncan, and Chase-Lansdale 2001). Moreover, although most of our discussion was on how parents' exclusion has negative effects on their children, we know that early childhood education and care (ECEC) has direct positive affects on children. Swedish, Danish, and French ECEC programs are excellent examples of social inclusion, but it is not clear how the *concept* of inclusion would advance that agenda.

In some respects, the social exclusion concept is certainly not new. There is a long history in the United States of dealing with the equivalent of social exclusion. In the nineteenth century, acculturation was a major function of the settlement houses. In addition, there were immigrant clubs and ward heelers who assisted with acculturation. In the 1960s and the War on Poverty there was concern about people being left behind, and the response involved the active participation of the poor in community action, empowerment, civil rights, welfare rights, and voting rights. In the 1980s and 1990s there was the Americans with Disabilities Act, and issues of mainstreaming children vs. responding to their special needs. In the 1990s, the Personal Responsibility and Work Opportunities Reconciliation Act excluded legal immigrants from the most important forms of social protection for poor children. Race has remained a major factor in social exclusion in the United States since the country was first established, and incarceration is clearly, by definition, equated with exclusion. One could argue that in Europe, in some sense, there has always been social exclusion of some groups. There were no immigrants permitted in many countries until very recently, and immigrants still cannot earn citizenship rights is some countries.

The final question raised was: Given all of these considerations, would this concept in fact be useful in policy terms? Is it, as John Hills suggested is the case in the UK, a code phrase, letting politicians deal with poverty without using the word? Is it another term for what previously was described as "the underclass"? In his discussion of the UK, Hills thought it might be a way of diverting attention from expensive cash benefits to cheaper services. (But if we look at the Swedish and Danish situations, where no one would question policy generosity, we see that more is spent on services than on their generous cash benefits!) However, Hills did note that embracing both an anti-poverty stance and a social exclusion stance has led the British government to a more generous position in relation to children.

Ultimately, our concern is with the conditions under which children flourish—and what it takes to achieve these conditions. How far does social exclusion go beyond material deprivation, and what would it take to obtain strong popular and political support for progress in that direction? What does social exclusion add to the discussion of child well-being—or could either term be used with the same results? The issue is, where do we want to go as a society with regard to children—not how we measure where we are.

Each of the final panelists (Nancy Folbre, Tom Corbett, Kristin Moore, and Irwin Garfinkel) enriched the discussion in a number of ways, but no one thought the group ready for consensus or closure.

Nancy Folbre stressed the need to redefine work as it relates to exclusion (what about elder care, childcare, or volunteering?). She urged looking at the exclusion process, noting that to focus only on measuring outcomes is to miss what is distinctive here. Americans, too, should stress rights, she said, perhaps using obligations as the concept.

Tom Corbett reminded participants, as he had throughout the meeting, that there *is* a long history of U.S. social policy dealing with exclusion (by other names). He mentioned efforts in recent decades to empower neighborhood service, self-help, and advocacy groups; the immigrant clubs of the nineteenth century; the War on Poverty's community action; and current delivery systems under welfare reform.

Kristin Moore talked about the need for conceptual clarity as a precursor to accurate measurement. She reminded participants that social inclusion is not the same thing as child well-being, and she questioned the value of one multidimensional construct, in contrast to examining the domains separately in policy work (e.g., health, income, poverty, or participation).

Irwin Garfinkel, like Tom Corbett, referred to a long-standing U.S. history of social exclusion based on race or immigration status (e.g., exclusion of Chinese). On the other hand, the United States can be proud of long periods of open immigration and its international leadership in offering public elementary education as a device to unify the society.

There was no formulation of a conference consensus, but what did emerge was some agreement that we in the United States do need to think more broadly than about an absolute poverty line. How can we best think about a richer concept? "Social exclusion" has apparently galvanized the EU and several European governments. Could it be of use here as we consider the closing out/lack of opportunity/obstacles encountered by children with handicaps, children of color, ethnic minorities, immigrants, or children in certain specified demographic groups (e.g., single-parent families, or the residentially segregated in impoverished neighborhoods)? If not "social exclusion," then what?

Note

1. This chapter combines Dr. Kamerman's Background Paper for the conference with the editors' Report of the Meeting.

References

Annie E. Casey Foundation. (2001). *Kids Count Data Book 2001.* Baltimore: Author.

Atkinson, A. B., and J. Hills, eds. (1998). *Exclusion, Employment, and Opportunity.* London: CASE Publications.

Berghman, J. (1995). "Social Exclusion in Europe: Policy Context and Analytical Framework." In *Beyond the Threshold: The Measurement and Analysis of Social Exclusion,* ed. G. Room. Bristol, UK: Policy Press.

Bradbury, B., and J. Markus. (1999) *Child Poverty Across Industrialized Nations.* Innocenti Occasional Paper 70. Florence: UNICEF Innocenti Research Centre.

Citro, C. F., and R. T. Michael, eds. (1995) *Measuring Poverty: A New Approach.* Washington, D.C.: National Academy Press.

Duffy, K. (1998). *Opportunity and Risk: Trends in Social Exclusion in Europe.* Human Dignity and Social Exclusion Project (HDSE). Strasbourg: Council of Europe.

Evans, M., S. Paugan, and J. Prelis. (1995). "Chunnel Vision: Poverty, Social Exclusion, and Debate on Social Welfare in France and Britain." STICERD Discussion Paper 115. London: London School of Economics.

Federal Interagency Forum on Child and Family Statistics. (2000). *America's Children: Key National Indicators of Well-Being 2000.* Washington, D.C.: Government Printing Office.

Haveman, R., and A. Bershadker. (1998)."The 'Inability to be Self-Reliant' as an Indicator of Poverty: Trends in the United States, 1975–1995." DP 1171–98. Madison: University of Wisconsin Institute for Research on Poverty.

Jencks, C. (1992). *Rethinking Social Policy.* Cambridge, Mass.: Harvard University Press.

Jencks, C., and P. E. Peterson, eds. (1991). *The Urban Underclass.* Washington, D.C.: Brookings Institution Press.

Katz, M. (1993). *The Underclass Debate.* Princeton, N.J.: Princeton University Press.

Klasen, S. (1998). "Social Exclusion and Children in OECD Countries: Some Conceptual Issues." Paris: Organisation for Economic Co-operation and Development. Processed.

Lenoir, R. (1974). *Les Exclus, un Français sur dix.* Paris: Seuil.

Magrab, P. R. (1998). "Social Exclusion and Children: A Brief Review of Selected Literature." Paris: Organisation for Economic Co-operation and Development. Processed.

Mejer, L. (2000). "Social Exclusion in the EU Member States." *Statistics in Focus,* Theme 3-1/2000. Luxembourg: Eurostat.

Mejer, L., and G. Linden. (2000). "Persistent Income Poverty and Social Exclusion in the European Union." *Statistics in Focus,* Theme 3-13/2000. Luxembourg: Eurostat.

Morris, P., G. J. Duncan, and L. Chase-Lansdale. (2001). "Welfare Reform's Effects on Children." *Poverty Research News* 5(4).

Paugam, S. (1995) "The Spiral of Precariousness: A Multi-Dimensional Approach to the Process of Social Disqualification in France." In *Beyond the Threshold: The Measurement and Analysis of Social Exclusion,* ed. G. Room. Bristol, UK: Policy Press.

Phipps, S., and L. Curtis. (2001). "The Social Exclusion of Children in North America." Processed.

Robbins, D. (1994). *Observatory on National Policies to Combat Social Exclusion.* 3rd Annual Report. Brussels: Commission of the European Communities.

Room, G., ed. (1995). *Beyond the Threshold: The Measurement and Analysis of Social Exclusion.* Bristol, UK: Policy Press.

Sen, A. (1992). *Inequality Reexamined.* Cambridge, Mass.: Harvard University Press.

Smith, A. (1776). *The Wealth of Nations.* Reprint, New York: Random House, 1993.

Townsend, P. (1962). "The Meaning of Poverty." *British Journal of Sociology* 13(3): 210–27.

UK Government (2001). *Preventing Social Exclusion.* London: Stationary Office.

U.S. Department of Health and Human Services. (2001). *Trends in the Well-Being of America's Children and Youth, 2000.* Washington, D.C.: Government Printing Office.

Social Exclusion: Cultural Roots and Variations on a Popular Concept

Chiara Saraceno

From "Poverty" to "Social Exclusion": An Incomplete Conceptual Shift?

In Europe in recent years, at both research and policymaking levels, there has been linguistic and conceptual movement from the concept of "poverty" to the concept of "social exclusion." The European Union (EU) has played a crucial role in this shift: first, because it created a public international space in which the latter concept has been proposed and debated; and second, because it introduced this concept institutionally, in its policy discourse as well as in its research policy—almost imposing it on diverse cultural and linguistic traditions.[1] As Paugam (1996, p. 7) wrote, social exclusion is the paradigm through which our society becomes aware of its own dysfunction and looks, possibly through confusion and a sense of urgency, for solutions. Further, in describing these dysfunctions, this paradigm has taken over at least two other competing ones: that of the underclass, which is prevalent in the United States, and that of *marginalidad*, which is prevalent in Latin America (Fassin 1996).[2]

This conceptual shift implies a change in perspective: from a static to a dynamic approach, from a one-dimensional to a multi-dimensional perspective, and from a distributional to a relational focus (e.g., Room 1995; Paugam 1996; Atkinson 1998a). To some degree, the emergence of the social exclusion concept has strengthened those conceptions of, and approaches to, poverty that stress that poverty involves not only a lack of fundamental resources, but also an inability to fully participate in one's own society (e.g.,

Townsend 1979). From this perspective, the concept of social exclusion is linked to the concept of social rights as relational rights, based on some kind of reciprocity, on mutual obligations (e.g., Room 1995). The concept of social exclusion emphasizes the individual's participation and involvement in society, and the community's customary way of life, as opposed to an emphasis on average income or basic needs, and a view of well-being as primarily financial. It shares with social Catholicism a view of individuals as being socially embedded (Daly 1999). Its analytic core is based on the structure of social relationships and social ties (Spicker 1997, p. 135). Its inherently comparative nature is apparent, in that it problematizes people's situations/conditions *vis-à-vis* the rest of society (Rustin and Rix 1997, p. 12). By focusing on social relationships, the social exclusion concept is better than the poverty concept at revealing mechanisms of marginalization and the processes associated with it, while acknowledging the excluded's agency.

In these and other respects, "social exclusion" emerges as a more dynamic, actor-oriented, multifaceted, and methodologically plural concept than "poverty." The sources of social exclusion may therefore be found, at the macro level, in the consequences of mass unemployment, mass migration, or deindustrialization; or they may be traced, at the micro level, in the particular experience of the (sometimes self-) exclusion of individuals and groups. These may lack feelings of membership in and loyalty to their communities, not only because of a scarcity of material resources or deprivation of social and legal rights, but also because the contexts people live in and/or their personal histories have not given them any motivation or chance to belong (Castel 1995). From this point of view, the concept of social exclusion could be understood as "postmodern." This is not because postmodern subjects have more sophisticated needs than modern ones (as Abrahmson [1997] seems to suggest), but because in contemporary societies it is more difficult to find the reasons for social integration. There has been an explosion of social "differences," which were, until recently, hidden or repressed (in the pseudo-universalistic ideal of a Eurocore, worker-centered citizenship), but so far there are no theories and practices capable of integrating these differences. In addition, economic growth without employment; technological change; and alterations in family patterns and behaviors systematically render a part of the population redundant, even when socially assisted.

Notwithstanding the wide popularity of the concept, we are still far from universal agreement on what social exclusion actually is. On the contrary, as it comes into more general use, the notion of social exclusion becomes somewhat vague, if not equivocal, as a scientific category (see also Frétigué 1999). The concept may be used to characterize situations or populations so different that it is sometimes hard to understand what they have in common. On the other hand, the concept may no longer be easily dismissed: not only because it has become the framework for public intervention at the national and supranational (particularly EU) levels, but also because it is a transversal notion in much ongoing research on the different phenomena and processes that affect the fabric of contemporary societies. These include the emergence of new risks in the labor market, the weakening of traditional communities and social ties, and the marginalization of whole social groups (see also Paugam 1996, p. 17). Through this, often comparative, research effort, a better understanding of what is covered under the term "social exclusion" is being developed, and both the potential and the internal ambiguities of the concept are being unraveled. Some of these contributions will be discussed below.

According to Levitas (1998, p. 27) the idea of social exclusion moves with seeming ease among discourses with different views of the world. The EU discourse on social exclusion, in itself, demonstrates this and other "political" advantages of social exclusion discourse. On one hand, this approach stresses the social rights dimension, which was the perspective that informed the work of the European Observatory on Social Exclusion (Room et al. 1992). (This emphasis was repeated in a recent Commission document [2000], which declared: "The extent of social exclusion calls on the responsibility of society to ensure equal opportunities for all.

This includes equal access to the labour market, to education, to health care, to the judicial system, to rights and to decision-making and participation.") On the other hand, these social rights seem to be interpreted in a very traditional way, and both "exclusion" and "inclusion" seem to refer almost exclusively to labor market participation. (That same document, in fact, argues: "Employment is the key route to integration and social inclusion; unemployment is the major factor of exclusion, particularly long-term unemployment and the increasing concentration of unemployment in households with no one in work.") Recent documents, coming from the Lisbon and Nice summits, oscillate somewhat between the (even too) broad approach and the restricted solution. Thus, social exclusion is seen to cover an increasing number of spheres and experiences; but at the same time, employment (or lack of it) continues to be pointed to as, if not the only form of social integration, certainly the main route to it—even given the risks of labor market instability and the large number of flexible positions.

The concept of social exclusion seems to have at least two different genealogies of linked terms and phenomena, which keep surfacing in a quite unresolved alliance in social exclusion discourse. There are poverty and material deprivation on the one hand, reviewed in the light of social rights thinking; and social disintegration, marginality, un-belonging, and uprootedness on the other hand. One level of analysis points to the social conditions by which individuals and groups are included in or excluded from relevant resources and social rights; the other points to processes by which individuals and social groups belong to, or are detached from, relevant and meaningful social networks, and share in values and identifications within a given community. Although both levels of analysis are important for understanding social exclusion, they are by no means always addressed jointly in social exclusion discourse. On the contrary, either the focus is on resources and social rights or it is on affiliation/disaffiliation dimensions (sometimes even further reduced to matters of psychological well-/ill-being).[3]

Yet, concern about moral and social disintegration—about the processes by which individuals and groups become detached from communities and their moral order, which are often associated with social exclusion (e.g., Castel 1995)—does not necessarily imply a concept of individual social rights. The recent debates over—and demands for—ethnic, community, or group rights, for instance, point to a radically different path towards social integration. Actually barring some individuals (e.g., women or the young) from possessing individual rights may be—and often is—advocated as a means of preserving social (family, community, ethnic) integrity (e.g., Sahgal and Yuval Davis 1992; Yuval Davis 1996; Okin 1989). On the other hand, access to social rights per se does not grant actual, meaningful membership in a community. Thus, in the most developed welfare states the homeless may be entitled in principle to housing and support, but many of them lack both the knowledge and the capacity to benefit from these rights because of their deep isolation and various personal traits. Sen (1985a, 1985b) addresses this issue under the concept of capability, understood as prerequisite for social participation and access to social rights. Sen's approach, although certainly nearer to the social exclusion than to the poverty approach, challenges both: neither the offering of resources nor the granting of rights is sufficient to avoid social exclusion if the specific capabilities and functioning of individuals are not addressed. (This perspective is particularly crucial with regard to children.) Moreover, while most definitions and uses of "social exclusion" imply that it occurs in connection with material deprivation of some kind (e.g., Castel 1995; Paugam 1997), that link is by no means necessary: one need not be financially poor to be socially excluded. The situation of many immigrants in Europe who are integrated into the labor market but lack many basic citizenship rights, and are perceived as extraneous to the communities they live in, is a case in point.

Furthermore, recent research has begun to question the empirical and theoretical validity of the relationship between the two concepts of poverty and social exclusion. Empirical data suggest a lack of self-evident linkage between unemployment and poverty, and also between poverty and social isolation and/or psychological ill-being. Not only do these vary among social groups and on the basis of duration (on economic distress or unemployment see Leisering and Leibfried 1999) but they also differ across countries according, inter alia, to social security systems, family arrangements, and cultures (Saraceno 1997; Gallie 1999; Gallie and Paugam 2000).

As a matter of fact, the origins and original subjects of any given social exclusion discourse should not be overlooked once it has been extended to other contexts. Both the national and cultural contexts and the actors focused upon highlight specific patterns of social exclusion and ways of understanding it. Thus social isolation and/or uprootedness appear to be more a feature of men's experiences of social exclusion than of women's: The former are readily seen as socially excluded when they are "long-term unemployed," because employment is perceived as their main route to both normality and social integration; when men lose the social ties they form through work, they are perceived as lacking social ties altogether. The fact that women may be excluded from employment and other forms of social participation, not because they are uprooted or have weak social networks, but because they are too strictly embedded in family networks and obligations, tends to be overlooked. Further, although welfare dependency is increasingly seen as a cause of social exclusion (or negative inclusion), dependency on one's own family resources is not, particularly in the case of women and the young; although, as Goodin (1996, p. 351) also observed, depending on one's family subjects one to the arbitrary will of others.

Actually, the dual, and ambivalent, role of family solidarity in protecting and restricting women (and the young, at least in southern European countries), illustrates the need for an integrated view of the two levels on which social exclusion occurs: that of (individual) social rights and that of community membership. Moreover, the complex networks in which many of the poor and long-term unemployed conduct their lives in Mediterranean countries defy conventional visions of the socially excluded as isolated (see also Gallie 1999). Community membership without individual rights may be as exclusionary as access to social rights without community membership, albeit in a different way. Of course, the severest exclusion occurs when access to both is denied. All this points to the need for a concept of social exclusion—and of its indicators— more attentive to context: both in terms of welfare regimes[4] and in terms of national, local, group-specific, and cultural understandings of such elements as patterns of inclusion and participation in a meaningful life (see also Svetlik 2000; Berman and Philips 2000).

Intellectual Roots of the Social Exclusion Discourse[5]

Silver (1994) identifies three different theoretical and political perspectives within which the concept (or metaphor) of social exclusion is developed. She calls these *paradigms*, as per Thomas Kuhn's use of the term,[6] and tracks differences in what they each regard as the causes of exclusion and in their guiding political philosophies. The three paradigms are *solidarity*, *specialization*, and *monopoly*. They dovetail, in some respects, with national discourses, for they may be traced, respectively, to French republican notions of solidarity, Anglo-American liberal individualism, and the European social democratic notion of conflict based on hierarchical power relations.[7] While Silver's reasoning and distinctions are not always clear, her thesis is insightful, not least in pointing out how different visions of the polity embody different concepts of social exclusion.

Within contemporary French discourse on social exclusion, the emphasis is on "social" and collective ties.[8] The risk of socially anomic behaviors and the need to offset the mechanisms that produce these are the core concerns of the French discourse on social exclusion, with its roots in the Durkheimian notion of social bonds and the relevance of normative integration. In other words, social cohesion (in the sense of dominant consensual values, mores, and social bonds) is foremost in this view. The socially excluded, defined as those who are outside the polity, are seen as suffering from some kind of inability in social relations, and rootlessness. According to Touraine (1991, 1992), social exclusion is typical of postmodern societies within which the issues are no longer hierarchy and inequality, but horizontal segregation and refusal to include. In this view, the hierarchy of traditional class structure was a way of including, even if through conflict. The refusal to acknowledge particular social groups is not merely a form of inequality; it is a form of non-membership, non-existence.

Thus, in the French policy discourse the focus is no longer on inequality and the means to correct it, but on integration, and insertion/re-insertion. The typical "socially excluded" individual in this view, and the ideal recipient of *Revenu Minimum D'Insertion* (RMI), an assistance program, is a family-less single person, often a man, experiencing various kinds of personal and social handicaps, who needs to be "socially reinserted" or "reintegrated." Re-insertion is to be achieved by various kinds of enabling activities, which may be perceived as empowering—but also involve attempts at control and placing the subjects under surveillance (e.g., Belorgey 1996; Barbier 1998).[9] At the same time, society, the state in general, and social workers in particular are seen as having a duty to actively seek out the socially excluded, to try to reweave their social bonds, and to offer them chances for "integration." In principle, the entire society is called upon to reintegrate itself by offering individuals the possibility of being inserted into solidarity networks and meaningful social contacts (e.g., Rosanvallon 1995). In the 1960s and 1970s, this concept still pointed to the existence of social groups and individuals who were characterized by a de facto exclusion, whereas the focus is now on the processes that lead to this situation, which in turn is perceived as threatening an increasing number of individuals and groups. In this perspective, the widely used, if contested, term "contract" (as in "insertion contract")—the key word in the French discourse—is nearer to the concept of a social contract than it is to that of an individual business contract. The concept of reciprocity, which stresses the community's (and social workers') responsibility as much as the recipient's agency, is central. Although in practice this concept of reciprocity, too, results in an asymmetrical relationship, it seeks to keep in check the strong asymmetry of the traditional social assistance relationship. Thus, the French idea of social exclusion does not principally emphasize recipients' obligations, as in the United States and the UK, but rather emphasizes their agency and negotiating power. It extends beyond income support or job insertion, encompassing measures aimed at combating disaffiliation and uprootedness (Milano 1995; Barbier 1996, 1998).

In the liberal tradition, and particularly in its Anglo-American variant, social exclusion is not an endogenous concept. Here, "the culture of poverty" has loomed large. In the 1960s, this concept offered a mirror in which the society could view itself, giving a rich account of the plight and experiences of those living at the margins, and connecting material deprivation with self-perception, identity, and ways of living. It also offered a theoretical rationale through which the poor could be blamed for their situation. In shifting focus from the deprivation itself to its symbolic and behavioral consequences, it turned away from excluding processes (and actors) and toward self-exclusion.

Concepts achieving prominence more recently in the UK and the United States are the "underclass" (Dahrendorf 1984; Wilson 1987; Smith 1992) and the "two tier society."[10] In the liberal tradition, the focus is as much on institutional barriers and forms of discrimination as it is on individual agency as the cause of social differentiation. If society's duty is to remove barriers, then that of the individual is to make the best of the options offered. Adopting the metaphor of social exclusion within this framework affords the opportunity to recapture the richness of the "culture of poverty" approach. The social exclusion focus on multiple dimensions of deprivation and the relevance of social networks and self-perception, together with its focus on actors, provides some of its noteworthy advantages in this regard. On the other hand, the idea of social exclusion draws attention to the social, as opposed to individual, mechanisms producing un-belonging—for instance, discrimination in the labor market, access to social security benefits, housing, or credit—or more generally, access to consumption (Atkinson 1998a). From this dual view comes a shared concern, both for the mechanisms producing the phenomenon of the working poor [11]—a particularly pressing issue in the United States and the UK—and the dependency produced by welfare state support, particularly among single mothers. In both countries, there is an understanding of inclusion as occurring mainly through paid work, so that it is necessary "to make work pay." However, the British tradition, informed by Marshall's theory of citizenship, recognizes that social exclusion also involves reduced access to social rights. This locates the British position closer to the social democratic one— the "monopoly paradigm," in Silver's terminology.

In the third paradigm, power relations, group monopolies, and the domination and exclusion of outsiders come to the fore. Powerful class and status groups, which have distinct social and cultural identities as well as institutions, use social closure to restrict the access of outsiders to valued resources (such as good jobs, good benefits, education, urban locations, and valued patterns of consumption) (Silver 1994, p. 562). While the liberal paradigm points to the risks of welfare dependency for the poor, the monopoly paradigm points to the material and cultural/symbolic privileges of insiders as causing exclusion of outsiders. Inequality and economic exploitation lead to exclusion, in this view; inclusion occurs mainly through access by outsiders to citizenship rights, which in turn must be monitored for their exclusionary potential. This discourse may apply to any kind of social barrier, including those between nation states and those between EU member states and other countries. The discourse on "fortress Europe" has its roots here, referring to external and internal boundaries and barriers that keep some groups from becoming insiders. In the liberal paradigm, social assistance rights (e.g., income support for the poor) are under scrutiny for their tendency to create exclusion through dependency, while in the monopoly paradigm, standard social rights—such as unemployment protection or pension benefits— are the main source of concern. In this perspective, these insiders' social rights must be scrutinized to ascertain if their protection creates barriers to entry for other groups. There are echoes here of the critique leveled against continental European welfare states— that they too strongly protect adult male, core workers (i.e., insiders) to the detriment of outsiders. Thus, in the monopoly paradigm, social inclusion implies not only extending access, but also transforming the social security and social protection system to make it more inclusive and more attuned, both to social and individual risks emerging throughout life, and to varieties of life circumstances (see Leisering and Leibfried 1999).[12]

The EU discourse on social exclusion has oscillated between these different paradigms over time, without clearly choosing among them. Thus, the EU stresses the social rights dimension, which was the perspective that informed the work of the European Observatory on Social Exclusion (Room et al.1992); but at the same time, it specifies employment as the main route to inclusion. This dual emphasis is confirmed in recent documents by the Commission on the European Social Agenda, and it has been incorporated to a degree in the document approved at the Nice summit (Commission 1993a, 1993b, 1993c, and 2000) in 2000. Thus a document of March 2000 declared: "The extent of social exclusion calls on the responsibility of society to ensure equal opportunities for all. This includes equal access to the labour market, to education, to health care, to the judicial system, to rights and to decision-making and participation." The European Social Agenda stresses that "Employment is the best protection against social exclusion . . . . Social policy has a crucial role parallel to that of employment policy; yet the relevance of other factors must be acknowledged, such as housing, education, health, information, communication, mobility, security and justice, culture and consumption."

This discussion shows that social exclusion is a politically flexible concept. Indeed, there are good grounds for claiming that social exclusion has been more developed as a discourse than as a concept: that is, the idea has been most used and articulated in the service of the language of politics. Hence it constitutes a relatively loose set of ideas that represent particular settings, rather than a concept with theoretical substance and coherence that transcends national and political contexts.

Unemployment and Social Exclusion: Contested Links

The wide popularity of social exclusion discourse has been prompted by the emergence of mass (male) unemployment. It is this deviance from the "normal" male pattern, around which so much of the social organization of industrialized countries developed, that is perceived as a social risk, certainly further heightened by other changes in what Crouch (1999) has defined as the postwar social contract. But family arrangements are also changing, particularly with the increasing fragility of marriage and the rise of single-parent (mostly single-mother) families; and the growing tide of immigrants from outside the borders of what used to be called the Western world. Both these phenomena bring into question long-standing arrangements in labor markets and systems of social protection, as well as in the organization of everyday life. As a matter of fact, concern over mass unemployment seems to obfuscate all other reasons for social and economic vulnerability. It is as though the weakening of male breadwinners—in the form of adult male unemployment—renders poverty unacceptable and a risk to social cohesion, notwithstanding the fact that the individuals most at risk of poverty and social exclusion are often children, housewives, and the elderly: individuals who, because of their age or position in the gender division of labor, do not even appear in the rolls of the unemployed. In fact, recent studies, both of poverty and of social assistance recipients, indicate that there exists a much broader range of social risks, many of which show remarkable continuity over recorded time, although their specific causes and circumstances may have changed. Now, as in the past, the end of a marriage exposes women and children to the risk of poverty and the need for social support, although separation is now more often the cause than death of a spouse; advancing age may still represent a risk, particularly for the older cohorts (and for women within them) and if associated with frailty. In addition to growing unemployment, immigration and adherence to nonstandard life styles increasingly represent new causes of poverty (Glotz 1994; Beck and Seewald 1994; Duncan 1984; Mejer 2000; Leibfried and Leisering 1999; Paugam 1997).

Moreover, social anxiety over not only the plight of individuals, but the threat to social cohesion posed by mass unemployment, poses risk: not only of equating the unemployed with the socially excluded, but of seeing the unemployed as needing special efforts to counter personal deficits or counteract negative tendencies. Many welfare-to-work and other employment policies, as well as in some cases the blurring of boundaries between social security and social assistance, arise from this anxiety.

Recent comparative research on the unemployed (e.g., Gallie 1999; Gallie and Paugam 2000) actually does not offer straightforward support to the hypothesis of a strong and univocal link between unemployment and social exclusion (in the sense of social isolation). The link is clearer with economic poverty, of course, but even in this case it varies greatly among countries, depending on the family arrangements of the unemployed and national systems of social protection (see also Haataja 1999). According to the study coordinated by Gallie and Paugam, the proportion of the unemployed in poverty (taking the 50% mean equivalised income line) varied from 8 percent in Denmark to 49 percent in the UK. These variations reflect, first of all, the effectiveness of systems of social transfers (unemployment indemnity) in the different countries. They also reflect, however, the country-specific ages and social profiles of the unemployed, and patterns of family arrangements. Thus, in the Mediterranean countries unemployment is heavily concentrated among the young; but in these same countries the young—as opposed to their contemporaries in other countries—live to a greater extent with their parents, and are thus partially shielded from poverty (see also Organisation for Economic Co-operation and Development 1998). Over two-thirds of young unemployed adults aged 20–29 live with their parents in Italy, Spain, and Portugal. The corresponding figures are 42 percent in the UK, 29 percent in Germany, and 14 percent in Denmark and Sweden. Of course, the level of financial support that the family provides depends upon its own level of resources, and the unemployed tend to be concentrated among the poorer families. The responsibility to support one's own unemployed due to lack of adequate social protection may cause financial stress and hardship for the whole family (see also Saraceno 2000). This situation is compounded by the lack, or scarcity, of support for families with dependent children in all southern European countries, which makes them more vulnerable to poverty than those in most Francophone and Scandinavian countries.

With regard to social isolation and psychological stress, the link is also far from evident. Certainly recent studies (Gallie and Paugam 2000; Gallie 1999; Mejer 2000) show that those who are unemployed not only have a higher risk of being poor, but also have a higher risk of having a low level of education and professional skills, of not owning a home or car, of not having the wherewithal for a week's holiday away. They appear generally more vulnerable to economic deprivation, and with lower human and social capital. Nevertheless, the hypothesis that unemployment causes social isolation is far from being confirmed by research. Both a comparative EU-wide study on the unemployed (Gallie 1999) and a cross-country and longitudinal study (based on Europanel data) on a number of European countries found that, with the partial exception of France, there is no evidence that unemployment reduces social networks. In each country, the social networks of the unemployed do not appear dissimilar from those of the employed. At the same time, there are substantial cross-country differences. In Mediterranean countries—where both unemployment and its attendant financial hardship are higher than in other countries—the unemployed show a higher degree of involvement with kin, friends, and neighbors than do the Danes or the Dutch; the German unemployed experience a comparatively higher level of social isolation from their friends' networks. Overall, the risk of social isolation appears to be heavily conditioned by broader country-specific patterns of sociability, rather than the experience of unemployment per se.[13] The clearest intracountry difference between the unemployed and the employed appears to be in participation in associative life, which tends to be reduced among the former in all countries, notwithstanding the existence of country-specific patterns. This might suggest that unemployment, particularly if it is long-term, reduces the range of social activities in which individuals are involved, particularly those activities that help people preserve their integration within socially acknowledged roles and citizenship norms. When the long-term unemployed have parental responsibilities, this may affect both their capabilities as parents and the range of meaningful networks and situations they can offer their children.

When unemployment is of long duration (over two years), studies find indications of a narrowing of the variety (not necessarily of the extent and intensity) of social networks, and also more psychological stress. Time appears, therefore, to be a crucial factor in social exclusion processes, although its impact might be different depending on social protection measures and patterns of informal and family support. As the study coordinated by Gallie and Paugam (2000) concludes, comparative variations in the link between unemployment and the risk of social exclusion may be accounted for, to a great degree, by variations in the character of the welfare state; but family cultures and arrangements, and patterns of sociability in certain societies are also of central importance. In the northern countries the system of social protection shields the unemployed not only from financial hardship, but also from loss of dignity and of human and social capital, allowing the unemployed to remain integrated into their social networks. In the southern countries, where both unemployment and poverty are much more widespread than in the northern ones, and social protection is meager, the unemployed appear to be protected from social exclusion through the financial and social support they receive from parents and friends. This, however, puts stress on these social supports, while leaving those who cannot count on them without resources. The risk of social isolation appears greatest in countries—such as the UK, France, and Germany—in which the system of social protection provides relatively low, uneven, and often stigmatizing financial assistance, and where informal social support is relatively weak.

We might add that an exclusive focus on employment as the main route to social inclusion does not allow for much understanding of the experience of children in social exclusion processes, except for predicting future outcomes. Both children's exclusion and their inclusion seem to be direct outcomes of the exclusion or inclusion of their parents from the labor market. It should be noted that this approach is increasingly reflected in national policies. This is particularly evident in countries, such as the UK and the Netherlands, where in the past, single mothers receiving social assistance were exempt from the requirement to take a job, in consideration of their main role as caring parents. Single mothers are now increasingly encouraged to take paid jobs; that is, to take up breadwinning as their main parental role (e.g., Van Dreuth, Knijn, and Lewis 1999). A mother who is employed may still be perceived as a possible liability in the upbringing of her children and a likely cause of their feelings of isolation and lack of connectedness. But when she is the only parent present, an unemployed mother is also, increasingly, perceived as a liability for her children if she receives social assistance: dependence on a husband is a sign of social integration, dependence on social assistance a sign of social exclusion. It should be noticed, however, that this does not always coincide with self-perceptions, and it depends heavily on subjective, as well as local and national, family and motherhood cultures. Thus, Dutch single mothers seem less willing to accept this shift in focus, because they share an idea of caring motherhood as a highly integrative activity. French single mothers who receive a benefit until their youngest child is three do not perceive themselves as being assisted because they are out of work, but because they are doing their duty as mothers (Aillet 1997/1998).

Finally, the idea that any job is better than no job (and particularly better than relying on social assistance) from a social inclusion point of view is at least over-simplistic. Atkinson (1998b) and Paugam (1997), for instance, argue that some jobs might be more socially excluding than social assistance itself, in terms of social and professional disqualification. Forcing a person to take any job may have serious effects upon his/her skills, and therefore also on his/her ability to stay in the labor market. This is particularly true when the unskilled bad job is also not a social security-protected one. From this point of view, Paugam distinguishes between "disqualified integration" in the case of people holding an unskilled—but secure and covered by social security—job, and "compromised integration" in the case of unskilled jobs in the informal economy with no social security coverage. Further, the reason that social assistance may result in social exclusion lies not so much in its hypothetical corrupting effect on beneficiaries,[14] but in the degree to which they are stigmatized by specific patterns of provision, weakening their social status and even their perceptions of themselves. Levels of generosity, degrees of universality, patterns of control and of enforcing specific behaviors have proven crucial in this respect (Saraceno 2002).

The Time Perspective and the Analysis of Social Exclusion

The relevance of a time perspective in the analysis of poverty has been acknowledged at least since Rowntree's (1901) pioneering studies a century ago. Rowntree, in fact, was well aware that the poor were not always poor throughout their lives. Rather, the chances of being poor for London's manual workers and their families were linked to specific life-course stages and circumstances: typically, being a child; having children in need of support; and being old (in pre-welfare state times). From a gender-sensitive perspective, we might add being fatherless or being a widow. Thus, any headcount in a given year says little about the life experience of the poor in terms of how long they have been poor, and how long they will likely remain in poverty. At the same time, head counts tend to under-represent the number of those who experience poverty over the life course. Both aspects of poverty—the fact that it is not a static phenomenon, and the fact that it may affect a larger population than is estimated by static headcounts—may be studied only on the basis of longitudinal data. This insight has been long, if unsystematically, present in postwar poverty research since at least the 1960s (e.g., Glatzer and Krupp 1975; Commissione di Indagine sulla Povertà 1985). Yet, until recently, longitudinal data was lacking, and Europe has lagged behind the

United States in providing it. As a result, the discourse on poverty continued to be based on headcount data, however sophisticated and differentiated techniques for "counting the poor" might be. Moreover, as Leisering and Leibfried (1999) point out, until recently even those studies of poverty that used a dynamic perspective shared the assumption that time was an aggravating factor in the dynamics of poverty and social exclusion. Poverty was seen as a cumulative process, where experiences, including that of receiving social assistance, and trajectories negatively reinforced each other. In this approach, concern for the multidimensionality of poverty combined with the possible labeling effects, not only of poverty (and unemployment) but also of social assistance, in offering a view of the poor as mere victims of society launched on a hopeless downward path. This same assumption more or less explicitly lies behind contemporary concerns over "welfare dependency," supported by research strategies and choices that have long favored the study of a specific subgroup of the socially assisted: those defined as being most marginal, either because of specific handicaps (deviant lifestyles, physical or mental handicaps, immigration) and/or because of the length of time they have been receiving social assistance.

U.S. research had already undermined the idea of poverty as a universally long-term and cumulative experience, since results of the important Panel Study on Income Dynamics (Duncan 1984) became known. From that study, it emerged that the portion of the population vulnerable to poverty was much greater and more heterogeneous than had been estimated by static measures, and that this group comprised individuals and families who experienced poverty once in their lifetimes; those who experienced it many times for varying periods; and finally, those who experienced poverty continuously, for lengthy periods, or possibly throughout their entire lives. The hypothesis of negative, cumulative, and mutually reinforcing processes certainly held for the last group, and was a possible risk for the second; but it did not hold at all for the first. The second group was possibly the most interesting from this point of view. It not only exhibited all the expected causes of vulnerability—female gender, inadequate education and professional skills, particular family composition and arrangements, lack of adequate means of social protection—but it also illustrated the variety of pathways by which one might enter, and leave, poverty. Illness, breakdown of a marriage, unemployment, or birth of an additional child might put a person or family below the poverty line; whereas employment, marriage, or a child exiting the household might raise one above it. This stress on the dynamics of poverty and on its variations was further developed, both empirically and theoretically, by Bane and Ellwood's studies (1986, 1994). An important contribution, although one not always fully acknowledged and integrated into mainstream life course poverty research, came from U.S. and European studies on women's gender-specific vulnerability to poverty: studies on the consequences of marital instability and divorce, and on women's vulnerability to poverty in old age, because of the combined effects of working within the home and social security regulations (e.g., Joshi 1989, 1992; Allmendinger, Brückner, and Brückner 1991). Attention to European life-course research in general, and life-course studies on poverty in particular, added an awareness of the structuring role of social policies. Overall, however, life-course research on poverty is still lacking in many European countries. The dynamic approach to poverty is particularly developed, and based on longitudinal data at the national level, in Germany, the UK, and the Nordic countries. Comparative studies are thus limited.

Leisering and Leibfried (1999), on the basis of their study of social assistance careers in two German cities over a six-year period, indicate that from the point of view of duration there are at least three distinct groups of social assistance recipients, with distinct paths into and conditions of poverty, as well as different vulnerabilities to social exclusion (see also Paugam 1997 for similar hypotheses on France).[15] These are: a) the *temporarily poor*, who have short, and sometimes single, spells of poverty—for example, in Germany in the 1990s these comprised mostly the unemployed and immigrants; b) the *repeatedly poor*, who, although often above the poverty line, fall frequently below it in times of economic insecurity and/or changing family circumstances or life prospects—here many low-income workers may be found; and c) the *permanent or long-term poor*, who comprise people who for some reason (age, gender, health, lack of skills, or a combination of these) do not succeed, or have no possibility of succeeding, in becoming financially self-sufficient. The various social groups vulnerable to poverty are differently distributed within these temporal patterns, and therefore are differently exposed to the risk of social exclusion. Leisering and Leibfried (1999, pp. 245–49) propose four main groups plus two additional, more cross-cutting ones. According to these two authors, the range of these types "exposes the diversity of conditions [that exist] between exclusion in a strict sense and full inclusion" (p. 246). The proposed groups are:

a) The relatively secure members of the middle class (often labeled as the "new poor") who are now more exposed to social insecurity than in the past, because of either family reasons (such as marriage breakdown) or labor market vagaries; they see claiming benefits as both temporary, and as a way to actively combat their situations.

b) People with permanently low incomes, living just above the poverty line, but always at risk of falling below it, since they lack a cushion of protective resources—either because of their structural position or their stage in life. Although they are integrated into society, their integration is always under threat, and they constantly run the risk of falling into the next category.

c) The long-term deprived, who suffer significant material or non-material deprivations, but are not necessarily and comprehensively excluded from participating in social life because of their embeddedness in family, kin, and community networks (see also Paugam 1997).

d) The long-term socially excluded, who are not only deprived of material resources but are also excluded from social participation, due to active social discrimination or the inability to cope, which render it difficult for them to be active members of meaningful social networks. The homeless, the mentally ill, and others whose lives have been seriously disrupted belong to this group; it has long dominated public imagination concerning the socially excluded or the Fourth World.

To these four types, Leisering and Leibfried add another two: e) People with an unsettled mode of existence, whose lifestyle on the edge of society is in part an expression of deliberate choice and who might be also be seen as risky "commuters" between a normal life course and social decline. These often use social assistance deliberately in a "strategic," if intermittent, way: not, as in the case of the first group, in order to bridge an occasional spell of misfortune or to re-orient their lives, but as a systematic way of supporting their chosen lifestyles. If the long-term socially excluded is the main reference group for much poverty discourse, "the unsettled" is the more or less explicit reference group when we point to the combined phenomena of social assistance dependency and social assistance scrounging. f) The new immigrants, who are by definition in a transitional situation. Depending on the circumstances, they may end up in one of the other groups, or exit poverty and social assistance altogether.

Thus, the longitudinal perspective offers ground both for an understanding of social exclusion as a succession, and accumulation, of breaks and disadvantages in an individual's life, and for more clearly distinguishing between occasional poverty and long-term deprivation, as well as between material deprivation and social isolation. This, in turn, helps us to understand the poor and those vulnerable to social exclusion as agents in their own right, and as bearers of interpretations and meanings concerning their circumstances—which must be taken account of not only in research, but also in policymaking.

Grappling with "Facts": A Revival of Social Indicators Research

As Berman and Phillips (2000) observe, social indicators are now back in vogue, and both national and international (EU, OECD, UN) institutions and social researchers are now involved in the effort of identifying and standardizing measurements of human well-being (see also Rothenbacher 1998). The most ambitious taxonomy was developed by the OECD in the early 1990s and covered "convergence, exclusion, equal opportunity, poverty and cohesion" (Vogel 1994, p. 252).

This development is taking place in the context of two others. First, there is a redefinition of the concept of the "level of living," and more, of the concept of "well-being," which lay beyond the development of the social indicators movement in the 1960s. The shift from attention to poverty and material deprivation, to attention to social exclusion, is part of this movement. Second, there is a growing interest in comparative, standardized data and indicators. This latter development is contributing, in crucial ways, to both conceptualizations and research. At the same time, there exists a kind of paradox: insofar as one of the reasons for redefining well-being and social inclusion/exclusion is attention to diversity—at the individual, community, local, and national levels—the aim to find common indicators and to set common standards seems at first sight ill-founded and possibly ill-conceived (see also Svetlik 2000). It might even be interpreted as an attempt at imposing, top-down, some kind of "universal" standard.[16] Yet the ongoing debate on social indicators offers, from the point of view of research, interesting terrain for a better understanding of what well-being, social inclusion, and social exclusion are—or might be—about.

In a report on social exclusion in the EU member states for Eurostat, Mejer (2000) presents a complex framework for analyzing social exclusion, synthesized in Figure 1.

Figure 1: A Framework for analyzing social exclusion

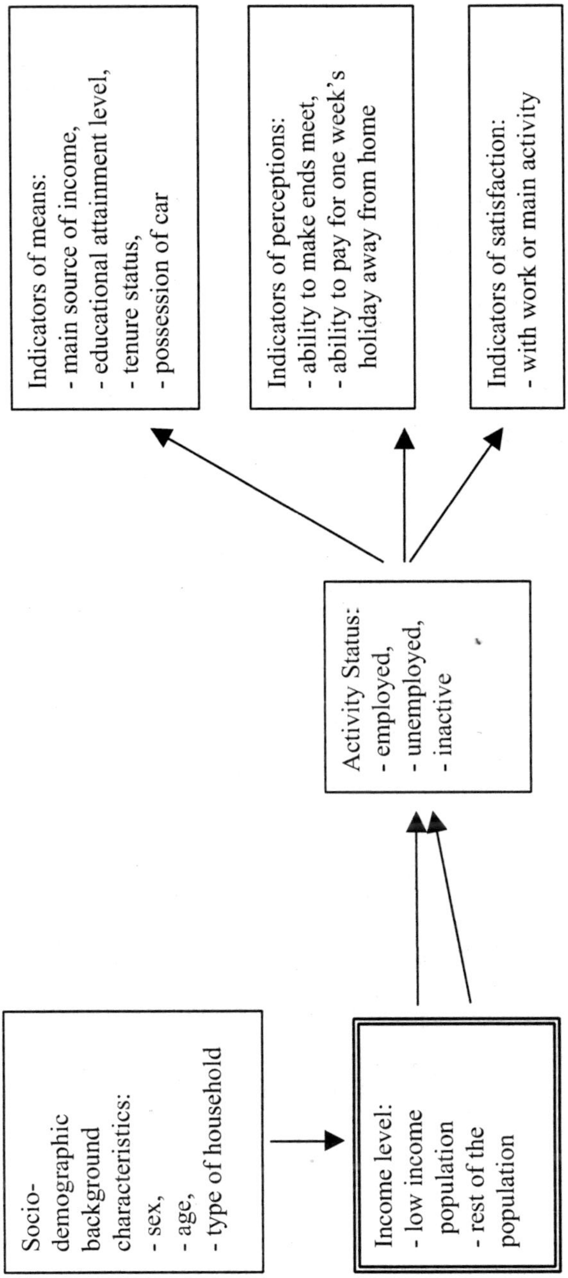

Socio-demographic background characteristics:
- sex,
- age,
- type of household

Income level:
- low income population
- rest of the population

Activity Status:
- employed,
- unemployed,
- inactive

Indicators of means:
- main source of income,
- educational attainment level,
- tenure status,
- possession of car

Indicators of perceptions:
- ability to make ends meet,
- ability to pay for one week's holiday away from home

Indicators of satisfaction:
- with work or main activity

In the guidelines for the preparation of the National Action Plans for inclusion and in the document supporting the creation of a subgroup on indicators within the Social Protection Committee (Mejer 2000) it is argued that seven indicators are already available for comparative purposes, and that others should be developed. The seven are:

1. distribution of income;
2. poverty rate before and after transfers;
3. persistence of poverty;
4. jobless households;
5. regional cohesion;
6. early school-leavers not in further education and training; and
7. long-term unemployment.

Health, housing, access to services and to training and education, and conditions of work are the areas which should be developed. The discussion is now open concerning not only the availability and reliability,[17] but the efficacy and cross-country significance of some of the seven indicators, from the point of view of social exclusion. For example, in Italy many jobless households might consist of a not-poor widow holding a survivor pension and an adult child still in education. Such a household is not necessarily poor nor socially excluded.

The issue of significance arises more readily in the case of comparative indicators. Yet the same problem is also present in national experiences. The very interesting debate that opened around the monitoring of the UK strategy to tackle poverty (Bradshaw 2001), for instance, points not only to the issue of the quality, availability, and national representativity of the indicators chosen by the UK government, but also to issues concerning the quality of indicators themselves: what they should measure and point to. Therefore, the debate addresses the issue of what social exclusion is supposed to be. For instance, Bradshaw (2001) argues that these indicators are both too narrow—in that they inadequately address issues of health and subjective well-being—and too wide, in that some of them are not related to poverty (e.g., smoking rates among adults or cocaine and heroin use among young people).

Harker (2001) in the same debate, although suggesting a number of areas/indicators that should be included in assessing social exclusion and monitoring success in reducing it, argues that measures of general well-being should not be confused with measures of poverty or social exclusion. Her criticism is particularly addressed to indicators such as the proportion of elderly people living with the fear of crime, life expectancy to age 65, or the proportion of people being helped to live independently. The concern seems twofold: on the one hand, there is widespread agreement that in order to grasp social exclusion, one needs indicators that go beyond material deprivation; on the other hand, there is concern about widening the range of areas and items included too much, at the risk of losing sight of social exclusion itself—which is understood as strictly linked to (even if wider and more multidimensional than), poverty and material deprivation. In the words of Harker (2001, p. 32), "Measures of poverty and social exclusion should be somewhere between income poverty and well being but focused on the 'bottom end'—in other words, the measures should reflect concern about where there are unacceptable differences in living standards and opportunities."

A quite different approach is taken by those who propose to insert the issue of social exclusion into the wider one of social quality. This term has been tentatively defined as "the extent to which citizens are able to participate in the social and economic life of their communities under conditions that enhance their well being and individual potential" (Beck, Van der Maesen, and Walker 1997, p. 3). This concept is intended to encompass both subjective and objective interpretations. Social inclusion/exclusion is one of the four elements that identify it, the others being socioeconomic security/insecurity, social cohesion/anomie, and empowerment/disempowerment. As a matter of fact, when addressing the issue of indicators for all these four elements, social exclusion/inclusion appears to be only one of them, but at the same time, cross-cutting and including them all. In the words of Berman and Phillips (2000, p. 333), who attempt a systematic approach toward the development of indicators for both social exclusion and social quality, "some of the domains for social exclusion necessarily have to be closely related to those of socio-economic security because social inclusion depends upon, among other things, a minimum level of the collective goods that confer socio-economic security. The definitional difference in these domains and indicators between the two dimensions relates to who is included. Moreover, social inclusion is not merely substantively co-terminous with socio-economic security, it also covers areas relevant to social cohesion," (and of course, also relevant to empowerment).

Within the "social quality quadrant,"[18] following Delanty's (1998) distinction between "Demos" and "Ethnos," Berman and Phillips identify two distinct sets of social exclusion indicators: one at the level of the nation-state (which they approximate to Demos) and the other at the Ethnos, community, level. Indicators at the level of the nation-state should measure the inaccessibility (through discrimination, ignorance, or inability) of rights and services to those who by definition of citizenship should have access to them. Indicators at the community level, instead, should measure participation and identification. "These domains are psycho-social in nature in the sense that they relate to the consciousness and significance of the interaction and relationship between a person and his/her identified community. Social exclusion in the community-individual relationship is a result of the weakness of social bonds" (p. 345). Thus individuals might be communally included but nationally excluded (e.g., immigrants living in tight ethnic communities, but also women included in family and kin networks, but excluded from social participation); or they might be nationally included but with no community membership (e.g., isolated immigrants or people who have left their rural communities); finally individuals might be both nationally and communally excluded, as in the case of the homeless, or of foreign immigrants having no citizenship rights and cut off from their communities.

We might say that this framework offers a way of integrating the two concepts of social exclusion that usually compete de facto in analysis: one that links social exclusion to a weakening, or absence, of social rights, and one that links it to the lack, or destruction, of patterns of belonging: these correspond, simplistically, to the British and the French traditions. What is perhaps missing, notwithstanding this broad perspective, is the sometimes exclusionary effect of rules of both national inclusion and community inclusion. We have already said that women might be excluded from social participation and even rights (e.g., to a decent pension) because of their "excess" of inclusion in family and kinship networks. Many rules concerning entitlement to social and political rights also effectively exclude groups who cannot fulfil the set requirements: for example, time requirements concerning residence or definitions of what counts as work. This dual risk is becoming increasingly apparent in the case of immigrants who, particularly among the young of both genders and women of all ages, may find themselves caught in the middle of two opposing definitions of and requirements for inclusion—in the nation states where they live and in their communities.

Conclusion

Chamberlayne (1997) regards the theoretical and methodological underdevelopment of the social exclusion concept as an opportunity. For her, it stimulates fresh thinking, calls into question assumptions and, in the European context, challenges national traditions in thinking about inequality, poverty, and difference. It also challenges traditions of social policy. Nevertheless, its conceptual looseness and shifting meanings, which render it perhaps more a metaphor than a concept, have their risks, at both research and policymaking levels. The more encompassing the concept, the greater the risk, not only of omitting something relevant, but also of accepting pre-judgements that remain unscrutinized. In his discussion of Doyal and Gough's (1991) contribution to the issue of "universal," cross national indicators of well-being,[19] for instance, Svetlik (2000, p. 81), argues that "the authors start from a specific theory, which includes certain value judgements made by the authors themselves. The main reference is made to the scientific community and to socially agreed documents." In other words,

they start from a shared idea of basic values. The recurrent nego-
tiations, in UN international conferences, over clear definitions
of these basic values, indicate not only the complexity but the
fragility of the consensus around them.

This acknowledgement, however, may suggest another way
of looking at social exclusion discourse at national and international levels: social exclusion is possibly much more a social policy
concept than a theoretical and research one. In the words of
Paugam (1996) that we cited at the beginning of this chapter, the
concept of social exclusion is a means for a society to assess its
performance and its risks with regard to social cohesion and individuals' well-being. As such, its meaning is not fixed and across
the board. Rather it is constructed in the specific patterns of a
community and state, in negotiated understandings about rights
and obligations, membership, and autonomy. The social exclusion
discourse as a policy discourse is part of this process of construction and negotiation. From this point of view, the existence of a
supranational discourse on social exclusion, in research but also—
possibly more importantly—in policymaking, is a way of expand-
ing, rather than simply imposing, basic shared values and standards.

Notes

1. In 1986, at the conclusion of the Second Anti-Poverty Program,
the European Observatory on Policies to Combat Social Exclusion was
instituted. When devising its Fourth Anti-Poverty Program (which was
never launched due to the opposition of some countries), the Commission explicitly stated that this would be a program against social exclusion, not "merely" against poverty (see Commission of the European
Communities 1993a, 1993b, 1993c; Robbins 1993). Social exclusion is
also the concept used in the framework of Targeted Social Economic
Research and in the Fifth Framework Research Program. The concept is
also used by Eurostat in its analysis of Europanel data, in which it also
attempts to develop a complex analytic framework (see Mejer 2000).

2. According to Fassin (1996), all three paradigms are mental maps,
with different interpretations of the basic divisions in society: high/low

in the United States (and partly the UK), center/periphery in Latin America, in/out in France.

3. In the latter meaning, the shift in focus from poverty to social exclusion may not simply represent a richer conceptual framework. It may also represent a shift in public discourse and concern: from concern about inequality in granting access to crucial resources to concern about social integration; from concern about living conditions and options to concern about social cohesion; from concern about the need to provide options and resources to concern about the need to keep in check deviant and socially dangerous behaviors; from concern about the adequacy of social protection to concern about the risks of social protection; from concern about the causes of unemployment to concern about the personal characteristics of the unemployed that may keep them from obtaining work.

4. I use the term "welfare regimes" rather than "welfare state," because the former implies the existence of a plurality of actors, and different balances among them, through which individual and household welfare and protection may be achieved. I think that this focus on interrelationship and changing balance between different actors and agencies is the main contribution of Esping Andersen's seminal work (1990), which stands even after the many criticisms addressed to it. Esping Andersen, in his most recent work (1999)—acknowledging some of these critiques—has further elaborated upon the crucial role of the family and its gender relations, both in the solutions offered and in the problems posed by the different regimes.

5. I rely here partly on an article I wrote with Mary Daly (Daly and Saraceno 2002).

6. According to Kuhn, a paradigm is "a constellation of beliefs, values, techniques and so on shared by the members of a given community" (Kuhn 1970, p. 175).

7. See Levitas (1998) for an alternative set of discourses on social exclusion. In the context of the British case, she identifies the following three discourses: a *redistributionist* discourse, the prime concern of which is poverty; a *moral underclass* discourse, which centers on moral and behavioral inadequacies of excluded people; and a *social integrationist* discourse, which focuses on paid work.

8. Although the term "social exclusion" gained popularity first and foremost in France, from where it was imported to other countries and languages, (e.g., Frétigué 1999), even in France it gained popularity only

in the mid-1980s, as an outcome of the concern for growing unemployment, instability of jobs, and the emergence of the so-called "new poverty." Previously, the term—first introduced by Lenoir (1974)—was strongly contested on political grounds, and in any case applied only to groups and phenomena perceived as marginal (see Paugam 1996, pp. 8–16; Frétigué 1999, chap. 3).

9. It is interesting that in France, where both the notion of social exclusion and its policy counterpart "insertion" were first and most thoroughly developed, the latter remains a very contested and indefinite term and practice, as many observers keep pointing out. See Belorgey (1996) and Barbier (1998).

10. This was first developed in Germany by Glotz (1984).

11. The phenomenon of the working poor is a paradox within the liberal paradigm, because those in paid work by definition are performing their duties, but are no better off for it. They represent the recurrent problem of the "deserving poor." It is possibly no accident that it is within this paradigm that proposals and practices for subsidizing low paid/low skilled jobs are most developed (starting with OECD economists), often as an alternative to minimum income provisions.

12. Leisering and Leibfried (1999) suggest that the concept of risk society developed by Beck (1992) is a better basis for social policies which prevent poverty and social exclusion in contemporary societies than concepts of the underclass or the two-thirds society.

13. These data are also confirmed by another targeted socioeconomic research study, based on a sample of fifty qualitative interviews with unemployed youth in each of six European countries: the Youth Unemployment and Social Exclusion project. See Kieselbach, T. et al. 2000.

14. Recent longitudinal research has challenged simplistic views concerning the generation of welfare dependency. Studies on welfare recipients in the UK and Germany, for instance, have offered no evidence of large numbers of people adopting social assistance as a permanent way of life. People become long-term recipients because they have characteristics that render them more vulnerable in the labor market, although these characteristics may vary according to the national context: for example, single motherhood in the UK and long-term male unemployment in Germany. At the same time, receiving social assistance may be part of a wider middle-term strategy towards strengthening one's own resources and capabilities and/or re-orienting one's own life. (Walker

and Shaw 1998; Leisering and Leibfried 1999; Leisering and Walker 1998).

15. The socially assisted may be taken as being fairly representative of the poor, only in so far as social assistance is universal. This is not always the case, not even in Europe. Thus, the degree to which these and other types are present is largely dependent on the degree of universality, and of generosity, of a given social assistance system. This issue has been the focus of a comparative study funded by the EU under the TSER program, coordinated by the author (Saraceno 2002).

16. Debating the new interest in and acknowledgement of "differences," Taylor (1998) points to a similar risk. He claims that in contemporary social policy, the group and community characteristics that are of interest are those that distinguish the positively perceived universals from some specific negatives—or the included, integrated citizen from the excluded alien.

17. For instance, there is a wide criticism of Europanel data on income and poverty, particularly from the point of view of representativity, because the national samples are small and the number of poor within them is even smaller.

18. Berman and Phillips (2000) point out that their list of indicators for all four dimensions greatly overlaps with the list of the OECD indicators, except for the powerment/disempowerment dimension.

19. According to these authors there are basic human needs, comprising physical health and human autonomy. A number of intermediate needs, which are required to meet the basic needs, are identified. They include: adequate nutrition, housing, nonhazardous work and physical environment, healthcare, security in childhood, significant primary relationships, physical and economic security, safe birth control and childbearing, and basic education.

References

Abrahmson, P. (1997). "Combating Poverty and Social Exclusion in Europe." In *The Social Quality of Europe,* ed. W. Beck, L. van der Maesen, and A. Walker. The Hague: Kluwer Law International.

Aillet, V. (1997/1998). "La orce symbolique de l'allocation de parent isolé." *Recherches et previsions* 50–51 (December 1997–March 1998): 7–16.

Allmendinger, J., H. Brückner, and E. Brückner. (1991). "The Production of Gender Disparities over the Life Course and Their Effects in Old Age—Results from the West German Life History Study." In *Age, Work and Social Security,* ed. A. B. Atkinson and M. Rein. New York: St. Martin's Press.

Atkinson, A. B. (1998a). *Poverty in Europe.* Oxford: Blackwell.

———. (1998b). "Social Exclusion: Poverty and Unemployment." In *Exclusion, Employment and Opportunity,* ed. A. B. Atkinson and J. Hills. London: CASE Publications.

Bane, M. J., and D. T. Ellwood. (1986). "Slipping Into and Out of Poverty: The Dynamics of Spells." *Journal of Human Resources* 21: 1–23.

———. (1994). *Welfare Realities: From Rhetoric to Reform.* Cambridge, Mass.: Harvard University Press.

Barbier, J. C. (1996) "Comparer insertion et workfare." *Revue Française des affaires sociales* 4 (October–December): 7–26.

———. (1998). "La logica del workfare in Europa e negli Stati Uniti: i limiti delle analisi globali." *Assistenza sociale* 1 (January–March): 15–40.

Beck, M., and H. Seewald. (1994). "Zur Reform der amtlichen Sozialhilfestatistik." *Nachrichtendienst des Deutschen Vereins für öffentliche und private Fürsorge* 74: 27–31.

Beck, U. (1992). *Risk Society: Towards a New Modernity.* Newbury Park, Calif.: Sage Publications.

Beck, W., L. van der Maesen, and A. Walker, eds. (1997). *The Social Quality of Europe.* The Hague: Kluwer Law International.

Belorgey, J. M. (1996). "Pour renouer avec l'esprit initial du RMI." In "Vers un revenu minimum inconditionne." *Revue du MAUSS semestrielle* 7 (1): 297–99.

Berman, Y., and D. Phillips. (2000). "Indicators of Social Quality and Social Exclusion at National and Community Level." *Social Indicators Research* 50: 329–50.

Bradshaw, J. (2001). "Poverty: The Outcomes for Children." In *Indicators of Progress: A Discussion of Approaches to Monitor the Government's Strategy to Tackle Poverty and Social Exclusion*. London: CASE Publications.

Castel, R. (1995). *Les metamorphoses de la question sociale*. Paris: Editions Fayard.

Chamberlayne, P. (1997). "Social Exclusion: Sociological Traditions and National Contexts."

Commission of the European Communities. (1993a). "Towards a Europe of Solidarity: Intensifying the Fight against Social Exclusion, Fostering Integration." Communication from the Commission. Brussels: Author.

———. (1993b). *The Future of Social Policy: Options for the Union. A Green Paper*. Brussels: DGV.

———. (1993c). *Social Protection in Europe*. Brussels: DGV

———. (2000). "Building an Inclusive Europe." Communication from the Commission. Brussels: Author.

Commissione di Indagine sulla Povertà. (1985). *La povertà in Italia*. Rome: Poligrafico dello Stato.

Crouch, C. (1999). *Social Change in Western Europe*. Oxford: Oxford University Press.

Dahrendorf, R. (1984). *The Modern Social Conflict: An Essay on the Politics of Liberty*. London: Weidenfeld and Nicolson.

Daly, M. (1999). "The Functioning Family: Catholicism and Social Policy in Germany and Ireland." *Comparative Social Research* 18: 105–33.

Daly, M., and C. Saraceno. (2002). "Social Exclusion and Gender Relations." In *Contested Concepts in Gender and Social Politics*, ed. B. Hobson, J. Lewis, and B. Siim. Cheltenham, UK: Edward Elgar.

Delanty, G. (1998). "Social Theory and European Transformation: Is There a European Society?" *Sociological Research on Line*. Available at: www.socres.online.org.uk/socresonline/3/1/1

Doyal, L., and I. Gough. (1991). *A Theory of Human Need*. London: Macmillan.

Duncan, G. J. (1984). *Years of Poverty, Years of Plenty: The Changing Economic Fortunes of American Workers and Families*. Ann Arbor, Mich.: Institute for Social Research.

Esping Andersen, G. (1990). *Three Worlds of Welfare Capitalism*. Cambridge: Polity Press.

———. (1999). *Social Foundations of Post-Industrial Economies*. Oxford: Oxford University Press.

Fassin, D. (1996). "Exclusion, underclass, marginalidad. Figures contemporaines de la pauvreté urbaine en France, aux Etats Unis et en Amerique Latine." *Revue Française de Sociologie* 36 (1).

Frétigué, C. (1999). *Sociologie de l'éxclusion.* Paris: L'Harmattan.

Gallie, D. (1999). "Unemployment and Social Exclusion in the European Union." In *European Societies* 1(2): 139–67.

Gallie, D., and S. Paugam, eds. (2000). *Welfare Regimes and the Experience of Unemployment in Europe.* Oxford: Oxford University Press.

Glatzer, W., and H.-J. Krupp. (1975). "Soziale Indikatoren des Einkommens und seiner Verteilung in der Bundesrepublik Deutschland." In *Soziale Indikatoren. Konzepte und Forschungsansätze III,* ed. W. Zapft. Frankfurt-am-Main, Germany: Campus.

Glotz, P. (1984). *Die Arbeit der Zuspitzung: Über die Organisation einer regierungsefähigen Linken.* Berlin: Siedler.

Goodin, R. (1996)."Inclusion and Exclusion." *European Journal of Sociology* 37 (1): 343–71.

Haataja, A. (1999). "Unemployment, Employment and Poverty." In *European Societies* 1 (2): 169–96.

Harker, L. (2001). "Measuring Wider Aspects of Poverty and Social Exclusion." In *Indicators of Progress: A Discussion of Approaches to Monitor the Government's Strategy to Tackle Poverty and Social Exclusion.* London: CASE Publications.

Joshi, H. (1989). "The Cash Opportunity Costs of Childbearing: An Approach to Estimation Using British Data." *Population Studies* 6.

Kieselbach, T., Beelman, G., Titzel, A., and Traiser, U. (2000). *Long-Term Unemployed Youth: A Qualitative Study on Risk of Social Exclusion in Six European Countries.* Brussels: Commission on the European Communities, DGXXII.

Kuhn, T. (1970). *The Structure of Scientific Revolutions,* 2nd edition. Chicago: University of Chicago Press.

Leisering, L., and S. Leibfried. (1999). *Time and Poverty in Western Welfare States: United Germany in Perspective.* Cambridge: Cambridge University Press.

Leisering, L., and R. Walker. (1998). "Making the Future: From Dynamics to Policy Agendas." In *The Dynamics of Modern Society: Poverty, Policy and Welfare,* ed. L. Leisering and R. Walker. Bristol, UK: Policy Press.

Lenoir, R. (1974). *Les exclus, un Français sur dix.* Paris: Le Seuil.

Levitas, R. (1998). *The Inclusive Society? Social Exclusion and New Labour.* London: Macmillan.

Mejer, L. (2000). "Social Exclusion in the European Union Member States." *Statistics in Focus,* Theme 3 (January 2000).

Organisation for Economic Co-operation and Development. (1998). *Employment Outlook.* Paris: Author.

Okin, S. (1989). *Justice and the Family.* New York: Basic Books.

Paugam, S. (1996). "Introduction: la constitution d'un paradigme." In *L'exclusion. L'etat des savoirs,* ed. S. Paugam. Paris: La Découverte.

————. (1997). *La disqualification sociale.* Paris: PUF Press

Robbins, D. (1993). *Social Europe: Towards a Europe of Solidarity.* Brussels: European Union, GDV.

Room, G. (1995). "Poverty in Europe: Competing Paradigms of Analysis." *Policy and Politics* 23(2): 103–113.

Room, G. et al. (1992). *Observatory on National Policies to Combat Social Exclusion.* Second Annual Report. Brussels: Commission of the European Communities.

Rosanvallon, P. (1995). *La nouvelle question sociale.* Paris: Le Seuil.

Rothenbacher, F. (1998). "European Scientific Socio-Economic Reporting: State and Possibilities of Development." *Social Indicators Research* 44: 291–328.

Rowntree, B. S. (1901). *Poverty: A Study of Town Life.* London: Thomas Nelson.

Rustin, M., and V. Rix. (1997). "Anglo-Saxon Individualism and Its Vicissitudes: Social Exclusion in Britain." In *Social Strategies in Risk Societies,* SOSTRIS Working Paper 1. London: University of East London.

Sahgal, G., and N. Yuval Davis, eds. (1992). *Refusing Holy Orders: Women and Fundamentalism in Britain.* London: Virago.

Saraceno, C. (1997). "Family Change, Family Policies and the Restructuring of Welfare." In *Family, Market and Community,* Social Policy Studies 21. Paris: Organisation for Economic Co-operation and Development.

————. (2000). "Italian Families under Economic Stress: The Impact of Social Policies." *Labour,* March.

————, ed. (2002). *Social Assistance Dynamics in Europe: National and Local Welfare Regimes.* Bristol, UK: Policy Press..

Sen, A. (1995a). *Commodities and Capabilities.* Amsterdam: North Holland.

————. (1995b). "Well-Being, Agency and Freedom: The Dewey Lectures, 1994." *Journal of Philosophy* 82(4): 169-221.

Silver, H. (1994). "Social Exclusion and Social Solidarity: The Three

Paradigms." *International Labour Review* 133(5–6): 531–78.

Smith, D. (1992). *Understanding the Underclass.* London: Policy Studies Institute.

Social Strategies in Risk Societies (SOSTRIS). (1997). *Social Strategies in Risk Societies,* SOSTRIS Working Paper 1. London: University of East London.

Spicker, P. (1997). "Exclusion." *Journal of Common Market Studies* 35(1): 133–43.

Svetlik, I. (2000). "Some Conceptual and Operational Considerations on the Social Quality of Europe." *European Journal of Social Quality* 1(1–2): 74–89.

Taylor, D. (1998). "Social Identity and Social Policy: Engagements with Post-Modern Theory." *Journal of Social Policy* 27: 329–50.

Touraine, A. (1991). "Face à l'exlusion." in *Citoynneté et urbanité.* Paris: Esprit.

———. (1992). "Inegalités de la société industrielle, exclusion du marché." In *Justice sociale et inégalité,* ed. J. Affichard and J. B. de Foucauld. Paris: Esprit.

Townsend, P. (1979). *Poverty in the United Kingdom.* Harmondsworth, UK: Penguin.

Van Dreuth A., T. Knijn, and J. Lewis. (1999). "Sources of Income for Lone Mother Families: Policy Changes in Britain and the Netherlands and the Experiences of Divorced Women." *Journal of Social Policy* 28 (October): 619–41.

Vogel, J. (1994). "Social Indicators and Social Reporting." *Statistical Journal of the United Nations* 11: 241–60.

Walker, R., and A. Shaw. (1998). "Escaping from Social Assistance in Great Britain." In *The Dynamics of Modern Society: Poverty, Policy and Welfare,* ed. L. Leisering and R. Walker. Bristol, UK: Policy Press.

Weitzman, L. (1985). *The Divorce Revolution: The Unexpected Social and Economic Consequences For Women and Children in America.* New York: Free Press.

Wilson, W. J. (1987). *The Truly Disadvantaged: The Inner City, the Underclass and Public Policy.* Chicago: University of Chicago Press.

Yuval Davis, N. (1996). "Women, Citizenship and Difference." Paper given at the Conference on Women and Citizenship, University of Greenwich, Greenwich, UK, July 16–18.

Against the Grain: "Social Exclusion" and American Political Culture

Janet C. Gornick

Introduction

One of the aims of the conference on social exclusion and children was to expose American social welfare researchers and policymakers to the European "social exclusion" framework, and to explore its meaning and applicability in a U.S. context. However, integrating social exclusion into research and policy analysis in the United States is not an insubstantial task, for two reasons.

First, the United States is characterized by a number of economic, demographic, and institutional realities that are, to some extent, unique. These differences hinder the task of importing European concepts and policies to the U.S., partly because they necessitate adjustments to the European framework, and partly because they shore up Americans' conviction that European perspectives are irrelevant in the United States. Second, and more significant, some of the defining elements of social exclusion cut against the grain of American political culture. ("Political culture" refers to the distinctive and patterned ways that people think about how political and economic life ought to be arranged.)

My aim here is to explore the barriers that impede "bringing social exclusion to the United States" and, in the process, to improve the prospects for meaningful dialogue between Americans and Europeans.

Multiple Paradigms of Exclusion: Social Solidarity and Social Rights

As Chiara Saraceno establishes in this volume, there are multiple interpretations of "social exclusion"—interpretations that vary over time and across place.[1] The concept of social exclusion emerged in the 1960s in France, where the term was coined and popularized in 1974 by Rene Lenoir, Secretary of State for Social Action in the Chirac government. According to Silver (1994), the original French usage of social exclusion stressed a "rupture of the social bond," that is, a breakdown in the tie between the individual and society. Rooted in French Republicanism, this construction of exclusion developed partly in opposition to British notions of poverty, and replaced individualistic concepts of poverty with concerns about fractured social solidarity. As Saraceno phrases it here, exclusion, from the French perspective, is equated with the "destruction of patterns of belonging."

In the original French view, social exclusion was largely attributable to failures of the state: excluded persons fell into categories that lacked social insurance protection. Therefore, the exclusion paradigm had direct implications for social policy reform. As Silver argues (1995), the exclusion framework led to demands for "a new personalized, participatory welfare state," one that would "rest on new principles of social cohesion, insertion, sharing and integration" (p. 64). The embrace of the exclusion concept in France laid the groundwork for new social programs introduced in the 1980s, including the initiation of the *revenue minimum d'insertion* (RMI, or minimum income). Advocates of the RMI on both the left and right adopted the language of solidarity and social ties (Silver 1995).

After its introduction in France, the social exclusion framework spread across Europe and beyond. Several national and supranational research and policy efforts adopted social exclusion as an organizing principle, which led to its rapid popularization. European Union efforts incorporated varied paradigms of social exclusion—exclusion is now written into the Maastricht Treaty—and ideas about exclusion moved on to development studies and an embrace by both the United Nations and the International Labour Organization.

The European Community advanced the concept of social exclusion when it established, in 1990, the *European Observatory on National Policies to Combat Social Exclusion*. Perhaps most significant was that the Observatory located exclusion within the paradigm of citizenship rights, contending that social exclusion "can be analyzed in terms of the denial—or non-realization—of social rights." The concept of social rights is embedded in social democratic ideology, and pervades much of European welfare state scholarship and public discourse, especially in the Nordic countries.

Social rights were laid out in the influential work of T. H. Marshall (1950), who extended citizenship to encompass three sets of rights: civil, political, and social. Marshall understood the *civil* element of citizenship to include the rights necessary for individual freedom, including the rights to free speech, thought, and faith. His *political* element referred to the right to vote and to seek political office in free elections. By *social* rights, or the social element of citizenship, Marshall referred to "the right to share to the full in the social heritage and to live the life of a civilized being according to the standards prevailing in the society" (pp. 10–11). In other words, Marshall's social rights grant individuals the right to economic welfare and social security—or, in popular terms, the right to live a decent life.

The social rights paradigm is different from the French notion of social solidarity; where the solidarity paradigm prizes group cohesion, the social rights paradigm seeks to alter power relations and equalize access. Yet there is commonality: like the solidarity paradigm, the social rights perspective has welfare state implications and is compatible with social exclusion. In social democratic thought, social rights justify the welfare state and, in turn, are granted and secured by law through the welfare state. Pateman (1988), for example, observes that "the moral basis of the welfare state lies in the provision of resources for . . . the 'social rights' of democratic citizenship" (p. 235). As Saraceno explains in this volume: "inclusion occurs mainly through access by outsiders to citizenship rights, which in turn must be monitored for their exclusionary potential." Again, the state can both include and exclude.

Social exclusion in most European settings can be located in relation to one or both of these paradigms: social solidarity on the one hand, and social democracy and social rights on the other. Silver (1994) observes that these paradigms are fluid, and that national discourses are often centered on internal debates between them. She notes that in France today, while the solidarity paradigm remains dominant, tensions between the solidarity and social democratic paradigms shape contemporary debates. Likewise with supranational discourses: Saraceno reports here that EU projects and programs have shifted back and forth between these paradigms, at times combining them.

While social exclusion is framed in a multitude of ways, drawing on diverse intellectual traditions, there are universal themes that crosscut nearly all usages. First, social exclusion is characterized as a process; it is more than an outcome or a collection of outcomes.[2] Second, exclusion is multidimensional and, as Saraceno notes, "methodologically plural." Third, exclusion is always relational, in other words, an individual or group must be excluded from some larger entity. Fourth, the primary causal factors underlying exclusion are found outside the excluded individual or group; according to Atkinson (1998), social exclusion "happens to you"; at the same time, inclusion emphasizes reciprocity.[3] Finally, social exclusion generally connotes some degree of permanence; it is a long-term affair.

"Social Exclusion" in the United States: Against the Grain

In the United States, most social welfare scholars have steered clear of the social exclusion framework altogether. While Silver (1995) identifies a few Americans who adopted discourses of exclusion—for example, Harrington (1962), Rainwater (1974), and Katz (1989)—recent mentions of social exclusion in American research and policy analysis are few and far between. Micklewright (this volume) searched for the term "social exclusion" in a variety of U.S. studies of child well-being, poverty, and welfare reform—and found it nowhere.

Why has the concept of social exclusion remained so marginalized in American social policy research and policy analysis? One reason is that the empirical realities that characterize the United States are, in some ways, unique. Compared to most European countries, Americans live with low wages, exorbitant poverty rates, extreme inequality, deeply rooted racial divisiveness, and high rates of single parenting. These realities are compounded by a limited and fragmented governmental system, weak unions, and a relatively unregulated market. Combating exclusion calls for inclusion, and inclusion in the United States is all the more complex in the context of diversity, economic insecurity and, by European standards, an unorganized labor force and a highly decentralized state.

Yet proponents of the exclusion concept face a more formidable barrier in the United States: fundamental elements of exclusion—the relativity, the external causation, the long time horizon—are at odds with aspects of American political culture. While public discourse in the United States *can* embrace process over outcomes (consider U.S. perspectives on equality), other elements of American political culture fit more poorly. Individualism and autonomy, core American ideals, are hard to reconcile with the relational perspective, and ideas about self-reliance mesh badly with locating the cause of hardship outside the individual. In addition, the promise of mobility, another cornerstone of American political culture, is hard to integrate with the component of social exclusion that connotes a long-term condition.

The poor fit of exclusion with American political culture is even more stark when we consider the two dominant European paradigms: social solidarity and social rights. Social solidarity is not a core value for most contemporary Americans. Although American political culture contains some communitarian elements, especially in conjunction with religious practice, individual and family responsibility are generally valued over social solidarity. The fit between American political culture and the social rights paradigm is even more problematic. While American political culture reveres *negative* rights—such as the right to be free of government interference—Americans are collectively skeptical of *positive* rights, which imply the right to have one's needs met, first and foremost, by the state.[4]

U.S. resistance to social and economic rights runs deep.[5] Bruce Porter, of the Canadian Center for Equality, observed in a 1991 paper on social rights and citizenship: "The United States has been and remains quite isolated internationally in opposing the recognition of social and economic rights." Porter notes that social and economic rights were originally contained in the 1948 Universal Declaration of Human Rights, along with civil and political rights. However, on the insistence of the United States, social and economic rights were excised and later placed in the separate International Covenant on Economic, Social and Cultural Rights. The United States has steadfastly refused to ratify the Covenant.

Long-standing struggles over economic rights in the United States have also taken place domestically. The U.S. Constitution did not lay a foundation for economic rights—as constitutions have in other countries—and the courts have ruled that "the federal government has no affirmative constitutional obligation to meet the material needs of its children and poor adults" (Summitt 2001). There are, however, other legal foundations for economic rights in the United States. Some economic rights have been legislated: for example, the Social Security Act of 1935 established legal entitlements to income transfers (for some categories), and the Fair Labor Standards Act of 1938 granted the right to earn a minimum wage. Moreover, some state constitutions (e.g., New York's) include an obligation to care for the needy. However, the U.S. courts have been a limiting factor, traditionally restricting the scope and application of both statutory rights and constitutional provisions (Summitt 2001).

American Alternatives: Poverty and the Underclass

The embrace of the social exclusion concept in the United States has been limited by real differences between the United States and Europe, exaggerated perceptions of American exceptionalism, and incompatible elements in political culture—especially the rejection of social and economic rights. This raises two questions: What have Americans pondered and measured instead? What is lost by rejecting the concept of exclusion?

Throughout the twentieth century, two interrelated American concepts have dominated social welfare research and related policy debates: those of poverty and the underclass. Americans have long turned their attention to poverty—in particular to *absolute poverty*, which assesses family resources compared to a threshold based on estimated need. Two recent developments have expanded U.S. poverty research. First, poverty scholars have theorized and operationalized new poverty measures: alternative measures extend the traditional indicator, typically by capturing a wider basket of resources and accounting for non-elective expenses. Second, spurred partly by expanded data availability, an ongoing wave of scholarship is complementing poverty measures with indicators of individual and family hardship, such as food insecurity, poor quality housing, and inadequate health care. While the new poverty measures and hardship indicators are useful—they add dimensions beyond income—they are fundamentally like their predecessors, measuring well-being against an absolute standard.

Clearly, it is imperative that U.S. researchers and policymakers continue to grapple with poverty and hardship from all angles: the underlying causes, the distribution, and the short- and long-term consequences. At the same time, the American preoccupation with poverty and hardship leaves core components of social exclusion unexamined. For the most part, analyses of poverty and hardship avoid questions of process; they are outcomes. Poverty and hardship also depart from dominant notions of social exclusion, to the extent that they are measured as static conditions; while dynamics have garnered much attention in recent years, point-in-time head counts remain commonplace.

The other American concept that falls close to European perspectives on social exclusion is that of the underclass. The term is often attributed to Gunnar Myrdal, who used it non-pejoratively to refer to those who had failed to benefit from the postwar economic boom because they lacked education and skills. Its usage surged in the United States in the 1980s, reviving old "culture of poverty" debates and finding proponents on both left and right. In American hands, Myrdal's economic determinism was weakened, and the concept was racialized. During the American "welfare wars," conservatives embraced the underclass idea and equated it with welfare dependency.

Like the concept of social exclusion, the concept of the underclass can be construed in diverse ways; it has been invoked to describe individuals, categories of individuals, behaviors, residential areas, and even structural barriers. Yet, in most formulations, the underclass perspective is closer to the exclusion framework than are the concepts of poverty and hardship. First, most—if not all—conceptions of the underclass are relational. Like "exclusion," especially the classic French interpretation, "the underclass" invokes broken or limited ties; both emphasize "unbelonging." The underclass is seen as disconnected, or left behind, from core institutions: the labor market, family, community, and political structures. Second, the underclass concept implies a *dynamic* component. Like the excluded, members of the underclass are characterized less by current condition and more by long-term prospects; the bleakness of the future is a common theme in their experience. Furthermore, the notion of cumulative disadvantage in members of the underclass is pervasive, as is characteristic of the excluded.

Nevertheless, replacing "social exclusion" with "the underclass," alongside poverty and material hardship, leaves American researchers and policy analysts a substantial distance from European exclusion paradigms. As a result, much is lost—intellectually and perhaps politically. The American alternatives differ from exclusion in at least three ways, and each has a cost.

First, the bar is set low in the United States. Poverty, hardship, and underclass membership limit American analysts, for the most part, to conditions that are more dire than those implied by most European conceptions of exclusion. The pull towards the bottom of the distribution is consistent with American ideas about social protections, public and private. The standard American view of social provisions implies that society's obligations are fulfilled once we lift our poorest citizens off the floor. Comparativists often observe that as Europeans ponder inclusion and "belongingness," Americans think more narrowly about poverty and deprivation. That characterization, albeit oversimplified, is consistent with much cross-national research on political culture and public opinion.

Second, American alternatives to exclusion often ignore questions about the processes through with societies exclude individuals. Undoubtedly, many American poverty analysts have theorized and measured the effects of social (macro-) factors on individual (micro-) outcomes. The key point is that the phenomena themselves—poverty, and even the underclass—do not *necessitate* inquiries about macro-level factors and processes, as social exclusion does *a priori*. Not surprisingly, many American scholars of poverty, hardship, and the underclass sidestep social etiology altogether.

Finally—and perhaps most significantly—American alternatives to exclusion fail to fully examine the role of government. While the European paradigms typically attribute exclusion to identifiable failures of the state, the American substitutes offer much less in the way of a critical policy framework. At times, American analyses of poverty and deprivation seem to focus attention everywhere but on social or labor market policy. (Consider the most visible anti-poverty strategy in the United States today: a concerted effort to alter poor people's marriage patterns.) The inclusionary potential of social policy, as well as its exclusionary features, too often escape scrutiny. Clearly, Americans reject state interventions partly because of a long-standing hostility towards government. But the absence of an intellectual framework that explicitly locates individuals, as does the exclusion framework, in relation to the states that govern them, can only compound Americans' tendency to underplay state solutions to poverty and hardship.

Conclusion

There is little question that daunting barriers would block any attempt to import European social exclusion paradigms to the United States wholesale. Clearly, the social rights perspective is sharply at odds with American political culture. The likelihood that Americans will embrace a framework of social rights is, for all intents and purposes, infinitesimal—barring the emergence of highly imaginative and extraordinarily effective political leadership.

Americans are more likely to accept an exclusion paradigm that invokes a breakdown in the ties between individuals and society. While social solidarity is not a core value in the dominant American political culture, the idea that everyone should "belong" resonates with many. Recent calls to "leave no child behind," now coming from both the left and the right, are based on Americans' valuing some variant of belongingness.[6]

American social welfare researchers and policy analysts would do well to work through the European exclusion paradigms and extract core components—the raised bar, the relational and process aspects, and most certainly the critical perspective on social policy—while, perhaps, setting aside the language of social exclusion. In this volume, Saraceno cites Paugam (1996), who wrote that "social exclusion is the paradigm on the basis of which our society becomes aware of its own dysfunctions and looks, possibly through confusion and urgency, for solutions." If European exclusion paradigms could inspire American scholars to look for solutions through new lenses, the intellectual and political benefits could be substantial.

Notes

1. For analyses of the multiple meanings of social exclusion, see Saraceno, Micklewright, Evans and others in this volume; also see Percy-Smith (2000) and Phipps and Curtis (2001). In two often-cited articles, Silver (1994, 1995) contrasts three paradigms of social exclusion

(Republicanism, social democracy, and liberalism), and locates each in a distinct intellectual tradition.

2. Perhaps most important in the U.S. context is that exclusion is always seen as distinct from poverty and other measures of individual or family resources. As Saraceno clarifies, "Social exclusion emphasizes participation, involvement, and the customary way of life, as against average income or basic needs/baskets of goods."

3. Saraceno clarifies that the reciprocity is of a certain kind: French exclusion discourse advocates a conception of reciprocity that stresses the community's responsibility as much as the recipient's agency. "Although in practice this conception of reciprocity, too, results in an asymmetrical relationship, it seeks to keep in check the strong asymmetry of the traditional social assistance relationship. Thus, the French idea of social exclusion does not principally emphasize recipients' obligations…but rather emphasizes their agency and negotiating power."

4. Americans do prize equality, but in a distinctly American way. In his analysis of American political culture in comparative perspective, Wilson (1997) writes of the United States:

> Equality is conceived of . . . in a manner that is congruent with negative rights. Scant support exists for the idea that the government should make rewards more equal or even guarantee a minimum annual income. Instead, Americans have interpreted equality as a starting condition from which subsequent inequality develops as the consequence of differences in strength of individual character. Unlike societies that presuppose inherent original inequalities and the need to structure the social order so that groups are made equal, Americans believe than men [sic] are created equal and that removing social barriers will allow individuals to maximize their potential through competition (p. 494).

5. Note that in the European citizenship literature, the terms "social rights" and "social and economic rights" are generally used interchangeably. Americans tend to refer to both as "economic rights."

6. I thank Larry Aber for linking the language of "leave no child behind" to social exclusion. The phrase was long associated with the Children's Defense Fund; George W. Bush appropriated the language during the 2000 U.S. presidential campaign.

References

Atkinson, A. (1998). *Poverty in Europe.* Oxford: Blackwell.

Harrington, M. (1962). *The Other America: Poverty in the United States.* Baltimore: Penguin.

Katz, M. (1989). *The Undeserving Poor.* New York: Pantheon.

Marshall, T. H. (1950). *Citizenship and Social Class.* Cambridge: Cambridge University Press.

Pateman, C. (1988). "The Patriarchal Welfare State." In *Democracy and the Welfare State*, ed. A. Gutman. Princeton, N.J.: Princeton University Press.

Percy-Smith, J. (2000). "Introduction: The Contours of Social Exclusion." In *Policy Responses to Social Exclusion: Towards Inclusion?*, ed. J. Percy-Smith. Philadelphia: Open University Press.

Phipps, S., and L. Curtis. (2001). "The Social Exclusion of Children in North America." Halifax, Nova Scotia, Canada: Dalhousie University Economics Department. Processed.

Porter, B. (1991). "Social and Economic Rights and Citizenship." Paper prepared for the Institute for Research and Public Policy, Victoria, British Columbia, Canada. Available at: www.equalityrights.org/cera/citizen.

Rainwater, L. (1974). *What Money Buys: Inequality and the Social Meaning of Income.* New York: Basic Books.

Silver, H. (1995). "Reconceptualizing Social Disadvantage: Three Paradigms of Social Exclusion." In *Social Exclusion: Rhetoric, Reality, Responses*, ed. G. Rodgers, C. Gore, and J. B. Figueiredo. Geneva: ILO Publications.

———. (1994). "Social Exclusion and Social Solidarity: The Three Paradigms." *International Labour Review* 133(5/6): 531–78.

Summitt, A. (2001). "The Case for Economic Rights." Detroit, Mich.: Guild Law Center for Economic and Social Justice. Available at: www.sugarlaw.org/projects/ecobill/caseforEBR.

Wilson, R. (1997). "American Political Culture in Comparative Perspective." *Political Psychology* 18(2): 483–502.

Social Exclusion and Children: A European View for a U.S. Debate [1]

John Micklewright

Introduction

"How has the concept of social exclusion been applied to the situation of children in Europe?" I confess to departing in three ways from this brief from the conference organizers.

First, I try to deal with the more fundamental issue of how the concept *should* be applied to children, as well as how it has been, and discuss whether this is worth doing at all. I hope this will interest European readers, as well as those in the United States, for whom the first version of the paper was intended.

Second, my coverage of applications in Europe is limited. I refer mainly to the use of the concept by the institutions of the European Union (EU) and by the UK government. These examples are certainly not representative of all such cases in Europe, either at the official level or in academia (although I do refer to a few of the latter). Nor does the UK have a special claim to coverage as the birthplace of the concept (which was, in fact, France). Nevertheless, if one comes to the European debate afresh, the EU and the UK are perhaps interesting because of the sheer prominence that the concept of exclusion now has in official pronouncements on living standards. The March 2000 meeting of the fifteen EU heads of government (the European Council) declared that " the number of people living below the poverty line and in social exclusion in the Union is unacceptable." Combating social exclusion is explicitly mentioned in the Amsterdam Treaty on Union. The UK under "New Labour " now has an annual government report on poverty and social exclusion, a Social Exclusion Unit reporting directly to the prime minister, and various other initiatives that stress problems of exclusion and the need for an inclusive society.[2]

The EU may hold some special interest for a U.S. audience because of its nature as a "union" of member states, with the conflicts that implies between governments at different levels, and the questions it raises about the definition of the society from which an individual may be excluded. The UK may also be of particular interest on the subject of social exclusion and children, because of the special position given to children by the Labour government in pronouncements and policies on both exclusion and poverty. Prime Minister Blair has vowed to end child poverty within twenty years, and Finance Minister Brown has taken a prominent role in the fight, labeling child poverty "a scar on the nation's soul."

Third, I have not confined myself to Europe. Rather than risk writing in a vacuum, I have tried to consider explicitly the possible application of the concept of social exclusion to the position of children in the United States. This is the subject of the last section of the chapter, where I connect back to themes discussed in earlier sections. Again, I hope that European readers may find that this stimulates them to reflect on the definition and application of the concept in their own countries.

The last thing I should note at the outset is that although I talk a great deal about measurement, I concentrate on ideas rather than numbers. I have resisted the temptation to fill up the chapter with tables comparing child well-being across Europe, whether from national analyses, those made by the EU, or those made by ourselves at UNICEF Innocenti Research Centre in our work on child well-being in industrialized countries.[3] In fact, this chapter contains no tables at all!

I begin with some discussion of the concept of social exclusion as applied in the EU and the UK to the population as a whole. What has it added, if anything, to the analysis of living standards and of policies affecting them? This is the subject of my section, "Notions of Social Exclusion in Europe." The child angle is the focus in the section, "The Child Dimension to 'Exclusion'." If we talk about exclusion of *children,* what particular aspects need to be considered, and does the current debate and analysis in the EU and the UK give sufficient recognition to them? By this point the chapter will display a rather fuzzy boundary between poverty and social exclusion, reflecting the application of the latter concept in practice, even if the two are (or can be argued to be) conceptually distinct.

Given the state of play in the United States on various topics—measurement of poverty, analysis of children's living standards, state versus federal responsibilities, welfare reform, "personal responsibility," politics and the economy—is there fertile ground for the discussion of social exclusion and children? Or, at least, does it seem so when viewed from Europe? These questions are addressed in the penultimate section, "Is the United States Ripe for 'Exclusion'?"

Notions of Social Exclusion in Europe

Chiara Saraceno's chapter gives an excellent account of the development of the concept of social exclusion in European thought, and of various lacunae that remain. But how has the concept been applied? The restriction of my discussion to the EU and to the UK must again be emphasized. I give no account, for example, of the French government's initiatives under an exclusion heading, such as the Revenu Minimum d'Insertion. (As already noted, France is the intellectual birthplace of the exclusion concept—see, for example, Renee Lenoir's 1974 work on *Les Exclus.*)

Social Exclusion in the UK

The UK government defines social exclusion as ". . . a shorthand term for what can happen when people or areas suffer from a combination of linked problems such as unemployment, poor skills, low incomes, poor housing, high crime environment, bad health and family breakdown" (Social Exclusion Unit 2001, p. 10).[4]

The words "can happen" are important. Social exclusion *can,* but does *not necessarily*, happen when there is a combination of the circumstances listed. Merely (!) suffering from the circumstances listed does not equate with being socially excluded: these are not sufficient conditions for exclusion. The circumstances mentioned are given only as examples, even if they are intended to cover many of the possibilities: hence, neither are they necessary conditions. Nor, in fact, is the fate that "can happen" actually described. So what we are left with is a description of examples of circumstances that may lead to exclusion, rather than a definition of exclusion itself—although it is fairly obvious that the implied fate behind the wording is one of being "shut out" from society in some sense.

This picking over of the UK government's description is not intended to ridicule the authors' chosen words. Rather, it is meant to illustrate that exclusion is a concept that defies clear definition and measurement—and that, as a result, is hard to use as a policy target in the conventional sense. Although the UK government's annual report on poverty and social exclusion contains a vast range of statistics on various dimensions of living standards, some of which are described in "The Child Dimension to 'Exclusion'," below, it does not try to count the number of excluded people, nor to indicate which of the chosen indicators relate to exclusion and which to poverty.

Social Exclusion in the EU

This lack of clear definition is found again in the EU's analyses of social exclusion. The concept has, in fact, a long history in EU parlance. As Tony Atkinson has noted: "Cynics have suggested that the term 'social exclusion' has been adopted by Brussels to appease previous Conservative governments of the United Kingdom, who believed neither that there was poverty in Britain nor that poverty was a proper concern of the European Commission" (Atkinson 1998, p. 1).

Whatever the genesis, the term appears to be here to stay in the EU, as the introduction to this chapter illustrates. The 1998

Eurostat Task Force on Social Exclusion and Poverty statistics considered social exclusion as ". . . a dynamic process, best described as descending levels: some disadvantages lead to some exclusion, which in turn leads to more disadvantages and more social exclusion and ends up with persistent multiple (deprivation) disadvantages. Individuals, households and spatial units can be excluded from access to resources like employment, health, education, social or political life" (Eurostat Task Force 1998, p. 25)

However, the Task Force did not define social exclusion precisely, arguing that this was not possible. Rather, it concluded that the statistical analysis of exclusion should start with those on lower incomes, on the grounds that this is where exclusion has the most severe consequences. It should then focus on the labor market given "the importance of employment as the core of the social tie, as the entrance to social protection, as it gives a social identity, social status, satisfaction, social contacts and prevents families from long term poverty." Finally, the analysis should consider the overlap between low income and a weak labor market position with various nonmonetary indicators of well-being, relating to dimensions such as skills and knowledge and access to health care, education, public transport, and state benefit systems—with both objective measures and subjective measures taken into account.

The Eurostat Task Force did not make recommendations and then look for data to implement them. The idea was—and is—that for practical purposes the European Community Household Panel (ECHP) would be used to investigate poverty and social exclusion on a comparable basis across EU member states. This important resource is an annual household panel survey operating in fourteen of the fifteen EU countries. ECHP started in 1993 and collects detailed information on nonmonetary indicators of deprivation, as well as information on incomes, the labor market, and standard demographic and household variables.

Eurostat has now started to publish detailed analyses based on its conception of social exclusion, notably with a report, *European Social Statistics: Income, Poverty and Social Exclusion* (Eurostat 2000). The chapter entitled "Social Exclusion" contains, for example, a series of tables showing the percentages of people in each country who cannot afford to eat meat or fish every second day, who cannot afford a week's holiday away from home each year, who cannot afford various durable goods, who report bad health, who meet friends or relatives less often than once a month, and so on. These tables distinguish between the poor, the non-poor, and the "persistently" poor—those who have been poor for three consecutive years. Other tables explore the links between these deprivations and the lack of work.

Note the implication in this form of presentation (and in the Task Force's conclusions that preceded it) that combinations of conditions constitute exclusion, as in the UK government's definition given earlier. Many commentators would disagree with this, however, arguing that one can be excluded as the result of a single condition alone.

Value Added to the Policy Debate

What do these attempts to measure things that are relevant to exclusion add to the policy debate? As far as the European Union is concerned, there is no doubt that the analyses by Eurostat of ECHP have started to shed much light on how disadvantage varies across member states. We are now beginning to know a great deal more about how living standards vary across the Union, how deprivation in terms of low income and lack of work is linked to deprivation in other dimensions, and how the strength of this link varies from country to country. But it is unclear whether the concept of exclusion is necessary to lend coherence to all this, and whether policy is being much influenced as a result.

On the policy side, as far as expenditures of the European Union institutions are concerned, "social exclusion" takes a backseat to "economic and social cohesion," the concept that drives development policy within the EU's borders.[5] (Aside from agricultural support, development policy dominates the very limited EU budget.) The Treaty on Union states firmly the goal of "raising of the standard of living and quality of life" within member states, and a reduction of the disparities in well-being among members is at the heart of the European project; this greater "cohesion" is a goal also stated explicitly in the Treaty. But greater cohesion has not to date been interpreted as "less exclusion." Rather, it has been taken to mean a reduction in differences in GDP per capita, with EU development policy trying to achieve this via (broadly speaking) investment in infrastructure targeted at low-income regions.

This situation reflects the principle of "subsidiarity" within the EU—the requirement that decisions be taken at the closest-possible level to the citizen. Subsidiarity means that most policy to combat poverty and social exclusion will remain a national, rather than an EU, responsibility—at least, in the case of policy that explicitly aims to redistribute, rather than to narrow, dispari-ties via catch-up growth.[6] However, this does not mean that the EU institutions' adoption of exclusion is of no consequence for policy. Union institutions can act as catalysts for policy change, helping to stiffen the resolve to act in individual member states, and cajoling and sometimes even obliging action at the national level. This process is known in EU parlance as "open coordina-tion." The December 2000 European Council meeting of heads of government followed up on the March meeting (referred to in my introduction) with the agreement that each member state would implement, by June 2001, a two-year National Action Plan (NAP) for combating poverty and social exclusion on the basis of jointly adopted objectives. NAPS are submitted to Brussels and will lead to a joint report by the European Commission and member states. It is hoped that Eurostat's analyses of exclusion will be one of the elements that inform national choices of targets. Another will cer-tainly be the report on indicators commissioned by the Belgian government during its presidency of the EU in 2001 (Atkinson et al. 2002).

The UK government, using the language of exclusion across the policy spectrum, emphasizes the need for what it calls "joined-up" policy—policy that results from collaboration between gov-ernment departments, and recognizes the links between problems as enumerated in the government's definition of social exclusion, quoted above (Social Exclusion Unit 2001, p.10). This emphasis on "joined-up" policy is said to contrast with earlier governments' initiatives that were seen to have dealt with each problem individually.

New Labour's determination to tackle deprivation in its many forms in the UK is clear. The second annual report on poverty and exclusion starts a section titled "Our Strategy" by noting firmly, "We are committed to eradicating child poverty in 20 years and halving it in 10, to providing employment opportunities for all those who can work, and to breaking the cycle of disadvantage which can perpetuate the effects of poverty throughout people's lives, from generation to generation" (Department of Social Security 2000, p. 4).

Few people would have problems signing up for goals such as these (the child emphasis within them is returned to below). But is the concept of *exclusion* essential to their selection, to the formulation of policy flowing from them, and to ensuring popular support so that policies can both be implemented and survive in the future?

Not everyone would immediately reply in the affirmative. Ending their major study of household living standards, *Resources, Deprivation and Poverty*, Brian Nolan and Chris Whelan make a strong case for continued emphasis on the concept of poverty in preference to that of social exclusion (Nolan and Whelan 1996, section 8.5). As they rightly point out, those who argue that exclusion is a more comprehensive concept than poverty, in relation to multidimensional disadvantage, may confuse the way that poverty is most often measured (via income) with the way in which it is conceptualized. Poverty can be defined in the broadest possible terms. For example, the definition adopted by the EU of the poor, as long ago as 1984, is those with "resources (material, cultural and social) [that] are so limited as to exclude them from the minimum acceptable way of life in the Member States in which they live" (Eurostat 2000, p. 11). (I shall discuss the focus on a *national* norm in the next section.)

Nolan and Whelan argue for the term "poverty" to be restricted to the lack of items (including participation in activities) viewed by society as necessities, where that lack is caused by insufficient income and other financial resources.[7] They are careful to emphasize that poverty defined in this way should not be the limit of concern about living standards, noting the need to assess aspects determined via non-market processes, such as publicly provided health care and housing. However, they question whether social exclusion has yet been defined and operationalized in a way that is much help in that additional assessment.

In neither the UK government's annual report on poverty and exclusion, nor in Eurostat's analyses, is it easy to point to anything concrete that would not have been there without the concept of social exclusion. In defense, the argument can be made that exclusion has sensitized researchers and policymakers to a much broader agenda. Proponents would say that it has shifted the debate on living standards away from description and to *processes* affecting changes in living standards, especially those that are not related to the level of resources an individual commands. (Nolan and Whelan admit the first possibility—the broadening of the agenda—but deny the logic in the second.) Some would argue that a focus on exclusion has also usefully emphasized the area-based nature of certain problems, and hence has stimulated area-based policies (e.g., in deprived inner-city areas).[8] Others would emphasize the dimension of individual perception implied by exclusion—excluded people feel excluded—contrasting this with traditional measures of deprivation based on objective measurement (although the Dutch school of subjective measurement of poverty should be recognized).

The value added by the concept of social exclusion will continue to be debated. On the concept itself, Tony Atkinson (1998) has tried to identify three common elements in the discussion, whatever definition of exclusion one might settle upon: relativity, agency, and dynamics.

• *Relativity.* This may seem obvious, but needs emphasis. Individuals are excluded from a particular society. Exclusion can only be judged by looking at a person's circumstances, relative to those of others, in a given place (and at a given time).

• *Agency.* People are excluded by an act of some agent. The emphasis on agency may help in the identification of the source of the problem, and hence with efforts to tackle it.[9]

• *Dynamics.* Exclusion may come about because of dim future prospects and not just because of current circumstances.

These three elements provide useful reference points for a discussion of the child dimension of exclusion, to which I now turn.

The Child Dimension of Exclusion

Discussion of exclusion among children needs to refer to their future prospects as well as their current living standards ("dynamics"). A decision must be made on the comparison group—other children or all persons—and on the geographical area for comparison ("relativity"). The issue of who excludes children also needs to be considered ("agency").

Children's Future Prospects

The idea that social exclusion may result from dim future prospects makes one think rather quickly about children. "Exclusion" may offer a useful label for the fate that awaits children who suffer from various disadvantages that threaten their capability to achieve in the future (as in Sen 1992). This includes disadvantage in traditional dimensions of "child development": education and health. It also includes teenage motherhood (although arguably this illustrates the "can happen" in the UK government's definition of exclusion—it would be wrong to label all teenage mothers as excluded). It could also include institutionalization. Children living in institutions suffer many disadvantages, including the obvious one of being excluded, literally, from normal family life, and parental attention and affection. Low income—especially persistent low income—is also on the list, although the "What Money Can't Buy" issues highlighted by Susan Mayer (1997) in the United States need to be remembered; this is something that underlines the importance of other direct measures of disadvantage.[10]

This concept of exclusion as it relates to children is central to the British government's presentation of social exclusion in the UK. Children are very high on New Labour's agenda in its efforts to tackle poverty and exclusion. Children are frequently the chosen entry-point into the whole debate: examples of childhood disadvantage, whether labeled as exclusion or poverty, are often mentioned first in the opening paragraphs of government reports. (Sometimes the same statistics appear to be treated as measures of poverty in one report, and of exclusion in another.) The emphasis is often on those disadvantages that threaten future life prospects. For example, seven of the thirteen indicators in the second annual report on poverty and social exclusion, intended to be used for monitoring progress among children and young people, involve measures of education or learning.[11] Teenage pregnancy is also covered. (Britain has the highest rate of teenage birth in Europe and one of the highest in the OECD. See UNICEF 2001a.)

The contrast with Eurostat statistics on poverty and social exclusion is marked. While the UK government has separate indicators for children and young people, working age adults, and the elderly, Eurostat's recent report based on ECHP (Eurostat 2000) focuses on measures of household living standards, which are then merely broken down by the age of the individual. That is, the percentage of persons in different age groups suffering from each disadvantage is given, but the definition of disadvantage is common across ages.

In this sense, children get no special place in the Eurostat analysis—there are no specific indicators that are intended to capture exclusion *among children*.[12] (Rather than being the result of a choice by Eurostat, this situation may merely reflect the position of a number of member states that do not regard child poverty as a major issue.) As a result, measures that relate directly to the future prospects of children are absent by definition. True, persistent low household income is reported (although only three years are covered by published analyses from ECHP to date) and this may indeed imply long-term disadvantage (even if the degree of causation is the subject of debate). But this measure cannot pick up everything. Nor does the incidence of long-term poverty shed light on the policy responses needed to combat disadvantage in education, health, and other areas of child well-being. By focusing on the links between low income and other general measures of household disadvantage as revealed in one survey, Eurostat's analysis of social exclusion is limited in what it can say about child exclusion.

Compared to Whom?[13]

Children can be defined as excluded only by considering their circumstances relative to those of others. As one 14-year-old girl in a UK family receiving state benefits said ". . . for me it's about not being part of things, not having the money to live normally like other people" (Roker and Coleman 1998, p. 17).

But are the things that this teenager considers she is "not part of" those things being done by her peers, or the things being done by the population at large? Are the other people who "live normally" other families *with children*, or are they other families in general? In other words, there is a reference group issue here.

The child angle is not typically prominent in discussion of relative living standards. Contrast this with efforts to establish an absolute poverty measure. The definition of an absolute poverty line has often started with consideration of the cost of subsistence for a family with children. This is true of Rowntree's (1901) work in England at the beginning of the twentieth century, and Orshansky's (1963, 1965) analysis, which underlay what became the official U.S. poverty line in the 1960s, as well as other later "budget standards" approaches. In this sense, children have featured prominently in attempts to define critical levels of living standards in absolute terms. On the other hand, discussion of relative standards has not had a child focus. The comment of Adam Smith, often quoted in discussions of relative poverty—that a person would be ashamed to appear in public in late eighteenth-century Britain if he did not sport leather shoes and a silk shirt—

is a remark more about parents' living standards than about those of their children.

If children are excluded from social participation by low living standards, the most important form of this may be exclusion from the lifestyle typically enjoyed by other children. In the case of income poverty, this suggests the use of a poverty line defined with reference to the average living standards of children in society, rather than to those of all people.

Bradbury and Jäntti (1999, 2001) show how child poverty rates change in industrialized countries covered by the Luxembourg Income Survey (LIS), when one switches from a poverty line of half the overall median to one of half the median of the "child distribution" (i.e., children ranked by equivalized household income). In all twenty-five countries considered, child poverty when assessed against the "child median" is lower, typically by about one-third. This is because the family income of the median child is less than the overall median (although as the authors point out the relativities between children and others are sensitive to the choice of equivalence scale).

Many people may object to the implication that exclusion of children would not rise if children as a group drifted down the overall income distribution, but the distribution of income within the group stayed the same. Children form part of society as a whole, and the overall median is the better societal norm. Or, drawing on the notion of perceptions that some commentators feel is an essential part of the concept of exclusion, if the child median were to fall well below the overall median, children would probably begin to perceive that their households lacked things that childless households did not.[14]

Arguments for a child-based reference standard might be stronger if child consumption were actually measured. The assumption typically made in applied work on living standards is that families pool their resources, so that in the calculations with the LIS that have just been described, each child is assigned the equivalized value of household income. However, there is considerable anecdotal evidence that the distribution of resources within households is not even. An Indianapolis single mother of two commented of her children, ". . . he wears the latest Nike brand shoes and she the latest Levi's. I like them to look nice, and here in the ghetto there are standards of dress. If they don't dress up to the standards, other kids tend to pick on them. I am not the only poor person who dresses her kids" (*New York Times*, October 18, 1999).

In this case, the children's exclusion in one dimension of their lives is prevented as a result of the intrahousehold distribution of resources being shifted towards them. However, something else must give somewhere in the family budget, and it is unlikely to be just their mother's personal consumption. As she also added, "they think I am richer than I am," noting that the gas had been turned off recently when she could not pay the bill, and that she also lacked money to fix her car. Losing the use of the car may be particularly important; it may exclude the children from participation in various activities and reduce their mother's ability to commute or search for work. (A telephone would be another example of an important public good within the family.)

More systematic evidence on children's individual living standards has been found by various authors. Middleton et al.(1997) interviewed mothers of British children and the children (aged over 5) themselves. The authors report that "parents are more likely to go without than children; one-half of parents who are defined as 'poor' themselves have children who are found to be 'not poor'" (p. 5). A large percentage of mothers, especially single mothers receiving social assistance benefits, said that they often or sometimes go without items or activities in order to provide things for their children. Middleton et al.'s research draws attention to potential inequalities between mothers and fathers, as well as between parents and children. This matters for children, because the impact on their living standards of higher family benefits may depend on which parent receives the extra resources. Recent research suggests that payments to mothers are more effective in raising expenditures on children's goods and services than payments to fathers. (See, for example, Lundberg, Pollack, and Wales (1997) and Phipps and Burton (1998).)

What is needed to assess child exclusion in the area of current living standards is systematic measurement of what children actually consume or do. Nolan (2000, p. 73) describes measures being added to the 1999 Living in Ireland Survey, the Irish part of ECHP. Mothers of children aged under 14 were asked whether lack of money over the previous year had meant children having to do without various things—for example a birthday party with friends, school trips, music lessons, or playing a sport. As far as children's future prospects are concerned, much measurement, by definition, should also be at the level of the child (such as the child's health or education) with the natural reference point being other children.

A final question here is, "which children?" in the definition of the reference group. One dimension of this is location, addressed below. But "communities" can be defined on other than a geographic basis, for example on ethnic lines (although obviously, there are often geographic concentrations of different ethnic groups). In a multicultural society, children may be part of a minority culture but not necessarily excluded, and in this case the issue then becomes one of inequality between communities. Put another way, is it exclusion from a *particular* community or from *any* community?[15]

Compared to Where?

Any discussion of relativity must address the issue of geography. Should the touchstone for comparison be local, national, or international?

Poverty measurement in the EU has focused on a *national* standard—see the 1984 definition of poverty in the Union given in the last section. Children in Portugal are poor in Eurostat's analyses if their household income is below 60 percent of the Portuguese median, Belgian children poor if below 60 percent of the Belgian median, and so on. Given the differences in average incomes across the EU, the resulting pattern of EU poverty rates contrasts markedly from those that would result from a common EU poverty line. For example, moving to a common EU line would raise the overall poverty rate in Greece in 1996 from 21 to 39 percent, and reduce that in France from 16 to 9 percent (Eurostat 2000, tables A.2.2.3 and A.2.2.3).[16]

If poverty were measured using a single EU poverty line, then this might reinforce calls for explicit EU-level redistributive policies, clashing with the typical perception of the implications of "subsidiarity." Of course, there is a potential contradiction here with policy on "economic and social cohesion" mentioned above, which aims to reduce income disparities within the Union by explicitly linking regional development funds to differences in regional GDP per capita. In terms of solidarity or cohesion within the Union, a common poverty threshold appears attractive, as it captures what convergence of incomes is all about: poorer parts of Europe catching up with the others.

On the other hand, "poverty" should be a term that is meaningful within each country, relevant to national sentiment and national policymaking. This reinforces the choice of national lines for EU poverty measurement. If relative poverty is about being excluded from things that others around you can participate in, then perhaps the basis of comparison should be brought even closer to where people actually live—to the region or state—with a spur to this shift in some countries provided by the devolution of programs of cash benefits and social services.

The shift to a state-level standard to measure poverty makes a considerable difference to the pattern of child poverty rates across the United States, as will be shown in the next section. It also makes a sharp difference in some European countries. This is true of Italy, where regional differences in average incomes are high. Switching from a half-national median income poverty line to a half-regional median line results in the child poverty rate in Sicily and Calabria, for example, falling from 45 percent to 19 percent (Rainwater, Smeeding, and Coder 1999). In the rest of southern Italy, the fall is less spectacular but still very substantial—from 27 percent to 16 percent. Nationally-based poverty lines reveal a poverty rate that is four times higher in the mid-south than in Lombardia in the north; state-based poverty lines show almost no difference between the two.

Italy is a good example of a European country where there is increasing demand for devolution of responsibilities in areas of policy that are important for child well-being: for example, health, accompanied by some form of fiscal federalism (see Granaglia 2001). However, a move towards sub-national poverty lines in Italy or anywhere else in Europe would, of course, run counter to any tendency to move in the opposite direction by using an Europe-wide yardstick in the EU.

There seem to be three criteria for selection of the appropriate geographic yardstick, of which two have so far been aired. The first is how differences are perceived and hence how exclusion is felt. The notion of participation in the "local community" argues for a sub-national reference point. But the region or state is probably a far too aggregated unit for this (it is standards in the ghetto that were referred to by the Indianapolis mother earlier in this section). Moreover, communities are aware of each other and have many common aspirations. Children in Calabria and Sicily watch the same television programs as those in Lombardia—and often the same ones as their contemporaries in other European countries or even in the United States. An argument of perception or participation does not inevitably lead to a sub-national reference point for assessing the exclusion of children.

The second criterion is the geographical organization of government and service delivery. For practical reasons—not those of principle—a sub-national yardstick may be a sensible one to emphasize, if the political reality is that national sentiment is not in favor of national standards, and policy responsibilities are heavily decentralized. However, in most European countries that national sentiment probably exists.

Third, there is the issue of international standards, and the reality of the wider world in which children are growing up. This is particularly important in the area of education. Knowledge, skills, and the ability to apply them are increasingly traded in a global marketplace, either directly through migration or indirectly through work for companies that trade internationally. Children are excluded from opportunities if their human capital is low by these standards.[17] The UK government's annual report on poverty and social exclusion looks too restrictive in this light: all seven of the education indicators for children refer to national standards only.

Of course, use of an international standard is only possible if something suitable is available. The assessments of learning achievement among children organized under the auspices of the International Association for the Evaluation of Educational Achievement provide one possibility for those countries participating in the surveys concerned. For example, results from the 1999 repeat of the Third International Maths and Science Study (TIMSS USGPO 2001) show the percentage of eighth-grade children scoring above the international median (and other quartiles of the international distribution, i.e., the distribution of scores in the pooled sample for all participating countries). (The UK scores in maths in the 1995 TIMSS are given in Social Exclusion Unit 2001, although the rationale for the international comparison is not made explicit.) Another perhaps even more attractive possibility is the new Programme for International Student Assessment (PISA) organized by the OECD (Organisation for Economic Cooperation and Development 2001). PISA is an ambitious undertaking designed to regularly monitor 15-year-olds in all OECD member nations for their "functional literacy," the ability to understand and to employ information in daily life.[18]

Finally, note that international comparisons may be used as part of an assessment of child poverty and exclusion, even if the answer to the "where" question is "in our country." Comparisons of child well-being with that in other countries provide benchmarks in terms of what is attainable, despite the natural reference population being the national one. We may believe that child poverty should be assessed using a national poverty line, but it is still of interest to know how child poverty compares on this basis with that in other countries using similarly defined national lines. If country X's child poverty rate is well out of step, then this suggests that something is going wrong. The UK government's recent presentation of poverty and exclusion among British children makes a number of comparisons of this type, calling attention, for example, to the fact that income poverty among children on a relative basis; the proportion of children in households where nobody works; and the extent of teenage motherhood are all high in the UK by international standards. This type of "benchmarking" is also becoming more important in the EU.

Who Excludes Children?

Exclusion of children can result from the actions of one or more of various agents—parents, schools, employers, or governments. We also need to consider the agency of children towards themselves, or other children.

Obviously, parents have an enormous influence on the well-being of their children. One implication is that parents must be major potential agents for their children's exclusion. Parents may fail to make sufficient effort to find work and hence to bring enough money into the household. They may fail to spend their income fairly or wisely. They may fail to take enough interest in the education of their children. They may fail to pay adequate attention to their children's health and nutrition. They may fail to help their children develop their social skills and contacts.

This may read like an onslaught on parents. But each sentence describing parental failures contains the word "may." The point is a simple one: given that parents and parenting skills *are* very important to children's progress, parents have the ability to encourage exclusion as well as to encourage positive progression. Parental failures leading to exclusion of children are typically inadvertent and may, of course, be exacerbated or ameliorated by other agents. But the conclusion must be that "social exclusion" is not a concept that removes from families all responsibility for their children's predicaments. Of course, the implication of recognizing parents as potential excluders—or includers—is that policy needs to help and work with parents.[19]

Schools exclude, sometimes literally—"school exclusions" (children being expelled permanently or temporarily from school) have been a considerable concern in the UK, and the number of truancies and exclusions is one of the child indicators in the government's annual report on poverty and exclusion. But schools may also be a source of exclusion simply through their failure to teach children to an adequate standard. Of course, school performance should in principle be measured in value-added terms, taking into account the backgrounds and ability on entry of children—and the financial resources that schools have at their disposal.[20]

Employers may exclude children and young people, either directly through their decisions in the youth labor market, or through the jobs held by parents. Employer "short-termism" (the application of a high discount rate to future incomes) makes firms less willing to invest in job creation, resulting in exclusion from the labor market (Atkinson 1998). This seems particularly relevant to the position of young people trying to get a foothold in the world of work. Short-termism may also exclude young people from on-the-job training and may result in proliferation of temporary "burger-flipping" jobs. Employers may be major sources of fringe benefits for parents, and children share in these benefits. Health insurance is probably the key one, which is especially important in countries with weak public health provision.

Governments, both national and local, can exclude. They may fail to provide adequate public services such as schools and health systems—whether through inadequate investment, inadequate current funding, or poor organization. They may fail to intervene in the labor market to: ease the entry of young people; give appropriate incentives to parents to move into work; promote day care for single (and other) mothers; or provide labor-market training for those in need. They may fail to provide an adequate cash-income safety net for families with children who cannot find work. (Note that consistency requires that "adequate" be interpreted in the relative sense discussed above.) They may fail to encourage alternatives to orphanages such as adoption or fostering when children enter public care. (The exclusionary nature of children's institutions is a concern, for example, in much of Eastern Europe. See UNICEF 2001b.)

Finally, there is the possibility of exclusion by other children, and of self-exclusion resulting from a child's own behavior. Being "sent to Coventry"—through the explicit decision of a group of children (e.g., a school class) not to talk to one member of the group—is an obvious form of exclusion from a particular community (note the reference group issue again). The same is true of being "left out" in a vaguer sense from one's peer group's activities.

Self-exclusion may take various forms. One example is truancy from school. Another, perhaps, is drug addiction, although even here there are clearly other agents at work, including drug-pushers. But some commentators define exclusion as resulting only from the action of others—for example Barry (1998) who distinguishes between "isolation," which may be self-imposed, and "exclusion." (Put another way, exclusion could be seen as a supply-side phenomenon, with isolation coming from the demand side), a view that is debatable. The young offender who is incarcerated is literally excluded by and from normal society through being locked away. But he or she chose to commit the offense —although, of course, society may have contributed to the pressures that led to that decision. Similarly, a child is formally excluded from school (sent home or expelled) as a result of the school's decision, but also as a result of his or her behavior. Although "child poverty" resonates with many people due to the assumption that the young are blameless, (in contrast to the feckless behavior assumed possible of adults) it is not clear to me that social exclusion should necessarily come with the same assumption when applied to children, especially teenagers.

Much of the above is obvious. In one sense, it says no more than that there are many influences on child well-being—which we knew already—and that attention needs to be paid to all of them. On the other hand, consideration of "agency" may usefully force attention onto each and every one of these influences—away from luck and genetics—and may stimulate thought about what to do about them.

Is the United States Ripe for "Exclusion"?

The phrase "social exclusion" does not occur in the U.S. government publication *America's Children: Key National Indicators of Well-Being 2000*. It is absent from the U.S. Department of Health and Human Services *2000 TANF Annual Report to Congress* and indeed is nowhere to be found on the Department's website. It does not occur in David Ellwood's excellent survey article on welfare reform (Ellwood 2000), and it does not exist in the CPS (2001) report, *Poverty in the United States 2000*. On this issue, the gulf between Europe and the United States appears huge.

I can think of two reasons for interest in introducing "social exclusion" into the debate on child well-being in the U.S. (or any another country). The first is "intellectual": a belief that this concept adds value in the definition and understanding of disadvantage in childhood, and in the formulation of policies to address this disadvantage. The second is "political": a belief that exclusion provides a language for discussing disadvantage that many more policymakers will sign up for than is the case with alternatives, not least because it avoids the P-word, "poverty" (see Atkinson's comment earlier on the cynical view of the EU's adoption of exclusion).

I don't always try to distinguish between the two in this section; I do discuss briefly several features of the United States that are probably relevant to both these motivations. The order is fairly random, except that I defer discussion of some broader aspects of U.S. society until the last. There are, no doubt, some naïve comments and some important omissions from the list, but I hope that this view from the outside will at least provoke thought, both in U.S. readers and in fellow outsiders regarding the situations in their own countries.

Measurement of Income Poverty

This is not an auspicious start. Exclusion is a relative concept, but the official U.S. poverty line—almost universally used outside as well as inside government—is not intended to measure a living standard that has any relationship to current societal norms. Contrast this with Europe, where it is common both in government and academia to measure income poverty with a line set as a percentage of average or median incomes. (For example, this is true of official measurement of poverty in Ireland, Italy, and the UK, and, as described earlier, the EU.) If measurement of even low income in the United States takes no account of distance from the average, what hope is there for a concept like exclusion, which has relativity at its core?

The problem is not so much that the U.S. line is an absolute one; calculations of a "minimum necessary income" can and often do take account of what is necessary for the society in question. Rather it is the persistence with a definition of "necessary" that is nearly forty years old. The original Orshansky minimum budget for a family of four in the early 1960s was in fact about half of the median net income of families of that type at that time—the ratio of average income that much "relative" poverty measurement in Europe focuses on. Now, however it represents not much more than one-quarter of the median net income.

All this is well-known; the mid-1990s saw a major review of the official poverty line by the National Research Council (Citro and Michael 1995). Nevertheless, as has been argued recently by Howard Glennerster, ". . . a European is struck by the relatively limited conceptual discussion of poverty in the U.S. even today. Many of the most recent papers on poverty in the U.S. continue to use the old official line as their starting point" (Glennerster 2000, p. 6).[21] Glennerster goes on to summarize the development of poverty measurement in Europe since the 1950s, in effect describing the increasing use of a relative concept that has paved the way for the move to the social exclusion concept.

Analysis of Child Well-Being

When a European researcher looks at what is available in the United States in terms of data and analyses of child well-being, it is quite easy to feel jealousy. The U.S. poverty line may not impress a European, but the data and analyses of children's economic welfare—and many other aspects of child well-being— often seem dazzling.

First, a great deal was discovered about the dynamics of income poverty among children in the United States, well in advance of analogous endeavors in Europe. The long-running Panel Study on Income Dynamics (PSID) has been the source for much of this. Pioneering research on income dynamics by Bane and Ellwood (1986) built on earlier use of the PSID (see, for example, Duncan et al. 1984; Hill 1981). Ten years later, Ashworth et al. (1994, p. 663) were able to comment that the distribution of the number of years during childhood spent poor was "quite familiar territory" in the United States. Would that it were in Europe! Panel surveys have now been developed and used in several European countries, for example Germany and the UK, and the European Community Household Panel (ECHP) provides a key new resource, as noted earlier (although it is planned to end well before any child's first seventeen years will have been tracked). But the United States still leads the way on what we know about low income patterns during childhood. Studies such as Duncan and Brooks-Gunn (1997), Duncan et al. (1998) and Mayer (1997) have done much to nail down the impact of low income in childhood on later life outcomes.

Second, both inside and outside government, analyses of the well-being of U.S. children already delve far beyond income into other areas—education, health (and health insurance), housing, and social environment—including the overlaps of these with income poverty. *America's Children: Key National Indicators of Well-Being* (Federal Interagency Forum on Child and Family Statistics 2000) would be a fine example for European governments to follow. There are many other examples, including the "Kids Count" state-level analyses of the Annie E. Casey Foundation and the Department of Health and Human Services' *Trends in the Well-Being of America's Children and Youth.*

The United States is therefore already collecting and analyzing a great deal of data on different aspects of childhood in which children have the potential to be excluded, and considering how these overlap with each other. "Child poverty" has long been seen as a multidimensional concept. Is all this good or bad news for the use of "exclusion" in the United States? On the one hand it is bad—one cannot look to social exclusion as a concept that will drive completely new collection and analysis of data on various areas of children's lives, as it has arguably done in some European countries. On the other hand it is good—the data are there, and there is much analysis on which to build.

Those signing up to the "intellectual" motivation for the use of exclusion would argue that the existing analyses and policies are no substitute for what could yet be attained. Those subscribing only to the "political" reason might argue that a banner of exclusion would allow the existing work to penetrate yet further into the policy world.

National versus State-Level Standards

If exclusion is to gain ground as a concept in the United States, then those who seek to push it will have to think hard about the geographical definition of the society from which children can be excluded, and how this relates to the level at which anti-poverty policy operates. Is it better to persist with a *national* definition of *poverty* (albeit with variation in the poverty yardstick, in line with some state-level prices, as recommended by the National Research Council review)? Or should the exclusion genie be let out of the bottle, with the risk that this leads to the use of state-level yardsticks?

In the U.S., as in some European countries (see the previous section), one sees large differences in state-level incidences of cash poverty among children when switching from a national to a state-level poverty line (when defined in conventional "European" terms). Rainwater, Smeeding, and Coder (2001, table 2.1) show the effect of moving from a line of half the national median income to one of half the state median. (In doing so, they also demonstrate that some U.S. researchers use relative poverty lines!) The average absolute difference in child poverty rates is 4.1 percentage points, and the correlation between the two rates is 0.53. For New Jersey and Arkansas, the richest and poorest states respectively with median incomes 25 percent above and 25 percent below the national figure, child poverty rates rise from 14 to 22 percent (New Jersey) and fall from 26 percent to 14 percent (Arkansas) with this change.

What I have labeled as a "risk" others might call an advantage. Rainwater et al. argue for state-level measurement: ". . . the state standards explored here come closer to the social standards that in fact operate when societies define some people as poor . . . . Moving from the national level to the state level would seem a step in the right direction" (Rainwater et al. 2001, p. 66). One argument Rainwater and his co-authors use is the practical one that "welfare reform" has led to the states having a bigger role in policy to fight child poverty. As they note, states now have "full latitude," subject to very few federal constraints, in their design of means-tested welfare support to families (TANF), including eligibility, benefit levels, and duration.[22]

I have stated the counter argument in general terms in the previous section. However, U.S. readers of the first draft of this chapter have pointed out that anyone wanting to promote the concept of exclusion in the United States would do well to recognize that in a federal vacuum, "states are where the action is" in the social welfare field. If a few key states were to be persuaded of the value of the exclusion concept—even if exclusion is defined in relation to a sub-national reference group—then this would help the concept percolate upwards and outwards.

Welfare to Work

There are three reasons why the concept of exclusion seems relevant to "welfare reform." One reason is the state versus national focus just discussed. The second is an emphasis on "personal responsibility," which I deal with at the end of this section. The third is the dynamic perspective to U.S. anti-poverty policy that the social exclusion concept illustrates, as it emphasizes the prevention of entry into poverty and the promotion of exits (rather than just paying benefits to the currently poor). There is raging debate, of course, on whether welfare reform has been effective in achieving its goals (summarized, for example, in Ellwood 2000). Welfare rolls have plummeted: the number of families on AFDC (Aid to Families with Dependent Children) and its successor, TANF, has been cut by more than half since 1993. Support for working families, via such measures as the Earned Income Tax Credit, has sharply increased, and more disadvantaged parents, especially single parents, appear to be working. On the other hand, there were concerns from the outset over what would happen were the economy to go into recession, concerns that the 2001 economic downturn have sharpened. There is evidence about the instability of jobs taken after exits from TANF; the plight of parents who cannot get work for whatever reason is clear; and the impact on child well-being as opposed to parental work status is uncertain.

However, this debate is not particularly relevant to the point at issue here, namely that U.S. policymakers and analysts are already well-attuned to a policy emphasis on "including" people into the labor market, the focus of much discussion of exclusion in Europe—some would say an excessive focus.[23] (Of course, the quality of jobs into which people are included remains an issue.) That could be useful for the fortunes of social exclusion as a concept in the United States. The UK case is particularly relevant here—some aspects of New Labour's social policy reforms in its anti-exclusion and anti-poverty strategy have clearly been influenced by the U.S. policy debate (see Glennerster 2000 for further comment on this).

Inner Cities and the Underclass

The U.S. poverty literature has paid much attention to problems of local communities, including the inner-city ghetto. This is highly compatible with the focus on area in some of exclusion literature, noted earlier in this chapter. (The papers in Power and Wilson 2000 provide a comparison of UK and U.S. work on urban disadvantage; Power's paper on the UK explicitly stresses exclusion, while Wilson's on the United States does not.) There is a natural child angle in this focus on area, given the importance to child development of local services such as schools, and high inner city youth unemployment.[24] Whether this compatibility makes exclusion more or less useful in the United States as an organizational concept for addressing problems of community disadvantage is a matter for debate; the arguments for and against are similar to those on the analysis of child well-being discussed above.

A related issue is that of the "underclass," also prominent in the U.S. debate on poverty since the 1960s. Nolan and Whelan (1996, p.153) quote Peterson (1991) as saying that this is a concept that can appeal to conservatives, liberals, and radicals alike. The same could be claimed of social exclusion. However, as Nolan and Whelan go on to note, there is wide agreement that only a subset of the poor could be considered to be in the underclass, whereas exclusion is typically intended as a broader concept than poverty. Again, one can see the U.S. experience of the underclass concept as cutting both ways.

Child Poverty, the Macroeconomy—and Politics

Child poverty measured with the official U.S. poverty line fell from a peak of 22.7 percent in 1993 to 16.2 percent in 2000.[25] Income poverty among children, measured by this yardstick, is now at its lowest level for twenty years. Welfare reform and associated policies to increase labor supply may be one factor, but another has been the strength of the U.S. economy, which from the early 1990s until 2001 experienced a period of unprecedented growth. As the economy now falters, child poverty can be expected to move back up, although whether it edges or leaps remains to be seen. (The reduced effectiveness of TANF as a safety net, compared to AFDC, may be one factor in this.) Does a falling child poverty rate make it harder to introduce discussion of "exclusion," and a rising rate make it easier? Arguments could be made on either side.

What about politics? Does the change in tenant at the White House make it easier to attract the Administration to exclusion, or harder? Perhaps a change in administration provides, in itself, an opportunity for pushing a fresh concept with policymakers. Or perhaps the new administration's concerns are not conducive to such a discussion.

Other Aspects of U.S. Society

This final sub-section was added following the conference for which the original paper was written, and is based on comments of the U.S. participants at that meeting. Besides the specific features of U.S. society and institutions that I mention above, are there more general aspects that need to be taken into account?

First, a note on history. It could be argued that in the past, the United States has been very inclusive in some senses, notably due to the arrival of large numbers of immigrants from different cultures and the need to absorb them into a "melting pot society." The early development of widespread public education (see Lindert 2001) was a strongly inclusive policy. More recently, however, exclusion as an official sanction for anti-social behavior has become very evident in extremely high levels of incarceration, especially among young black men. Social exclusion is seen here (by some) as a *solution* to a problem.

Second, if social exclusion is seen as stemming solely from the actions of others, it will jar badly against U.S. emphasis on personal responsibility. Not for nothing was the welfare reform legislation of the Clinton administration entitled "The Personal Responsibility and Work Opportunity Reconciliation Act." Inevitably, for some people, "social" may imply that society is to blame. I argued earlier that the definition of social exclusion should be broad enough to allow agency of the individual, at least in a contributory role, although I also noted that some commentators rule this out.

Third, and following on from the above, Americans' tolerance of inequality is generally higher than that of Europeans; the lack of any relativity in the measurement of income poverty discussed earlier is just one manifestation of this.[26] Another is the less well-developed welfare state. The rhetoric of U.S. politics on occasion seems to encourage the language of inclusion in discussion of distributional issues, as in the Bush administration's education proposal, described as the "No Child Left Behind Act" of 2001. But the typical U.S. interpretations of equality of opportunity and access to the American Dream are probably not sympathetic to the entry of "social exclusion." The opposition in some sectors of U.S. society to a broad concept of human rights encompassing economic, social and cultural fields (so-called "positive" rights), which is subscribed to by most European countries, is not encouraging in this respect.

Finally, what may be perceived as "European ideas" are not always well-received in the United States. Several Americans have expressed to me the view that, like it or not, the fact that "exclusion" has taken Europe by storm should be kept quiet by anyone trying to promote the concept in the United States.

Conclusions

My conclusions relate to both the concept of social exclusion itself, including its application to children, and the possible expansion of the concept to the United States in the analysis of child well-being.

Does the concept of social exclusion offer added value over the concepts of multidimensional poverty or deprivation? If it does, it is as a complement rather than as a substitute, and that is how it is used most of the time in Europe. "Poverty" will continue to have a resonance that "exclusion" may never achieve, as well as being something that is easier to define. Social exclusion's emphasis on *process* seems useful. The application of the concept to children needs more thought, but the headings suggested by Atkinson—dynamics, relativity, and agency—offer a good route forward.

The same headings are useful for thinking about possible added value in the United States. The U.S. literature on child well-being is good on dynamics but less so on relativity and, arguably, agency. Relativity, it seems to me, is a nettle that will have to be firmly grasped by anyone seeking to promote the concept of exclusion in the United States, and as part of this some serious thought will have to be given to the geographical dimension.

The problems in defining the concept could help it gain currency in the United States in the same way that (as it has been argued) it has in Europe: exclusion meaning "all things to all people" (Atkinson 1998, p. 6). But one needs to be prepared for that possibility.

Finally, some reflection on the past may be worthwhile: Would "exclusion" have usefully deepened and widened the attack during President Johnson's "War on Poverty," producing the "joined-up policy" that is the current aim of the British government? Or would it have helped in the U.S. debate on welfare leading to the 1996 reforms?

Notes

1. In revising the conference paper I have benefitted greatly from the comments of the discussants Tim Smeeding and Jane Waldfogel, and of many other participants at the conference. Very helpful comments were also made by Tony Atkinson, Tania Burchardt, John Hills, Julian Le Grand, and Brian Nolan. The opinions expressed in this chapter are personal and should not be taken as representing those of the United Nations Children's Fund, UNICEF.

2. Initiatives of successive Irish governments under the Irish National Anti-Poverty Strategy (NAPS) would have provided another example of prominent use of the concept of exclusion in an English-speaking country. The first sentence of the NAPS refers to tackling both poverty and social exclusion, and the strategy is overseen by a cabinet committee on "social inclusion," chaired by the prime minister (see www.welfare.ie/dept/reports/naps/index).

3. These include UNICEF (2000, 2001, 2001a, 2002) comparing

different dimensions of childhood disadvantage across all OECD countries; Micklewright and Stewart (1999, 2000, 2001) who focus on the EU; and Bradbury, Jenkins, and Micklewright (2000, 2001) who look at a selection of industrialized countries, including the United States. (For more details see the UNICEF IRC website, www.unicef-icdc.org.)

4. This definition is also given on the Social Exclusion Unit's website (www.cabinet-office.gov.uk/seu/index) and in the government's new annual report on poverty and social exclusion (Department of Social Security 1999, 2000).

5. See European Commission (2001), the second periodic report on cohesion that is required of the Commission by the Treaty on Union. "Social exclusion" receives little mention.

6. See Atkinson (1998, pp. 142–43) for a positive view on the redistributive function of EU institutions given the principle of subsidiarity and for discussion of how this relates to the Social Chapter of the Treaty on Union.

7. Nolan and Whelan's empirical work was based on Irish household survey data and their conception of poverty has in effect been reflected in the central target of the Irish government's National Anti-Poverty Strategy, which is a reduction in the numbers of "consistently" poor—those with low income *and* lacking necessities (see Nolan 1999, 2001).

8. Area-based policies are an important plank in the UK government's strategy to tackle exclusion. Glennerster et al. (1999) review the debate on this subject.

9. An analogy may be made here with recent attempts to integrate the concepts of human development and human rights (United Nations Development Programme 2000). The nonfulfillment of economic, social, and cultural rights implies that someone has violated the rights of another, either actively or through having failed to take some action. This, it is argued, provides focus for consideration of why human development may falter.

10. Attempts in Europe to separate out the independent effect of low income in childhood on life chances include Gregg and Machin (2001) and Hobcraft (1998) for the UK, and Büchel et al. (2001) for Germany. Some may label long-term or recurrent poverty itself as exclusion. However, as Atkinson (1998) argues, although persistent poverty may greatly increase the risk of exclusion, time spent poor in the past should not be equated with ex-ante expectations.

11. Four of the first six reports published by the Social Exclusion Unit dealt with disadvantage among children and the young (truancy/school exclusion, teenage pregnancy, out-of-school/out-of-work youth, and young runaways).

12. Some measures are not defined for children at all. For example, the indicator for social interaction with friends and relatives outside the household is only defined for those aged over 16.

13. I draw here, in part, on chapter 2 of Bradbury, Jenkins, and Micklewright (2001).

14. The concept of the child income distribution is very useful, however, when comparing the dynamics of child poverty across countries. Bradbury, Jenkins, and Micklewright look at mobility out of the bottom fifth of the child income distribution for seven industrialized countries (Bradbury, Jenkins, and Micklewright 2000 and 2001). The advantage is one of standardization: in year one exactly 20 percent of children in each country are defined as having low income.

15. I am grateful to Tony Atkinson for this observation.

16. Rates using an overall EU line are not given separately for children. For this see Immervoll et al. (2001). See also Atkinson (1998a) for discussion of EU versus national lines.

17. At the very least, reference points for education should be national—I can see no argument at all for counting children in Calabria and Sicily as excluded from educational opportunities only by reference to a standard for southern Italy.

18. Information on TIMSS and published reports can be found at www.timss.bc.edu and on PISA at www.oecd.org/els/pisa.

19. The worst forms of exclusion through parents may require state action. Those children at risk of various forms of parental abuse are placed on the Child Protection Register in the UK; the number of re-registrations on the register is one of the child indicators in the official annual poverty and social exclusion report.

20. Barry (1998, p. 13) argues that schools exclude if their selection policy results in children of a homogenous social background, on the grounds that much research shows that "children with middle class attitudes and aspirations constitute a resource for the rest."

21. Glennerster does, however, note that the Luxembourg Income Study, which has done so much to extend the international dimension of poverty analysis in the United States and elsewhere, is the brainchild of an American (Tim Smeeding)!

22. Meyers et al. (2001) show the differences across states in a range of policies to support families with children, showing that these exist not only in AFDC/TANF.

23. It might argued that U.S. policy places more emphasis on "pushing" than on "including," making the similarity less strong. However, European readers aware of the reduction in generosity of welfare benefits in the United States may be surprised, as I was, by the current extent of incentives now given through support to working families.

24. Area effects on child well-being can even include the propensity to commit crime. Ludwig, Duncan, and Hirschfield (1999) use data from a randomized housing-mobility experiment in Baltimore to show that moving between low-poverty and high-poverty areas has an effect on the criminal behavior of U.S. teenagers.

25. Child poverty rates are given at: www.census.gov/hhes/poverty/histpov/hstpov3. The Census Bureau website also gives results based on experimental measures that implement the Citro and Michael recommendations. These show somewhat larger drops in child poverty than the official rate over 1993–98, ranging from 5.4 to 6.1 percentage points (Table E definitions) compared to 3.8 points with the official measure.

26. See Evans (1993) for an international comparison of attitudes to income differences within each country, showing U.S. respondents to be the least likely to agree that they are too large.

References

2000 TANF Annual Report to Congress. (2000). U.S. Department of Health and Human Services, Administration of Children and Families. Washington, D.C.: Government Printing Office.

Ashworth, K., M. Hill, and R. Walker. (1994). "Patterns of Childhood Poverty: New Challenges for Policy." *Journal of Policy Analysis and Management* 13: 658–80.

Atkinson, A. B. (1998). "Social Exclusion, Poverty and Unemployment." In *Exclusion, Employment and Opportunity*, ed. A. B. Atkinson and J. Hills. London: CASE Publications.

————. (1998a). *Poverty in Europe*. Oxford: Basil Blackwell.

Atkinson, A. B., B. Cantillon, E. Marlier, and B. Nolan. (2002). *Social Indicators: The EU and Social Inclusion*. Oxford: Oxford University Press.

Bane, M. J., and D. T. Ellwood. (1986). "Slipping Into and Out of Poverty: The Dynamics of Spells." *Journal of Human Resources* 21: 1–23.

Barry, B. (1998). *Social Exclusion, Social Isolation and the Distribution of Income*. CASEpaper 12. London: CASE Publications.

Bradbury, B., and M. Jäntti. (1999). *Child Poverty across Industrialized Nations*. Innocenti Occasional Paper 70. Florence: UNICEF Innocenti Research Centre.

————. (2001). "Child Poverty across the Industrialised World." In *Child Well-Being, Child Poverty and Child Policy in Modern Nations*, ed. K. Vleminckx and T. Smeeding. Bristol, UK: Policy Press.

Bradbury B., S. J. Jenkins, and J. Micklewright. (2000). *Child Poverty Dynamics in Seven Nations*. Innocenti Working Paper 78. Florence: UNICEF Innocenti Research Centre.

————, eds. (2001). *The Dynamics of Child Poverty in Industrialised Countries*. Cambridge: Cambridge University Press.

Büchel, F., J. R. Frick, P. Krause, and G. Wagner. (2001). "The Impact of Poverty on Children's School Attendance—Evidence from West Germany." In *Child Well-Being, Child Poverty and Child Policy in Modern Nations*, ed. K. Vleminckx and T. Smeeding. Bristol, UK: Policy Press.

Citro, C., and R. Michael, eds. (1995). *Measuring Poverty: A New Approach*. Washington, D.C.: National Academy Press

Current Population Reports. (2001). *Poverty in the United States: 2000*. *P60-214*. Washington, D.C.: Government Printing Office.

Department of Social Security. (1999). *Opportunity For All. Tackling*

Poverty and Social Exclusion. Cm 4445. London: Stationary Office.

————. (2000). *Opportunity For All. One Year On: Making a Difference.* Cm 4865. London: Stationary Office.

Duncan, G. J., R. D. Coe, and M. S. Hill. (1984). "The Dynamics of Poverty." In *Years of Poverty, Years of Plenty: The Changing Economic Fortunes of American Workers and Families,* ed. G. J. Duncan, R. D. Coe, M. E. Corcoran, M. S. Hill, S. D. Hoffman, and J. N. Morgan. Ann Arbor, Mich.: Institute for Social Research.

Duncan, G. J., and J. Brooks-Gunn, eds. (1997). *Consequences of Growing up Poor.* New York: Russell Sage Foundation Press.

Duncan, G. J., J. W. Yeung, J. Brooks-Gunn, and J. R. Smith. (1998). "How Much Does Childhood Poverty Affect the Life Chances of Children?" *American Review of Sociology* 63(3): 406–23.

Ellwood, D. T. (2000). "Anti-Poverty Policy for Families in the Next Century: From Welfare to Work—and Worries." *Journal of Economic Perspectives* 14(1): 187–98.

European Commission. (2001). *Unity, Solidarity, Diversity for Europe, Its People and Its Territory. Second Report on Economic and Social Cohesion.* Luxembourg: Office for Official Publications of the European Communities.

Eurostat Task Force. (1998). *Recommendations on Social Exclusion and Poverty Statistics.* Document CPS 98/31/2. Luxembourg: Eurostat.

Eurostat. (2000). *European Social Statistics: Income, Poverty and Social Exclusion.* Luxembourg: Office for Official Publications of the European Communities.

Evans, G. (1993). "Class Conflict and Inequality." In *International Social Attitudes: The 10ᵗʰ BSA report,* ed. R. Jowell, L. Brook, and L. Dowds. Aldershot, UK: Dartmouth Publishing.

Federal Interagency Forum on Child and Family Statistics. (2000). *America's Children: Key National Indicators of Well-Being, 2000.* Washington, D.C.: Government Printing Office.

Glennerster, H. (2000). *U.S. Poverty Measurement and Poverty Studies: The Past Twenty-Five Years.* CASEpaper 42. London: CASE Publications.

Glennerster, H., R. Lupton, P. Noden, and A. Power. (1999) *Poverty, Social Exclusion and Neighbourhood: Studying the Area Bases of Social Exclusion.* CASEpaper 22. London: CASE Publications.

Granaglia, E. (2001). "The Italian SSN and the Quest for Accountability." Paper presented at the conference, The Welfare State, Poverty and Social Exclusion in Italy and Great Britain. University of Siena, Italy, April 6–8.

Gregg, P., and S. Machin. (2001). "Childhood Experiences, Educational Attainment and Adult Labour Market Performance." In *Child Well-Being, Child Poverty and Child Policy in Modern Nations,* ed. K. Vleminckx and T. Smeeding Bristol, UK: Policy Press.

Hill, M. S. (1981). "Some Dynamic Aspects of Poverty." In *Five Thousand Families: Patterns of Economic Progress,* ed. M. S. Hill, D. Hill, and J. N. Morgan. Ann Arbor, Mich.: Institute for Social Research.

Hobcraft, J. (1998). *Intergenerational and Life-Course Transmission of Social Exclusion: Influences of Childhood Poverty, Family Disruption, and Contact with the Police.* CASEpaper 15. London: CASE Publications.

Immervoll, H., H. Sutherland, and K. de Vos. (2001). "Reducing Child Poverty in the European Union: The Role of Child Benefits." In *Child Well-Being, Child Poverty and Child Policy in Modern Nations,* ed. K. Vleminckx and T. Smeeding. Bristol, UK: Policy Press.

Lenoir, R. (1974). *Les Exclus, un Français sur dix.* Paris: Le Seuil.

Lindert, P. (2001). "Democracy, Decentralization, and Mass Schooling before 1914." Working Paper 104. Davis: University of California at Davis Agricultural History Center.

Ludwig, J., G. Duncan, and P. Hirschfield. (1999). "Urban Poverty and Juvenile Crime: Evidence from a Randomized Housing-Mobility Experiment." Georgetown Public Policy Institute, Georgetown University, Washington, D.C. Processed.

Lundberg, S. J., R. A. Pollak, and T. J. Wales. (1997). "Do Husbands and Wives Pool Their Resources?" *Journal of Human Resources* 32: 463–80.

Mayer, S. E. (1997). *What Income Can't Buy: Family Income and Children's Life Chances.* Cambridge, Mass.: Harvard University Press.

Meyers, M., J. Gornick, L. Peck, and A. Lockshin. (2001). "Public Policies that Support Families with Young Children." In *Child Well-Being, Child Poverty and Child Policy in Modern Nations,* ed. K. Vleminckx and T. Smeeding. Bristol, UK: Policy Press.

Middleton, S., K. Ashworth, and I. Braithwaite. (1997). *Small Fortunes: Spending on Children, Childhood Poverty and Parental Sacrifice.* York, UK: Joseph Rowntree Foundation.

Micklewright, J., and K. Stewart. (1999). "Is the Well-Being of Children Converging in the European Union?" *Economic Journal* 109: F692–F714.

———. (2000). *The Welfare of Europe's Children: Are EU Member States Converging?* Bristol, UK: Policy Press.

———. (2001). "Child Well-Being in the EU—and Enlargement to

the East." In *Child Well-Being, Child Poverty and Child Policy in Modern Nations*, ed. K. Vleminckx and T. Smeeding. Bristol, UK: Policy Press.

National Center for Education Statistics (2001). *Pursuing Excellence: Comparison of International Eighth-Grade Mathematics and Science Achievements From a U.S. Perspective, 1995 and 1999.* Washington, D.C.: Government Printing Office.

Nolan, B. (1999). "Targeting Poverty: Lessons from Ireland on Setting a National Poverty Target." *New Economy* 6 (1): 44–49.

————. (2000). *Child Poverty in Ireland.* Dublin: Oak Tree Press.

————. (2001). "The Evolution of Child Poverty in Ireland." In *Child Well-Being, Child Poverty and Child Policy in Modern Nations*, ed. K. Vleminckx and T. M. Smeeding. Bristol, UK: Policy Press.

Nolan, B., and C. Whelan. (1996). *Resources, Deprivation and Poverty.* Oxford: Oxford University Press.

Organisation for Economic Co-operation and Development. (2001). *Knowledge and Skills for Life: First Results from the OECD Programme for International Student Assessment (PISA) 2000.* Paris: Author.

Orshansky, M. (1963) "Children of the Poor." *Social Security Bulletin* 26 (July): 3-13.

————. (1965) "Counting the Poor: Another Look at the Poverty Profile." *Social Security Bulletin* 28 (January): 3-29.

Peterson, P. E. (1991). "The Urban Underclass and the Poverty Paradox." In *The Urban Underclass*, ed. C. Jencks and P. E. Peterson. Washington, D.C.: Brookings Institution Press.

Phipps, S. A., and P. S. Burton. (1998). "'What's Mine Is Yours?,' the Influence of Male and Female Incomes on Patterns of Household Expenditure." *Economica* 65: 599–613.

Power, A. and W. J. Wilson. (2000). *Social Exclusion and the Future of Cities.* CASEpaper 35. London: CASE Publications.

Rainwater, L., T. M. Smeeding, and J. Coder. (2001). "Poverty across States, Nations, and Continents." In *Child Well-Being, Child Poverty and Child Policy in Modern Nations: What Do We Know?*, ed. K. Vleminckx and T. M. Smeeding. Bristol, UK: Policy Press.

Roker, D., and J. Coleman. (1998). "The Invisible Poor: Young People Growing Up in Family Poverty." Paper presented at the conference to mark the centenary of Seebohm Rowntree's first study of poverty in the University of York, York, UK, March 18–20.

Rowntree, B. S. (1901) *Poverty: A Study of Town Life.* London: Thomas Nelson.

Sen, A. (1992) *Inequality Reexamined.* Cambridge, Mass.: Harvard University Press.

Social Exclusion Unit. (2001). *Preventing Social Exclusion: Report by the Social Exclusion Unit.* Available at: www.cabinet-office.gov.uk/seu/index.

UNICEF. (2000). *A League Table of Child Poverty in Rich Nations.* Innocenti Report Card 1. Florence: UNICEF Innocenti Research Centre.

————. (2001). *A League Table of Child Deaths by Injury in Rich Nations.* Innocenti Report Card 2. Florence: UNICEF Innocenti Research Centre.

————. (2001a). *A League Table of Teenage Births in Rich Nations.* Innocenti Report Card 3. Florence: UNICEF Innocenti Research Centre.

————. (2001b). *A Decade of Transition.* Regional Monitoring Report 8. Florence: UNICEF Innocenti Research Centre.

————. (2002). *A League Table of Educational Disadvantage in Rich Nations.* Innocenti Report Card 4. Florence: UNICEF Innocenti Research Centre.

United Nations Development Programme. (2000). *Human Development Report 2000.* New York: United Nations Publications.

Social Exclusion and Students with Special Educational Needs [1,2]

Peter Evans with Suzanne Bronheim, John Bynner, Stephan Klasen, Phyllis Magrab, and Stewart Ranson

Introduction

This chapter will provide an overview of the work being carried out at the Organisation for Economic Co-operation and Development, Centre for Educational Research and Innovation (OECD/CERI) in the field of social exclusion as it applies to children. In particular, it will focus on disabled and disadvantaged children and young people, since these populations are most likely to be at risk of exclusion and are targets of significant OECD activity (e.g., OECD 1995, 1996, 1998, 1999, 2000).

The concept of social exclusion was first popularized in 1974 in France by René Lenoir, the then Secretary of State for Social Action; it was used to refer to the "physically disabled," the "mentally disabled," and the "socially maladjusted." Lenoir recognized the needs to improve conditions for those the economy was leaving behind, and strengthen social cohesion.

More recently, the concept of social exclusion has expanded to include those with disadvantages, and has taken on a more elaborated meaning both inside and outside France (Ebersold 1999, OECD [www.oecd.org/cer/obj5/docs]). It has now become one of the most important themes of contemporary social debate in many OECD countries, because of the challenge that exclusion presents to social cohesion.

In contrast to poverty and unemployment, which focus on individuals and households and were central to earlier discussions on exclusion, social exclusion in its current form has taken on a

broader significance; it is concerned with the "inability to participate effectively in economic, social and cultural life and, in some
characteristics, alienation and distance from mainstream society"
(Duffy 1995). The concept of social exclusion thus focuses on the
relationship between the individual and society and the dynamics
of that relationship.

The main groups who are potentially subject to being socially
excluded remain unchanged, and include those from disadvantaged
backgrounds and those with disabilities. But the results of disadvantage are no longer viewed as being passed exclusively through
families, leading to restriction of life chances and impediments to
development. Instead, the concept of social exclusion shifts the
responsibility to society, which is seen as erecting obstacles to the
progress of particular individuals and groups, and even to citizenship itself. When looked at in this way, social exclusion can "be
seen to be present in almost any of the domains of modern living,
including education, employment, community life and citizenship
to which individuals or groups fail to gain access or exclude themselves from" (Bynner 1999).

Such an approach also lies comfortably with other descriptions that emphasize a rights-based approach. Room (1995),
for instance, talks of the "denial or non-realisation of civil,
political, and social rights of citizenship." A rights-based approach, which was the model driving the inclusion movement
in the United States, also has much in common with the capabilities approach developed by Sen. This "calls for efforts to
ensure that people have equal access to basic capabilities such
as the ability to be healthy, well-fed, housed, integrated into
the community, participate in community and public life, and
enjoy social bases of self-respect" (Sen 1992; also see Klasen
1999).

Much of the current debate has focused on adults, but children and young people, too, are in danger of becoming excluded.
Thus, extending the idea of social exclusion to children requires
further consideration and is best considered in the context of the
Convention on the Rights of the Child.

Defining Social Exclusion among Children

Under what circumstances can one say that a child is suffering from social exclusion? Applying the capabilities approach used by Sen (1992, 1999), we can define social exclusion as the inability to participate in, and be recognized by, society. A slightly stronger version would also include the terms of such participation and recognition in the definition. In particular, one may want to include the concept that participation in society, and recognition of people by society, has to be in terms of equality or equal opportunity. This would ensure that equality was inherent in the notion of citizenship, as well as the protection of human dignity necessary for all social interactions.

Failure of the ability to participate in, and be recognized by, society, is not only theoretically important. Attitude surveys have determined that European citizens consider participation in society a necessity of life. Using data from the Eurobarometer survey, Golding (1995) shows that 65 percent of EU citizens regard "feeling recognised by society" as an absolute necessity. Other indicators of participation are ranked very highly as well, which suggests that participation is indeed an important and valued capability that should be open to all citizens.[3]

One way to refine this capability failure would be to define more specific rights and capabilities that are necessary in order for the child to be able to interact equally in, and be recognized as an equal by, the rest of society. Berghman (1995) distinguishes between four types of integration and participation: civic integration relating to the democratic and legal system (and, for example, the legal status and treatment of children in general and minority, foreign, or disabled children in particular); economic integration mainly related to employment; social integration related to the inclusion in the public safety net, and family and community integration relating to networks or, to what some observers have recently termed "social capital."

A related starting point, focusing specifically on children, would be the UN Convention on the Rights of the Child (UNICEF 1989), which has been signed and ratified by the majority of countries in the world. The rights that may be relevant to social inclusion and exclusion are the following:

• Article 2: "States Parties shall respect and ensure the rights set forth in the present Convention to each child within their jurisdiction without discrimination of any kind, irrespective of the child's or his or her parent's or legal guardian's race, colour, sex, language, religion, political or other opinion, national, ethnic or social origin, birth, property, disability, birth or other status. . . ."

• Article 3: "In all actions concerning children, . . . the best interests of the child shall be a primary consideration. . . ."

• Article 7: "The child shall be registered immediately after birth and shall have the right from birth to a name, the right to acquire a nationality, and, as far as possible, the right to know and be cared for by his or her parents."

• Article 9: "States Parties shall ensure that a child shall not be separated from his or her parents against their will. . . ."

• Article 17: "States Parties . . . shall ensure that the child has access to information and material from a diversity of national and international sources, especially those aimed at the promotion of his or her social, spiritual, and moral well-being. . . ."

• Article 23: "States Parties recognise that a mentally or physically disabled child should enjoy a full and decent life in conditions which ensure dignity, promote self-reliance and facilitate the child's active participation in the community. States Parties recognise the right of the disabled child to special care. . . ."

• Article 27: "States Parties recognise the right of every child to a standard of living adequate for the child's physical, mental, spiritual, moral, and social development. . . . States Parties . . . are to assist parents to implement this right . . . ."

• Article 28: States Parties recognise the right of the child to education . . . and on the basis of equal opportunity shall, in particular make primary education compulsory and available free to all; encourage the development of different forms of secondary education, . . . make them available and accessible to every child, and take appropriate measures such as the introduction of free education and offering financial assistance in case of need; . . . take measures to encourage regular attendance at schools and the reduction of drop-out rates . . . ."

• Article 29: "States Parties agree that the education of the child shall be directed to the development of the child's personality, talents, and mental and physical abilities to their fullest potential; . . . [and] the preparation of the child for responsible life in a free society, in the spirit of understanding, peace, tolerance, equality of sexes, and friendship among all peoples, ethnic, national, and religious groups and persons of indigenous origin."

• Article 30: " . . . A child belonging to a minority or who is indigenous shall not be denied the right, in community with other members of his or her group, to enjoy his or her own culture, to profess and practise his or her own religion, or to use his or her own language."

• Article 31: "States Parties recognise the right of the child to rest and leisure, to engage in play and recreation; . . . States Parties shall respect and promote the right of the child to participate fully in cultural and artistic life and shall encourage the provision of appropriate and equal opportunities for cultural, recreational, and leisure activities."

Failure in meeting any of these rights, for whatever reasons, could then be seen as evidence of social exclusion, as all of these rights deal with the ability of the child to interact with society on equal terms.[4] The advantage of basing discussions of social exclusion and children on the Convention is the public and political acceptance the Convention has gained through its signatories, ratification, and the monitoring processes that have accompanied it.

One should point out, however, that the Convention on the Rights of the Child is not in all cases consistently following a capabilities approach as suggested by Sen (1992, 1999). In particular, some parts of the Convention merely call for equal opportunities and nondiscrimination, which may be interpreted as less than calling for equal capabilities.[5]

Also, the Convention singles out physically and mentally disabled children as having rights to special support to achieve a full

and decent life in dignity and self-reliance and with active participation of the community (Article 23). Children who are not
disabled but otherwise disadvantaged by birth, background, or circumstance are not specifically mentioned, and all children are not
specifically granted the right to a full or decent life and active
participation in the community. As argued above, it is unclear why
nondisabled disadvantaged children (or, for that matter, all children) should not enjoy these same rights.[6]

The mentioned clauses of the Convention on the Rights of
the Child deal with a variety of aspects of children's lives. Many
of the mentioned clauses relate to legal rights of inclusion (including nationality, nondiscrimination, growing up with parents,
access to media, and respect for own culture and language) and
can generally be met through appropriately passed and enforced
legislation. Others, particularly Articles 23, 27, 28, 30, and 31,
deal with the interaction of economic and social forces and governmental action where governments are asked to correct exclusion that may otherwise be created as a result of economic or
social forces (see also Klasen 1999).

Such a capabilities- or rights-based approach to child development differs sharply from a utilitarian concern of maximizing
wealth or consumption. Article 29, about the goals of education,
highlights this contrast. While a utilitarian approach to education
would promote education in ways that raise the sum total of
achievement in the education system, and thus would target resources on those best placed to make use of them, a rights-based
approach calls for maximizing the potential of each child, regardless of whether this will or will not further growth, technological
development, or the position of the country in the global marketplace. Thus the focus of educational and other policies, if they are to
deal with social exclusion, has to deal with the capabilities of those
most disadvantaged, rather than those who are able to use the system
most effectively. An emphasis on educational policies aimed at combating social exclusion will have to focus heavily on the distribution
of resources access and achievements, rather than averages, and
OECD/CERI has begun work on these issues (Evans OECD 2000).[7]

Intrinsic and Instrumental Issues

The rights- or capabilities-based approach used above in defining social exclusion carries with it a focus on the *intrinsic* problems associated with social exclusion. If social exclusion is a violation of rights or capabilities, this immediately implies that a society that tolerates social exclusion is *intrinsically* deficient if it fails to grant basic rights or capabilities to its citizens, in this case to its children. The use of the Convention on the Rights of the Child, signed and ratified and thus accepted by the majority of the world, nicely illustrates this intrinsic importance.

At the same time, there are several types of *instrumental* reasons why the treatment of children should receive close scrutiny. First, socially excluded children may grow up to be adults who are similarly suffering from social exclusion, which we should worry about for intrinsic reasons. Thus, combating social exclusion among children can help combat the social exclusion of adults.

Second, socially excluded children may, as a result of their exclusion, suffer from deficiencies in other important capabilities, such as the ability to be healthy, well-educated, well-housed, or well-nourished. This clearly reduces the well-being of those suffering from exclusion, but may also have larger societal implications (e.g., due to the positive externalities of health and education). In addition, social exclusion may have close empirical relationships to other social problems that threaten the stability and prosperity of society at large—such as crime, violence, social pathologies, societal divisions, racism, or xenophobia.

Third, there is the additional worry that socially excluded children will pose a threat to the future well-being of society, as they may become a social and economic burden to society or, worse, generate considerable social disruption if they have little stake in the existing order. In addition, to the extent that social exclusion is transmitted intergenerationally, social exclusion of children may create ever-deeper divisions within society that amplify across generations.

Fourth, there may even be situations where one cannot speak of social exclusion among children, but in which the particular situations children find themselves in may promote social exclusion among adults. For example, one can think of educational arrangements in which children with learning difficulties or other disadvantages are well-integrated and do not suffer from social exclusion, but in which their needs are insufficiently taken into account, leaving them poorly catered for. These four points are expanded upon below.

It is important to point out that the intrinsic and instrumental reasons to be concerned about social exclusion have very different moral standings. While the intrinsic arguments against social exclusion rise and fall with the acceptance of their philosophical basis (such as a capability-based or other rights-based approach), the instrumental considerations rise and fall with the veracity of the linkages postulated, which is largely an empirical question. This has important implications for a research agenda on social exclusion. A research agenda focused on testing the linkages between exclusion and other desirable welfare criteria implicitly accepts the instrumental approach; one that accepts the intrinsic arguments, such as the rights or capabilities approach suggested above, can immediately move to policy questions related to social exclusion.[8] In practice, even an approach highlighting the intrinsic problems associated with social exclusion should also be concerned with the instrumental issues. If social exclusion causes other social ills, which themselves are intrinsically problematic, this should add to the worry of those who care about social exclusion for intrinsic reasons.

As noted above, children, as members of families, may also suffer from the social exclusion of their parents. The restriction this places on their development provides the basis of their own exclusion later in life. This means that the outcomes of their early experiences at home and in school, and through which their positions in adult society are ultimately determined, need to be a focus as well. Such a sequence is illustrated by the list below:

- poor acquisition of the basic skills of literacy and numeracy
- poor educational attainment through school
- early leaving from education without qualifications
- early labor market entry problems, including jobs without training
- casual work and unemployment
- teenage pregnancy
- trouble with the police
- alcohol abuse
- criminal convictions
- poor physical, and especially mental, health

Each outcome is both an indicator of social exclusion early on, and a predisposing factor for social exclusion later. This brings the idea of risk and protective factors into the picture. Thus, for example, success at preventing educational failure through intervention in preschool preparation is a source of protection against the later risk of exclusion in the adult labor market.

Such a process is continuous, in the sense that one outcome leads to another, and it is also to a degree cyclical in its effects, in the sense that its outcomes are mutually reinforcing and may be damaging to achievements earlier in life. For example, the experience of family conflict at a particular stage of childhood may not only hold back the child educationally, relative to peers, but he or she may regress to earlier levels of cognitive performance and behavior (Bergman and Magnusson 1991; Caspi et al. 1996).

The broad definition of social exclusion advanced here involves restriction of access to the capabilities essential to functioning in adult life. Through the early stages of childhood, first the basic building blocks and then the capabilities themselves are developed. Principally these are reflected in educational outcomes associated with cognitive development, such as literacy and numeracy in childhood and educational qualifications in the teens—the basis of *human capital formation* (Becker 1975). But along-

141

side these are the psychological and social resources, underpinning the *social* and *cultural capital* components of human development. In total, these add up to what Côte (1996) describes as "Identity Capital"—the key protector against adult social exclusion in late modern society.

Figure 1 illustrates how early precursors in a child's life translate into particular social exclusion externalities or outcomes via the medium of capability. The former include material elements of the child's home, and parental characteristics when the child is born, together with such individual characteristics as gender, ethnicity, or disability. From birth onwards, the child is subjected to both the positive and negative aspects of the services directed towards him or her. These comprise in early life the health and early education services, then schooling; then, in adolescence, the education service, youth service, and vocational advisory service. In adulthood services broaden further, embracing all the institutions of the state: social welfare, employment, housing, transport, health, and the judicial system. It is in these institutions that the obstacles, as well as opportunities, for the individual's access to capabilities—and ultimately identity capital—reside (Bynner 1999).

Inclusive education, for example, may draw children with special needs into mainstream schooling. Large class sizes, on the other hand, may mask the difficulties of individuals who, through lack of parental support, are unable to keep up with the rest of their peers. There are both physical and educational resources that play a part here, but also the more hidden, but nevertheless highly potent, psychological and cultural resources on which identity capital is built. The labeling of children as dull or stupid excuses teachers in large classes for dismissing such children as lost causes. Gender and ethnic stereotyping may, in subtle ways, reinforce their marginalization.

Longitudinal studies (e.g., Bynner 1999) show that as children move through education, the gap between the educational haves and have-nots gets wider; progress is enhanced for some, while others are held back. The consequence is social exclusion for the

FIGURE 1: PROCESS OF SOCIAL EXCLUSION OR INTEGRATION

MATERIAL FACTORS
Family poverty
Geographic location

FAMILY FACTORS
Parents' education
Parental interest and support
Social class

PROVISION OF SERVICES
Education
Social services
Housing
Transport
Health

INDIVIDUAL
Aptitudes/Motivation
Gender
Disability

ACCESS TO OR OBSTACLES TO OPPORTUNITIES FOR

CAPABILITY

PARTICIPATION AND PROGRESSION

OCCUPATION
INCOME
FAMILY LIFE
HOUSING
HEALTH
COMMUNITY

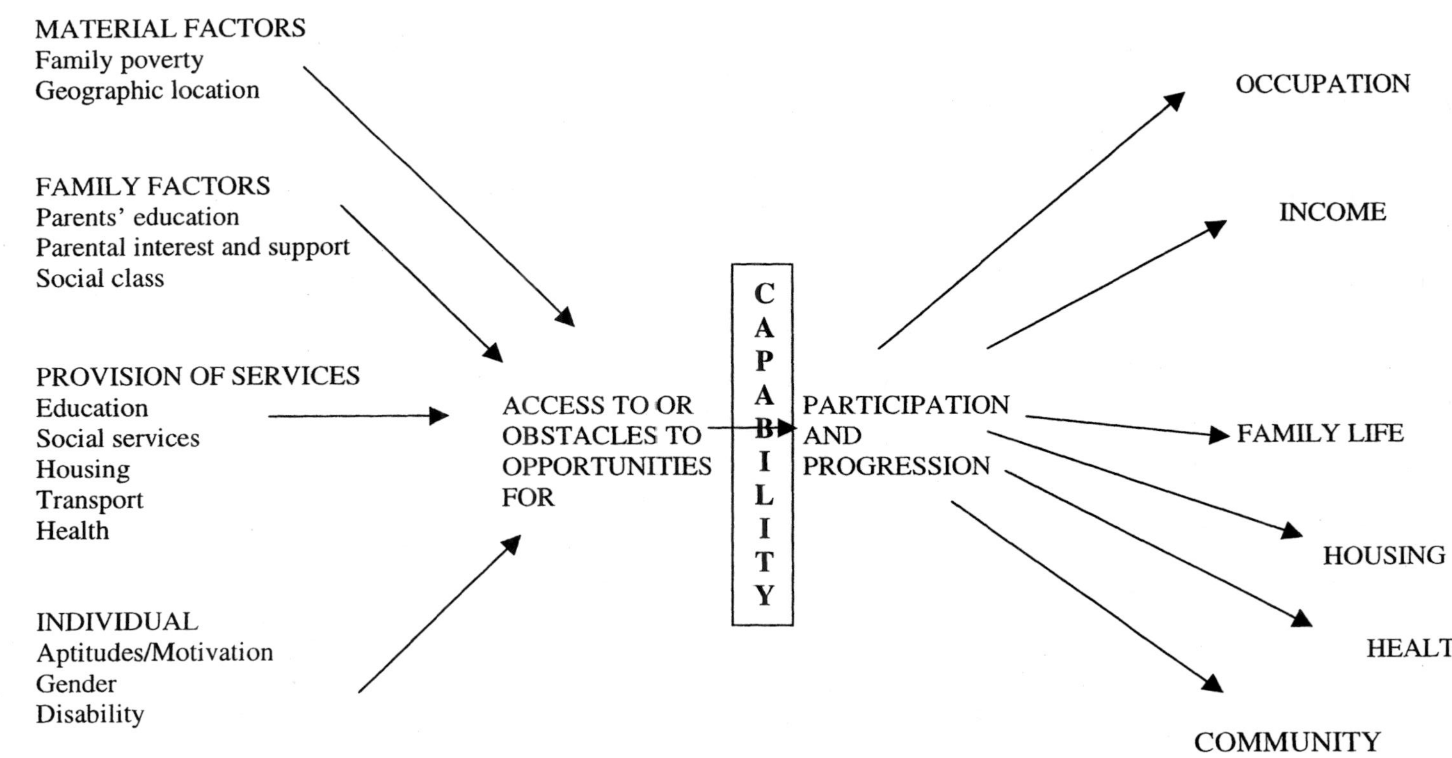

143

former and full participation in citizenship for the latter, as illustrated on the right-hand side of Figure 1. The forms of status through which such citizenship is expressed include occupation, income, family life, housing, health, and community (including social and political participation). The social exclusion process may be conceived as one in which the probability of access to such outcomes is much reduced, or disappears altogether.

In the following sections, data collected in a number of countries is used to elaborate upon the significance of childhood components of social exclusion.

The Research Approach

The OECD is approaching the problem of studying social exclusion, as it applies to children, from several points of view, using literature from different research traditions. It is clear from what has been said above that the concept of exclusion requires a broad approach that will look at issues as they cover the development of the whole child. This approach is commensurate with that taken in earlier OECD studies on both children at risk and those with disabilities (OECD 1995, 1996, 1998, 1999, 2000).

For this study, three complementary approaches are being developed. These are:

1. Quantitative data based on the gathering of internationally comparative statistics and the development of indicators for disadvantaged and disabled students, to gauge the extent of the problem and the response being made by education systems;

2. Data derived from international longitudinal studies to understand more fully the nature of the causes; and

3. Qualitative case studies to describe the complexities and processes of potential holistic solutions.

Although these data are incomplete in many ways, they do give some indication of the current situation.

Statistics and Indicators on Students with Disadvantages, Learning Difficulties and Disabilities

What is the extent of the problem? Following the capabilities approach advocated by Sen (1992, 1999), a starting point for understanding the potential extent of childhood social exclusion and governments' responses is to look at efforts being made to create equal capabilities in students with disabilities or disadvantages. The data reported here cover provision for education systems only, but nevertheless are critical to the discussion. The international comparisons are based on additional resources made available by countries to schools, to allow students with various forms and causes of learning difficulties to more effectively access curricula—and hence to avoid social exclusion. Such information is important to data-driven policy development.

All OECD countries provide, to a greater or lesser extent, for students who have difficulties in learning, by identifying categories of students with disabilities or disadvantages who are in need of extra support. Unfortunately, direct comparisons between countries using these categories are not possible, because systems have been developed independently within each country.

However, what is in common is the fact that countries provide extra resources for these children. This is the basis of the model that has been developed at the OECD/CERI in order to make valid international comparisons. Countries are asked to identify all their children who receive additional resources (this might be in the form of extra teachers, for instance) and then to categorize them according to three agreed-upon cross-national categories, which for reasons of neutrality are called here A, B, and C.

Briefly, category A is operationally defined to include those children whose difficulties in learning are perceived to be due to organic impairment—such as partial vision or physical disability. Category B includes those children who are having difficulties in learning but where no particular reason can be identified. Category C covers those children whose difficulties stem clearly from social disadvantage. (For a fuller description see OECD 2000.)

Figure 2 shows the proportions of students in primary and lower secondary education who receive additional resources to help them access the curriculum. As can be seen, there is wide variation between countries, with the United States supporting the most, some 42 percent, and Turkey the least, less than 1 percent. Figure 2 also shows how these students break down into cross-national categories A, B, and C. The proportion in cross-national category A is represented by gray bars, B by black bars, and C by white bars. Again, there are large differences between countries for all three categories. Such variation suggests that there are differences between countries in the ways that they try to overcome the effects of inequalities, and this could, in principle, have an impact on school outcomes through the processes described above, and hence on exclusion. It is important to note that a considerable number of students are involved.

Figure 3 shows the place where disabled students (category A) are educated—in either special schools (light gray bars), special classes (black bars), or regular classes in mainstream schools (dark gray bars). It Italy almost all disabled students are included. In contrast, in Switzerland nearly all disabled students are excluded. It is clear that there are substantial differences between countries, with potentially differential impacts on educational outcomes, because of the different curricula followed and the experiences of individual students according to the place of education. Here again, there is a source of the exclusion of substantial numbers of children, one that also applies differentially across countries and would contravene Article 29 of the Convention on the Rights of the Child, if it could be shown that the education provided does not develop abilities to the fullest potential.

Figures 4a, 4b, and 4c show that boys and girls appear to receive differential treatment. In all countries, more boys find

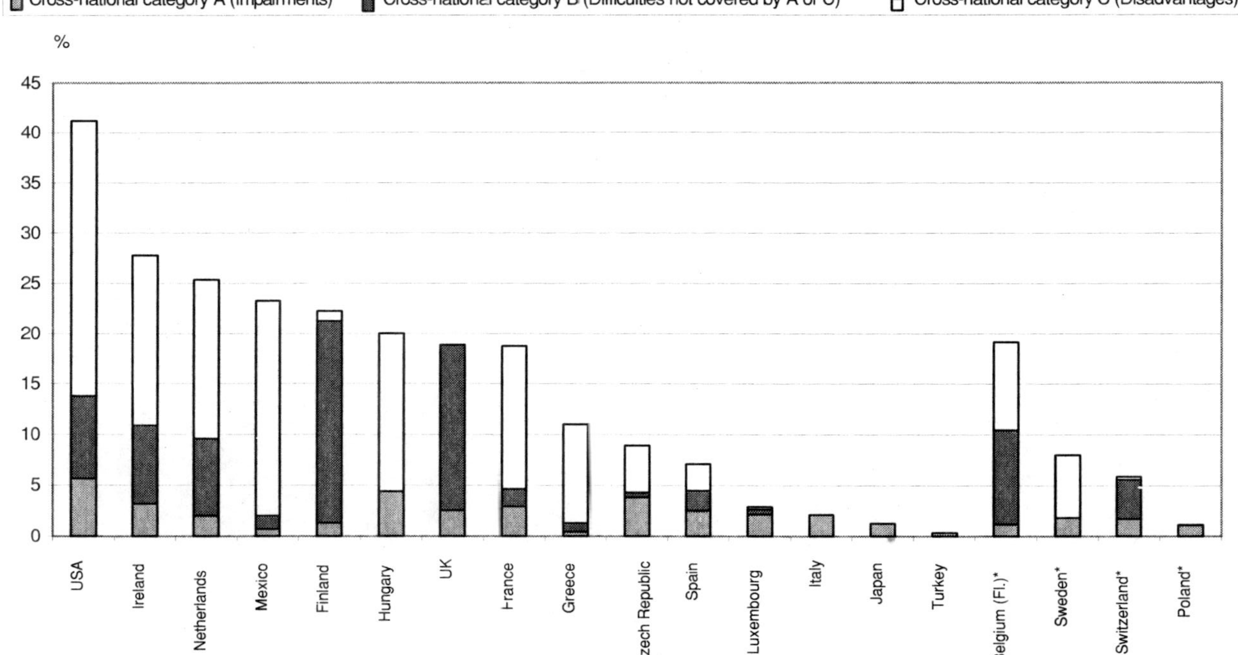

Countries are ranked in descending order according to the percentage of students receiving additional resources. * Countries with partially missing data are placed on the right-hand side. Source: OECD.

147

Figure 3: Distribution of Students in Cross-National Category A, by Special Schools, Special Classes, and Regular Classes

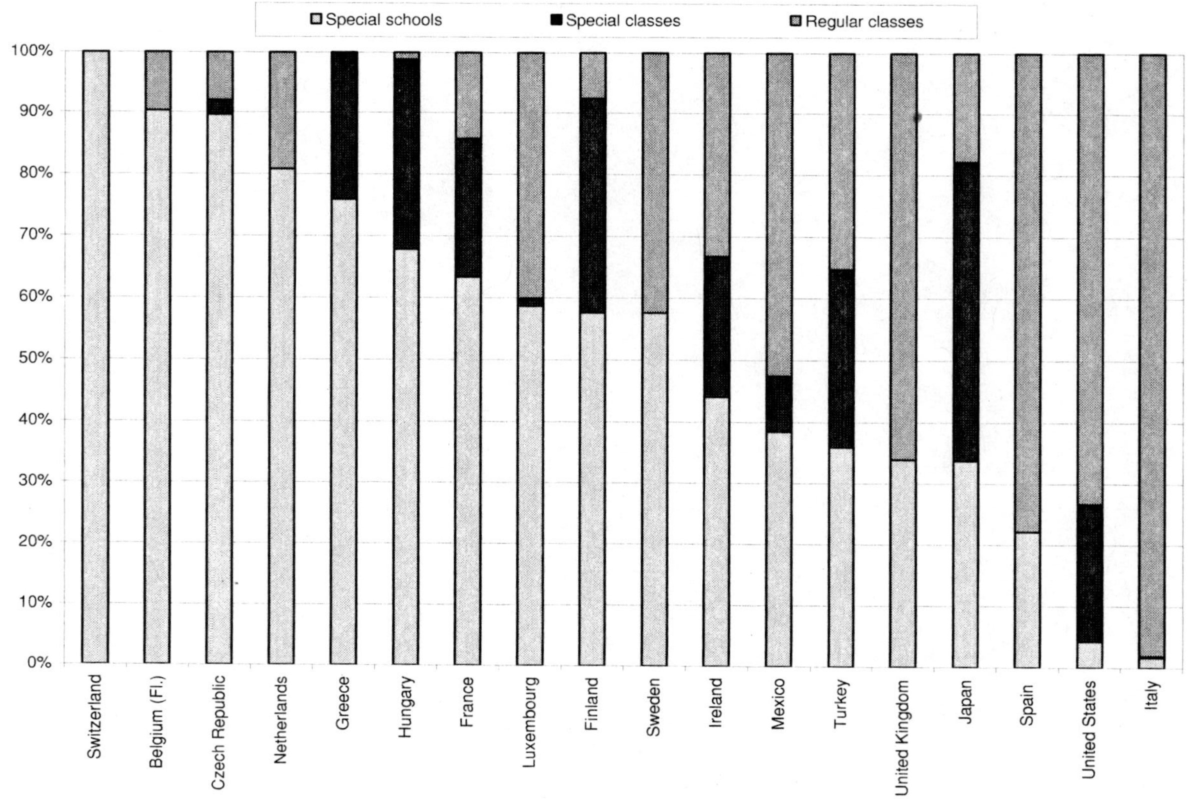

Countries are sorted in decending order according to the proportion of students in special schools.

Source: OECD

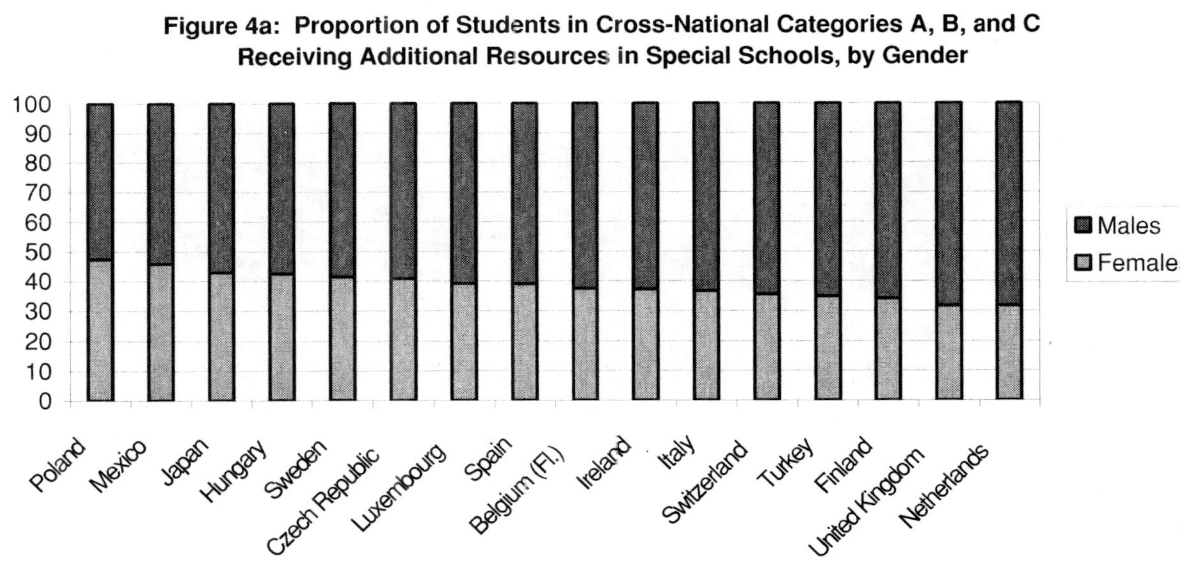

Figure 4a: Proportion of Students in Cross-National Categories A, B, and C Receiving Additional Resources in Special Schools, by Gender

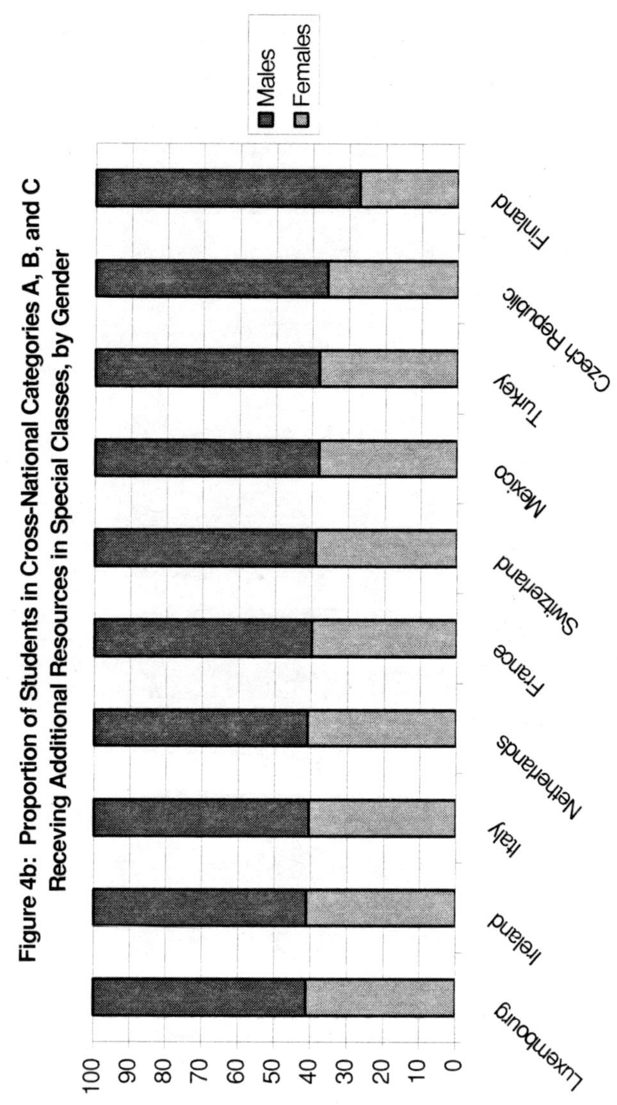

Figure 4b: Proportion of Students in Cross-National Categories A, B, and C Receving Additional Resources in Special Classes, by Gender

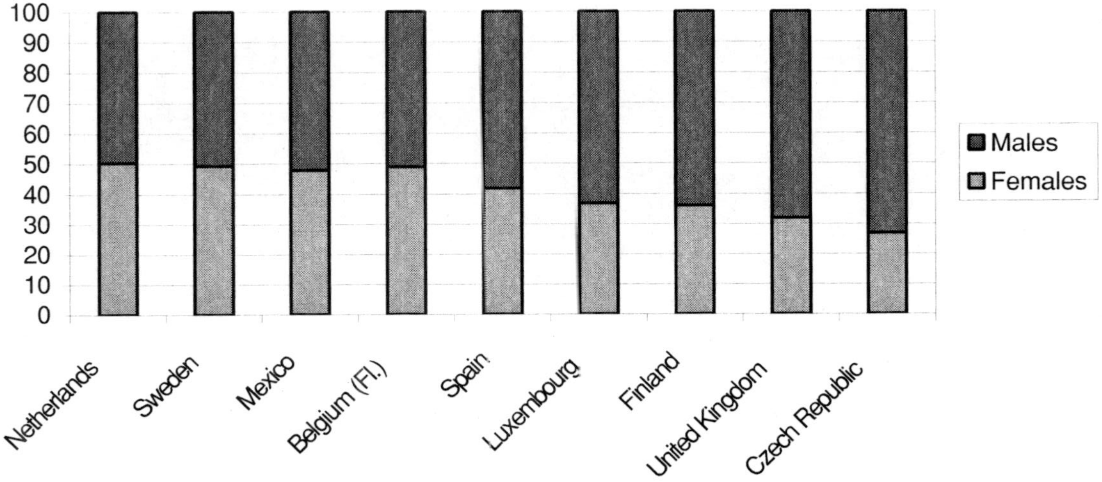

Figure 4c: Proportion of Students in Cross-National Categories A, B, and C Receiving Additional Resources in Regular Classes, by Gender

themselves in some form of special provision (such as special schools, special classes, or extra help in integrated classes), than do girls. It has been argued above that boys tend to be more sensitive to negative environmental consequences than girls, and these findings may simply reflect this result. On the other hand, whether special schools or classes are the answer is another question, because these facilities themselves tend to hinder inclusion (e.g., in the labor market) and could serve to exacerbate further the problem of exclusion as described above, thus contravening the Convention articles concerned with gender equality (e.g., Article 2).

Although in need of further development, these statistics and indicators give a broad indication of the extent of the problem as seen by OECD countries. In the next section data, taken mainly from longitudinal studies carried out in a number of countries, are used to throw light on the range of processes and factors thought to be key elements in leading to the difficulties requiring the additional resources identified above.

Illustrations from Longitudinal Research

A full understanding of social exclusion depends on longitudinal research involving long-term follow-up of individuals from early life onwards. There are a limited number of studies that meet this criterion fully. Most have been done in the UK, New Zealand, the United States and Sweden (e.g., Wadsworth 1991; Silva and Stanton 1996, Bynner, Ferri, and Shepherd 1997; Ferri 1993; Fergusson et al. 1989), see Exhibit 1 for brief notes on the studies included. Full details are supplied in Bynner (1996). These involve the collection of information from large samples of individuals over long periods, ideally from birth into adult life. Alongside these studies are those that comprise narrower investigations of children in high-risk situations—such as growing up in public care— or monitoring the outcomes of children who have experienced different kinds of interventions to combat risk.

The life histories captured by the longitudinal data can be used retrospectively to identify the circumstances and experiences early in life that precede particular problems in adulthood. They can also be used prospectively, to identify children at risk of social exclusion in adulthood and the accumulation of risk as they get older (Rutter 1988; Brooks-Gunn, Phelps, and Elder 1991; Caspi et al. 1990). The analysis of data from cohort members' children gives the added opportunity of finding out the extent to which social exclusion processes are repeated from one generation to the next (e.g., Gregg and Machin 1997; Gregg et al. 1998, Chase-Lansdale et al. 1991).

EXHIBIT 1: LONGITUDINAL RESEARCH RESOURCES
(FROM BYNNER 1999)

Denmark: *Project Metropolitan.* **This was based on a cohort of 12,270 boys born in the metropolitan area of Copenhagen in 1953, who have been followed up nine times since 1983. The study began when the boys were 13 years old; all the data about their earlier lives came from administrative records.**

Great Britain: *National Survey of Health and Development (1946 cohort).* **This began with a perinatal mortality study of 16,000 births in one week in March 1946. A stratified sub-sample of 5,382 cohort members (single legitimate births) was followed up subsequently. Over 3,000 cohort members are still participating, with the last data collection taking place when they were 43 years old.**

Great Britain: *National Child Development Study (1958 cohort).* **This began with a perinatal mortality study of 17,000 births in a single week in March 1958, subsequently followed up at ages 7, 11, 16, 23, and 33.**

Great Britain: *1970 British Cohort Study (BCS70).* This began with a birth survey of 17,000 babies born in one week in April 1970. Data have been collected subsequently at ages 5, 10, and 16.

Great Britain: *Cambridge Study of Delinquent Development.* This started with 411 boys aged 8 in 1961. These have been followed up since in nine waves. Of the original group, 408 are still in the study.

New Zealand: Dunedin *Study of Education, Psychology and Health.* This started in 1972 and comprises follow-up of 1,037 cohort members into adulthood, with data collected at birth, age 3, and subsequently at two-year intervals.

New Zealand: *Children's Survey on the Development of Anti-Social Behaviour and Substance Abuse.* This started with 1,265 individuals born in a Christchurch urban area in New Zealand. They were followed up at 4 months and then annually thereafter

Sweden: *Malmö Study.* This started in 1938 with a sample of 1,500 children in the third grade of school (average age 10). The sample has been followed up though six surveys into adulthood, with over 1,000 individuals still participating.

Sweden: *Evaluation through Follow-up.* This study, based in Gothenberg, brought two separate longitudinal studies together in 1991: the *Individual Statistics Project* conducted by the Department of Educational Research at the University of Gothenberg (ISP) and *Evaluation through Follow-up* conducted by the Department of Education in Stockholm University (UGU). Overall, it involves follow-up (minimum start at age 10) of five birth cohorts—1948, 1953, 1967, 1972, and 1977—involving over 50,000 individuals.

Sweden: *Individual Development and Adaptation.* **The Psychology Department of Stockholm University has carried out another longitudinal study, following 1,393 children who were aged 10 in 1965. There have been eight waves, the last of which was in 1992.**

Sweden: *Project Metropolitan.* **This started in 1964 with a sample of over 15,000 13-year-olds in Stockholm who were followed up at regular intervals. Government administrative data, including criminal convictions, is linked to the respondents' records up to the age of 30. (Currently suspended).**

United States: *National Longitudinal Study of Youth.* **This began with multiple cohorts, aged 14, 15, 16, 17, 18, 19, 20, and 21. These have been followed up annually since 1979. Since 1986, children of mothers who were cohort members have been tested on a number of behavioral and cognitive measures every two years, and the mothers have been interviewed.**

United States*: Kauai Longitudinal Study.* **Based on 1,311 pregnancies in Hawaii, with 1,000 children followed up at regular intervals. Of the original group, 615 were still participating at age 18 and 545 at age 30.**

Importance of Early Learning

It has long been established that the early stages of life, even the first year of growth, are of enormous importance in development. During the first year of life, brain development is rapid and extensive, and vulnerable to environmental influence. Early stress has been shown to have a negative impact on brain function. Low birth weight, similarly, has been shown to carry health and education risks in adult life (Wadsworth 1991; Silva 1996). The first signs of the risk potential of these occurrences are evident almost as soon as they are measurable. For example, in the 1970 British Birth Cohort study, even at 22 months social gradients in cognitive development were appearing, though the overall dispersion of performance around the mean was also large. At 42 months, the dispersion had been reduced and the gradients were larger. With every additional month of life, children with parents in unskilled manual jobs fell behind those whose parents were in nonmanual occupations. Every step up the class scale carried a benefit in terms of enhanced opportunities that were manifest from the day the child was born (Feinstein 1998).

It seems that what takes place before a child starts school may be as important, if not more important, as what happens afterwards. Figures 5a and 5b put this into perspective for the development of literacy and numeracy skills from birth to adulthood, as revealed by the 1958 British birth cohort study (NCDS) and the 1970 British birth cohort study (BCS70).

The graphs show the percentages of variation in men and women's literacy and numeracy scores at age 37 that can be explained by a whole range of background characteristics measured from birth to age 33. Notably, there is a huge escalation in the percentage of variation explained through the preschool and primary school years, and then a leveling off from about age 11 onwards, with only small additions to the percentage explained from then on. This demonstrates the importance of early years' experience in accounting for variation in adult outcomes; but it is also evident that much of the variation remains unexplained. Part of the unexplained variation can be attributed to measurement error. A substantial proportion, however, is also attributable to individual life experiences (e.g., employment and leisure) that are not predictable from early circumstances and experiences (Bynner and Steedman 1995; Parsons and Bynner 1998). More generally, the graphs tell us that although there is a high degree of predictability of capability from earlier capabilities, circumstances and experiences, there is a great deal that is not predictable. Failure to acquire the basic skills—a key risk factor in social exclusion—is predictable only to a certain extent. Some socially excluded adults

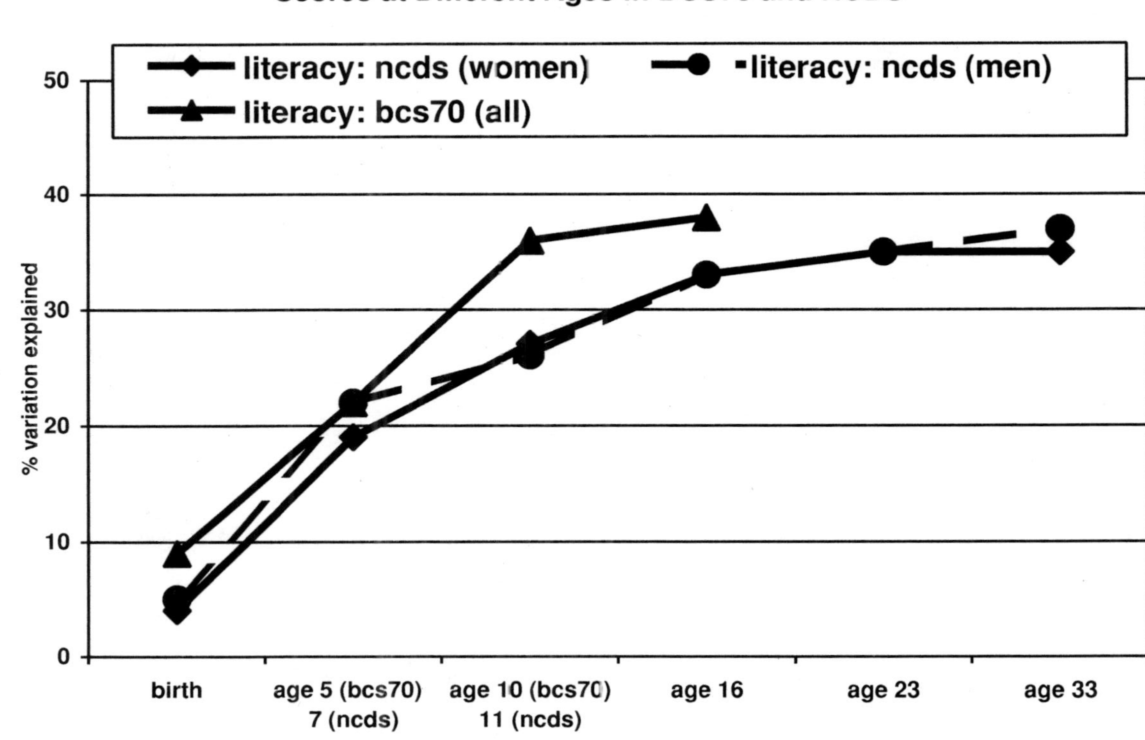

Figure 5a: Percentage Variation Explained in Adult Literacy Scores at Different Ages in BCS70 and NCDS

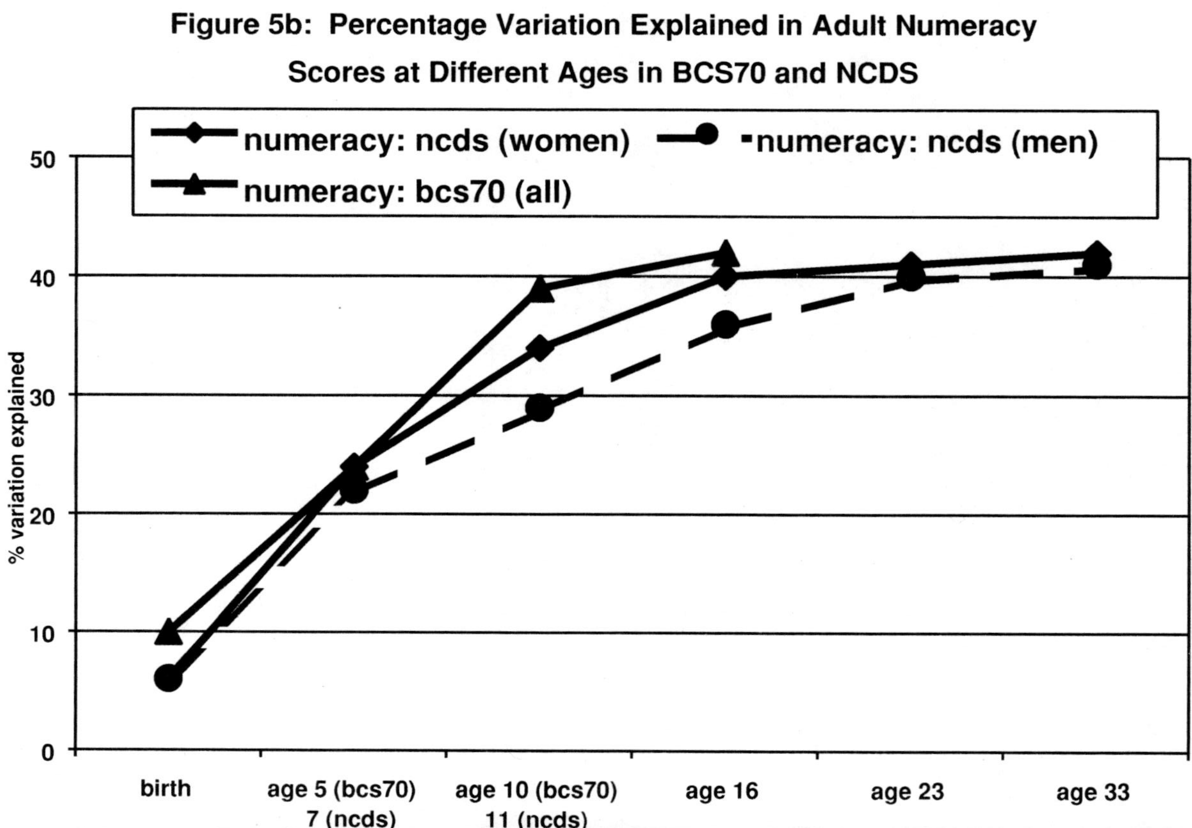

Figure 5b: Percentage Variation Explained in Adult Numeracy
Scores at Different Ages in BCS70 and NCDS
numeracy: ncds (women)
numeracy: ncds (men)
numeracy: bcs70 (all)
% variation explained
50
40
30
20
10
0
birth
age 5 (bcs70) 7 (ncds)
age 10 (bcs70) 11 (ncds)
age 16
age 23
age 33

do not show evidence of risk in childhood, and similarly many children for whom social exclusion would be expected later on in life manage to make the necessary adjustments to achieve success in adult life. As we shall see later, although many people are trapped by disadvantage, many escape from it (Pilling 1990).

Risk and Protective Factors

Reviewing all the predisposing conditions for the social exclusion outcomes mentioned earlier, a common set of features with some variations across particular outcomes can be identified. These are listed below under four broad headings (Exhibit 2): child factors, economic factors, parent factors, and school factors. One of the key findings from statistical modeling that has attempted to identify the individual effects of these characteristics and their combined effects (e.g., Gregg and Machin 1997; Kiernan 1995), is the key role of poor educational achievement, which is typically associated with all of them.

Child Factors

As disability prompted the original concerns about social exclusion, it makes sense to use it as the benchmark against which to set other risk factors. The long-term outcomes of disability, whether physical or mental, are well established from longitudinal studies. Disabled children, when they reach adulthood, are less likely than the able-bodied to be in full-time employment, to have a partner, to have children (this is mainly true of men), to own their homes, or to express satisfaction with life. Educational qualifications ameliorate these outcomes only to a limited extent. In an analysis of 1958 British Birth Cohort study data, half the 33-year-old men in the lowest qualification group, who at age 7 had learning disabilities, had never had a partner and lived in rented housing. This compared with one-fifth of those without the learning disability. Twice as many were also out of employment at the time of interview. Women with learning difficulties appeared to have been

Exhibit 2: Childhood Risk Factors

Child Factors	Economic Factors	Parent Factors	School Factors
Low birth weight Physical and mental disability	Poor living conditions	Low aspirations for child and lack of interest	Preschool support poor or absent
Poor visual-motor skills	Rented social housing in economically rundown areas	Troubled relationships within family, especially between parents and between parents and children, and family breakup	Inadequate transition from preschool to primary school
Poor early cognitive development	Overcrowding	Lack of adult role models for child	Home-school relations weak
Poor grasp of basic skills: reading and number work	Free school meals for children	Lack of social controls	Poor leadership
Temperamental difficulties—hyperactivity, impulsiveness and attention (HAI) disorder Aggressivity Lack of attachment to adult role models	Low family income	Frequent changes of career and parental absence	Low teacher commitment to child
Behavioral problems		Father long-term unemployed	Manual working class intake
Poor school attendance		Lone parent	Council estate intake
Low self-esteem		Parents with alcohol, drug or psychiatric problem	Poor monitoring of children's progress

just as disadvantaged with respect to employment as the men, but far more of them had partners and children. At the higher qualifications levels these differences persisted, but were reduced in size.

Some of these disabilities arise from conditions accompanying or arising from birth. Although children born pre-term do not necessarily appear to suffer any lasting ill effects, low birth weight (as measured by weight for gestational age) has shown up in a number of studies as a long-term risk factor (Wadsworth 1991; Silva 1996). Such children are twice as likely to die in the first 28 days of life (Blair and Ramey 1997). Long-term physical outcomes are reflected in respiratory illness and cardiovascular disease (Wadsworth 1991). Those surviving frequently experience early learning difficulties and behavioral disorders. The Dunedin birth cohort study showed, for example, that there was often language delay, which hindered the development of reading skills (Silva 1996).

Other risk factors associated with early life include poor diet, which is also often associated with early learning problems (Wadsworth 1991). There is a poor grasp of visual-motor skills and below-average performance on copying design tests, when children first enter primary school. Later cognitive achievements, including vocabulary, reading, and numberwork, are also stunted relative to other children (Silva 1996). Temperamental difficulties including hyperactivity, impulsivity, and attention deficit disorder are also risk factors, as are behavioral problems, lack of attachment to adult role models, and poor school attendance. These play a role, particularly, in relation to outcomes associated with later criminality.

Economic Factors

Material risk factors often lie behind many of the individual (child) risk factors, interacting with biological factors in the production of the personal characteristics associated with risk. They are less susceptible directly to intervention, so serve particularly in the identification of populations (of families and of children) where intervention may be necessary. They include the situational effects of living in poor conditions in areas that are generally dis-advantaged, but—particularly at the level of individual family life—poor-standard rented accommodation, overcrowding, and low family income, often manifested by the children's need for free school meals. Hobcraft (1998), using longitudinal data from the 1958 British Birth cohort study, demonstrates the impact of per-sistent poverty on a range of adult social exclusion outcomes at age 33, including poor qualifications, low income, teenage preg-nancy, and depression. Duncan and Brooks-Gunn (1997) refine the picture further, concluding—from a number of U.S. and Canadian longitudinal studies—that poverty has large effects on children's ability and achievement, but not so much on behavior, mental health, or physical health measures. The latter are more strongly affected by family breakdown, but this too can affect edu-cational attainments, even when poverty is taken into account. They also conclude that the main impact of poverty occurs in early childhood rather than in adolescence. McLeod and Shanahan (1990), using the same data source as some of the Duncan and Brooks-Gunn authors—the U.S. National Longitudinal Study of Youth—also concluded that persistent poverty has an effect on mental illness, but only the kind involving internalization of symp-toms (e.g., depression). It also affects boys more than girls.

Socioeconomic status or social class, as assessed from parent's occupation, is a surrogate for many economic indicators. Those families at the bottom of the social class scale are most likely to have children at risk (Wadsworth 1991; Silva 1996). Timms's analy-sis of Project Metropolitan data collected in Stockholm extends this finding, demonstrating that social mobility downwards is a risk factor particularly for maladjustment in adolescence and later mental illness (Timms 1991, 1995)

Parent Factors

Factors connected to parents include parents' own lack of education, lack of parental interest and support as reported by teachers, or indications that the teachers do not know whether the parents are interested. This is often coupled with parents' low aspirations for the children. Material disadvantages in the parents' own childhood also emerge as important factors in their children's development, demonstrating continuity of social exclusion risk from one generation to the next (Gregg and Machin 1997). Poor relationships within the family, especially between parents and children, and lack of social controls on the children are another set of risk factors, as are family breakdown, frequent changes of career and parental absence (Kiernan 1995, 1997; Chase-Lansdale et al. 1995). On the other hand there is little evidence that mothers' employment—in isolation from other factors—has deleterious effects (Silva 1996).

Many of these parental problems arise through difficulties in the parents' own lives—expressed through the path of exclusion on which many find themselves. Thus labor market problems brought about by poor educational achievement impel many young women into early pregnancy. Those growing up in public care are particularly prone to this course (Quinton and Rutter 1988). Long-term unemployment of fathers not only limits family income, but reinforces a role model that in some families challenges the importance of educational and occupational achievement. Parents with criminal convictions or psychiatric problems add another set of predisposing conditions for childhood risk.

School Factors

Preschool experiences are important, especially those that lay the foundations of primary education. Being ready to attend, and attending, nursery school or play group can be part of this (Osborn and Millbank 1987; Bynner and Steedman 1995). Absence of such preschool preparation can be a risk factor, especially in families where the parents' own educational resources are limited. In school itself, the main risk factors have to do with being in a low stream, and experiencing remedial education. The social-class composition of the school population also features, as does the geographical location (e.g., inner-city, high-rise rented housing).

One of the more surprising findings is the lack of identifiable school and classroom effects in most analyses. Counterintuitively, even class size appears to have negligible effects on children's attainment. Preschool intervention programs, such as the U.S. Head Start (e.g., Schweinhart, Barnes, and Weikart 1993) can often demonstrate their efficacy, but as Bailey (1997) points out, success is generally associated with overall program quality rather than the specifics of organization and curriculum. In terms of risk factors, what seems to be significant is an overall disjunction between the capability of the family to provide the child with the necessary educational preparation and support, and the expectations of the education system. Middle-class families have little difficulty in keeping in step with what the system expects of them, but many less advantaged families have great difficulty in doing so. Effective programs are those able to bridge the gap.

Vulnerable Groups

Taken on its own, no single risk factor in the list above is likely to set the social exclusion process going. It has been repeatedly stressed that risk factors go together, either in tandem or one leading to another. It is in combination, therefore, that their potency for impeding children's cognitive and behavioral development becomes apparent. Rutter (1990) argues that risk and protection are better seen as processes or mechanisms than factors or variables; it is the interactions between the two at particular life stages, or over an extended period of time in a particular location, that determine the direction the child's development will take.

Certain geographical locations, especially in the inner cities, are likely to show higher than average concentrations of risk, centered on poor housing, family poverty, and low-achieving schools. But the most clearly vulnerable children are those whose key family relations are weak or absent. Children growing up in public care are the most obvious example, followed by children with absent parents, parents with alcohol or drug problems, and those with criminal records (Robins and Rutter 1990). Children with disabilities, especially those growing up in difficult material circumstances, are also particularly vulnerable. Early intervention, as in the U.S. Head Start, can target cognitive skills, and be directly backed up by the kind of social support the child may be lacking. The U.S. High/Scope Perry Preschool project, based on random allocation of children to a preschool program for comparison with a control group, was able to demonstrate lasting reductions in social exclusion outcomes for the intervention group over a period of twenty years (Schweinhart, Barnes, and Weikart 1993). The later the intervention takes place, the more work will have to be done in changing the direction of a well-established risk trajectory.

Protective Factors

Garmetzy (1993) draws on an early model by Birch and Gussow (1970) to stress the cyclical nature of the processes of risk and protection, tracing the effects of family poverty on children: first, via poor maternal health and inadequate services; second, through social deprivation and environmental inadequacy; and third, through child malnutrition and poor health. These predispose the child to school failure that, in turn, increases the likelihood of long-term unemployment. The consequence is family poverty and the repetition of the cycle.

The antidote to vulnerability is breaking the cycle through protection. But this involves more than just countering those factors identified with risk. Risk factors point to children where intervention may be needed; protective factors suggest the form the intervention needs to take. Garmetzy (1985) identifies three types of protector:

• *Child-based:* concerned with such characteristics as personality, autonomy, self-esteem and positive social orientation

• *Family-based:* concerned with cohesion, warmth and an absence of discord

• *Community-based:* concerned with availability of external support systems that encourage and reinforce a child's coping efforts.

Rutter (1990) makes the point that protection, like risk, is less of a fixed factor than a process that counteracts the negative developmental processes arising from multiple risks. Such processes support Garmetzy's concept of protectors and the opening up of opportunities. Timing is also critical if these interventions are to have the most impact. In the early years, success depends on recruiting the family—especially the mother—into the role of educator. Guralnik and Neville (1997) argue that for parents to do this effectively, their information needs have to be met (this is especially the case for children with disabilities). They also need social support, not only from professionals, but from others in a similar situation to their own. Professional social support is most effective when it is informal and mirrors as closely as possible the person's social world.

Life-Course Patterns

The examination of risk and protective factors in social exclusion draws attention repeatedly to their connectedness and interdependency. This challenges the psychiatric approach to adjustment problems in adolescence and their outcomes in adulthood. Psychiatrists rely on diagnosis in terms of recognized categories of personality disorders (e.g., the DSM-IV-TR classification of the American Psychiatric Society). The alternative (developmental) approach (Rutter 1990) conceives such problems more as interactions among personal characteristics (capabilities, temperament, gender, ethnicity); the immediate social environment (relationships); and the institutions to which the individual relates (such as family and school). The significance of each in the social exclusion process will vary from one age to the next, from one individual to the next, and from one social situation to the next. Nevertheless, broad patterns of such relationships that result in social exclusion can be established from longitudinal data. Two patterns are examined here: origins of education and employment problems; and behavioral problems, criminality and mental health.

Origins of Education and Employment Problems

It has long been established that disadvantaged circumstances in childhood adversely affect school performance later. The 1946 birth cohort study supplied some of the early evidence of this, and in such books as *The Home and the School,* James Douglas, the principal author, also identified parents' aspirations as important factors in children's educational development (Douglas, 1964; Douglas and Ross, 1968). Analysis of data from a range of longitudinal studies enables us to track the origins of children's educational difficulties. We can exploit the full strength of the longitudinal data, over even longer periods of time (Bynner and Steedman 1995; Parsons and Bynner 1998; Wadsworth 1991; Silva and Stanton 1996).

Central to educational achievement is the acquisition of the basic skills of literacy and numeracy. Exhibit 3 sets out the factors involved in the process at each of the main educational stages, illustrating the role of these skills in mediating the effects on educational achievement of circumstances and experience.

The key early risk factors that emerge from the range of variables that have been studied are difficult material circumstances in the home (including low income, social rented housing, overcrowding, and the need for free school meals for the children). These are often associated with lack of parental interest and aspiration, and absence of support at home for early learning. There is an association with consistently poor performance in cognitive tests: from visual-motor tests such as copying designs, through early reading and mathematics tests right through to qualifications. Behavioral problems and poor school attendance also emerge as significant factors, as the children move through primary school and in particular, secondary school. Early school leaving follows, accompanied by difficulty in gaining employment. Any work that is obtained is usually low-grade, often casual, and rarely offers training. At every stage, cognitive outcomes mediate the effects of earlier circumstances and experience—serving the dual func-

Exhibit 3: Origins of Education Difficulties and Protection Targets

Life Stage	Risk Factors	Main Outcomes	Protection Targets
Preschool	Disadvantaged home background Parents' education poor No preschool preparation—mother not reading to child	Visual-motor skills weak Limited vocabulary	Preschool preparation Family disadvantage
Early Primary School	Visual-motor skills poor Disadvantaged home background Parents' interest low	Reading skills weak Math skills weak	Primary curriculum Family disadvantage Family literacy Home-school relations Pupil-teacher ratio
Late Primary School	Cognitive skills weak Disadvantaged home background Parents' interest low	Reading skills weak Math skills weak	
Early Secondary School	Disadvantaged home background Reading poor Mathematics poor Non-exam/ low-level exams Behavior problems Parents' interest low	Reading skills weak Math skills weak Examination potential low	Secondary curriculum School/class organization Examinations policy Home-school relations Student behavior Teacher expectations
Late Secondary School	Reading poor Mathematics poor School attendance poor Behavior problems Teacher expectations low	Reading skills weak Math skills weak Public examinations not taken	
Post-16	Basic skills poor Early leaving of full-time education No qualifications No work-based training Unemployment	Reading skills weak Math skills weak No academic qualifications No vocational qualifications	Further educational curriculum Youth training First employment Work-based training Employers Unemployment Leisure life
Adulthood	Literacy and numeracy poor No further education or training No continuous employment unemployment	Literacy poor Numeracy poor No further vocational qualifications No professional qualifications	Basic skills education Further education and training Work-based training Unemployment Parent education

tion of risk outcome and risk producer. Thus, any targeting that fails to address centrally cognitive developmental processes, and the means by which they are enhanced or impeded, is unlikely to be of lasting value.

We must conclude that critical elements of preschool preparation are missing for children who experience cognitive difficulties and end up educationally backward. In particular, the constructive play that underpins the development of visual-motor skills is absent; this then impedes early reading. Without early reading, mathematics development is similarly stunted. Such children enter secondary school well behind their peers and experience great difficulty in catching up.

Behavioral Problems, Criminality and Mental Health

The factors that predict behavioral and psychological difficulties in children are very similar to those that predict basic education difficulties, although the latter are implicated more heavily in the former than *vice versa*. In adolescence and early adulthood these may convert, in Farrington's words (1987) into a constellation of "socially deviant features . . . including drinking, [use of] drugs and reckless driving, sexual promiscuity and aggression of which criminality is only one element." The common history is similar to that for educational failure, and includes large families, poor housing, fathers with erratic job histories, broken homes, and parents convicted of crimes. The main differences that mark out criminality have to do with temperament and relational factors, first at home and then within school.

A number of studies have identified children who tend to be most prone to risk in this respect (Graham and Bowling 1995). Such children are often hyperactive and show impulsiveness and attention disorders (HIA). These are often accompanied by early aggression and poor peer relationships (Bergmann and Magnusson 1991; Stattin and Magnusson 1989). These characteristics, which may be genetically based (Rutter et al. 1997, 1998), are related to, but distinct from, the conduct disorders of early childhood

(Farrington et al. 1990). HIA is typically accompanied by cognitive problems, whereas conduct disorders need not be. The existence of these HIA characteristics helps to explain why not all siblings of a delinquent child have the problems in adolescence that result in delinquency and adult crime (e.g., Caspi et al. 1996; Moffitt and Harrington 1996; Wadsworth 1991).

Analysis of data from the Dunedin birth cohort study in New Zealand distinguished between "life course" persistent and "adolescent situation specific" offenders, and examined the early childhood characteristics of the two groups (Moffitt and Harrington 1996). The defining characteristics of the life course persistent group had to do with temperament coupled with adverse family conditions, low cognitive ability, low self-esteem, and low attachment to parents. The situational delinquents showed none of these temperamental characteristics, and little evidence of the adverse family conditions. In other words, much situational delinquency was part of "normal growing up" even though it could often lead to trouble with the police and ensuing problems.

Studying the effect of family disruption, set against that of parental deviance, reveals another interesting feature of the early antecedents of delinquent behavior. A study (referred to earlier) by Quinton and Rutter (1988) compared children growing up in state care with a control group, in terms of these characteristics. Family disruption, rather than the parental deviance, was a critical factor for both sexes, but especially for girls.

Such findings are part of a body of evidence suggesting that certain temperamental characteristics in children are often associated with poor family relations, to which is added the pressure of low incomes and family breakdown. But is it the breakdown as such that is crucial, or what leads up to it within the family? A number of studies using 1958 birth cohort study data have addressed questions concerning the consequences for children of divorce (e.g., Ferri 1976; Elliot and Richards 1991; Chase-Lansdale et al. 1995; Kiernan 1997). Elliot and Richards (1991), for example, demonstrate convincingly that for most developmental outcomes, the problem behaviors *precede* divorce and relate mainly to difficulties that existed in the family before the divorce occurred. Kiernan (1995) found that differences in educational and career outcomes were much reduced when pre-existing family conditions were taken into account, whereas early partnership and parenting difficulties appeared to connect to the divorce itself. She concludes that "we should be as concerned about the conditions that preceded divorce and sometimes lead to divorce, such as poverty and economic uncertainty, as well as with the consequences of marital breakdown."

What seems to happen in such families is that children with temperamental difficulties add to the existing tension in the family, exacerbating negative relations. The children with temperamental difficulties show low levels of attachment to their parents, which further weakens the parents' often ineffective social controls. In consequence, the child enters primary school ill-prepared. Another set of relational problems, comparable to that in the family, follow—but this time between teachers and children. The child's behavior in the classroom is a source of stress for the teacher, who will tend to exercise every effort to inhibit the child's disruptive effects, and consequently appears in the child's eyes in an authoritarian role. Exclusion from school may follow. The irony is that frequent standoffs between teachers and such children may endow them with heroic qualities in the eyes of other children, strengthening their self-esteem and consequently reinforcing the problem behavior. There is a strong tendency for juvenile delinquents who are convicted of offences to have shown such characteristics as children. They exhibit a form of alienation throughout their school careers, which often originates in alienation within their own families (Rutter et al. 1997).

Such maladaptive patterns can be usefully viewed in terms of failures in adaptive capacities and coping behavior, with their outcomes reflected in behavioral disorders and criminality. They may also result in psychological difficulties, of which anxiety and depression are the most common, particularly among girls. In their review of these kinds of outcomes in adolescence, Ebata et al (1990) emphasize, along with all the other factors reviewed here, the significance of the social context in triggering the maladaptive and sometimes regressive responses that lead to mental illness. A changing family situation, with new relationships to be negotiated, or with children too young for a key transition—such as from primary to secondary school—can operate cumulatively to heighten stress. Educational performance, including the degree of motivation, is also typically implicated in the production of this stress and the reaction to it (Roeser, Eccles, and Freedman-Doan 1999).

Protective Patterns

What can reverse these processes, in other words, protect against risk? In relation to education, the right-hand column of Exhibit 3 identifies the key protective factors, identified from studies of individuals in longitudinal studies who managed to overcome early disadvantage and lead successful adult lives. Pilling (1990) selected a sample of adults, aged 27, from the 1958 birth cohort study, who as children had met all the criteria of disadvantage, yet had reached the top bands of educational achievement by age 16. As adults they had achieved high incomes and high status jobs, and owned their own homes. These were matched with another sample of adults who as children had similarly met all the criteria of disadvantage and had not succeeded in adult life. Both samples were interviewed, using a mixture of quantitative and qualitative techniques. The main discovery was that the achievers had experienced family cohesion, high parental aspirations and high parental interest in their progress, and that schools or particular teachers had shown "strong commitment" to them over an extended period of time. It is important to note, however, that the earlier the disadvantage occurred, and the longer it had persisted, the lower was the likelihood that these factors would counter it.

The Kuai study carried out by Werner (1989) in Hawaii, similarly tracked down the 540 members of her cohort study at age 30, to find out who had succeeded against predictions and what had protected them. One in three of her original 1,000-strong cohort had a delinquent record. Two-thirds of those who had experienced risk factors (impairment, chronic poverty, parents with no education, troubled family environment—boys more than girls) developed serious learning and behavior problems by age 18. One-third developed into caring adults. She found that half the stressful life events that significantly increased the likelihood of a criminal record or an irrevocably broken marriage by age 30 took place in infancy and early childhood. Of those who had overcome the risk, the most common characteristics were, for both sexes, high levels of achievement orientation. In early childhood, problem-solving skills and communication skills were prominent; in middle childhood, alternative caretakers to the parents had an important role; and intrapersonal factors such as internal locus of control and self-esteem were significant in adolescence. For all these factors, boys were less resilient than girls in early childhood and in late adolescence; in middle childhood and adolescence girls were more vulnerable.

Protective factors in the Kuai study included dispositional attributes such as activity level, sociability and intelligence; affectional ties within the family that provided emotional support in times of stress; external support systems at school, work, or church that rewarded the individual's competence and provided a sense of meaning; and internal locus of control. Good social relations with other children, and better reasoning and reading skills, were also prominent.

Such findings dovetail with conclusions drawn from evaluations of preventative interventions meant to reduce the risk of criminality. In reviewing the results of such studies, Graham notes the value of home visits to engage parents in preschool education. Therapeutic programs, such as High/Scope, aim to help families cope with children's aggressive behavior, and help families stay together and avoid the risk of the child being taken into public care. Successful approaches through the schools targeted aggressive behaviors such as bullying, and the strengthening of home-school relations (Graham 1998). Casework, including individually-based therapy and counseling in isolation from the child's social context, were generally found to be ineffective.

It is clear that there are many routes and sources that may lead to children experiencing adjustment and learning difficulties, with potentially disastrous outcomes in terms of failure and exclusion. In the next section, case studies provide descriptions of country responses at the community level, which were intended to take on some of the complexities identified above.

A Case Study Example of a Country Approach

In this section, a UK example of developments intended to tackle social exclusion in children is briefly reported. For a somewhat different U.S. initiative, see Bronheim et al., 1999.

The United Kingdom [9]

Education Action Zones have been implemented by the current government as a way to tackle social exclusion through community development. There is a special concentration on tackling underachievement and raising educational standards that are often linked to other problems, such as truancy, exclusion from school and crime. Education Action Zones (EAZs) are being implemented to provide new solutions to these problems, by developing new forms of governance to enable capacity building and social inclusion to evolve over time. EAZs are supposed to develop action plans to improve educational outcomes, through interlinking strategies that will bring together schools, families, business, and health and social services in a coordinated approach (e.g., see OECD 1996, 1998) to improve learning and teaching.

In the schools now organized into EAZs, educational standards have often been low, with significantly reduced achievements in comparison to other local education authorities in England as a whole. This is especially true for boys. There are generally negative attitudes to learning, with 30 percent of 16-year-olds not proceeding into training or further education. The post-16 dropout rate in EAZs can be double the local figure.

This approach is in the tradition of developing learning communities, and hence improved governance through the renewal of civil society. In addition to creating learning communities and improving community governance, some of the features of this approach include the development of lifelong learning, partnership across sectors, participation, and improved consultation and dialogue with the citizens involved.

EAZs frequently suffer from geographical isolation, for example in the case of housing areas on the edges of urban developments that have poor transport and communication facilities. Rural isolation is also common, especially if parents do not have cars. The areas are often seriously deprived in terms of social amenities, access to shopping facilities, libraries, and sporting facilities. There is often substantial poverty. Unemployment is common. Children often are hungry or without appropriate clothes. Children also often suffer from ill health that can lead to a variety of problems, including learning difficulties, restricted emotional development, poor mental health, criminality, and teenage pregnancy.

Single-parent families and absent male role models are common. Mothers, therefore, must have a number of jobs to raise adequate resources and to keep their families together. There are few male role models in the nursery and primary schools, and many EAZs are looking at ways of bringing males into schools as teachers or assistants.

These factors lead to low standards in education, and hence to potential exclusion through factors such as inertia and restricted experiences, parochiality, hopelessness about the future, low educational aspirations, disaffection, and community anger.

This work on EAZs is also based on a new agenda, or new culture, for learning and education in the UK. The key components of this, which are being practiced in EAZs, are the following:

• *Learning for Capability and Active Membership in Society*

Education has been driven by too narrow a conception of the competencies that people need to acquire. The challenge is to reconceive the purposes of education as preparation for living and becoming active citizens.

Education has been shaped by a mistaken division between knowledge and practice. The point of learning is practice. Learning now needs to be connected to the wider experiences of people and the purposes that are to shape their lives. The relevance of education to the lives of people is the challenge facing educators at every level.

• *Valuing the Whole Learner—Recognizing All the Needs of All the Learners*

Learning has been mistakenly envisaged as a narrow cognitive process, with thinking and feeling separated out. The research of Goleman (1996) and others is illuminating the significance of emotional well-being, and the health and quality of relationships, for learning and fulfilling one's potential. Educators are learning to recognize the importance, not only of developing basic cognitive skills and competencies, but also of addressing the social and emotional health of each person to enhance self-esteem, motivation, and well-being.

• *Learners are Capable*

Education has been undermined for many because of flawed assumptions about capacity and intelligence. The research of Gardner (1993) is transforming our understanding of human ability and potential. In this model, intelligence is thought of as being far more diverse and broad-ranging than in more traditional approaches. Intelligence is not viewed as a fixed internal characteristic of individuals; instead, each individual is accepted as able and with a different portfolio of abilities that require careful nurturing to develop that person's talents to full potential. Intelligent behavior is learned (Perkins 1995) through experience, hard work, and developing capacities for critical self-reflection. Achievement in all areas of learning needs to be celebrated.

• *Involving the Family*

The more holistic view of the learner that the new education strives to achieve is reflected in the practice of involving parents and families. This also requires focusing support on the family unit to encourage and bring out the best in both parent and child through family learning and the development of positive parent-child interaction.

• *A Pedagogy of Active and Flexible Learning*

If learners are to become active members of their communities, then institutions need to become crucibles of active learning, enabling people to see the purpose of education by reconnecting learning and practice. Grounding education in investigative learning and reflective problem-solving motivates people to become involved in their learning. Gardner's research has revealed that individuals learn in different ways. Music, color, and movement are as important in teaching as traditional forms of knowledge transmission.

• *Curriculum Extension and Enrichment*

The new education is grasping the importance of encouraging and supporting learning beyond the classroom. As the work of Macbeath (1999) has emphasized, achievement depends upon encouraging self-directed learning out of classroom and school hours. The DfEE[10] has reinforced the importance of extracurricular provision for achievement in school: through curriculum enrichment (such as sport, drama, and photography) and curriculum extension (study support opportunities provided before and after school and during holiday times).

• *Multi-Agency Working*

Addressing the needs of the learner and the family leads to a much more integrated approach to education, one that involves family support, health, and social services in a coordinated approach.

• *Engagement with the Wider Community*

The new pedagogy that relates learning to practice and social purpose, together with the inclusion of families, provides the context for engagement with the wider community. An education that includes adults in their own learning, as well as in support of the education of the young, creates a broader agenda supporting education for lifelong learning.

EAZs are faced with overwhelming problems and require radical innovations. Additional funding, although helpful, is not enough. Therefore, many are basing their new pedagogy—intended to improve the capabilities of an active citizenship—around four key themes: reconnecting learning to living through preparation for active citizenship; understanding all the needs of the learner, particularly emotional well-being; enriching understanding of human capability and potential; and active learning for developing responsible as well as reflective learners.

Learning to Learn in the Learning School

The learning school places dialogue at the center of its management strategy for change, helping colleagues to unify around shared purposes. This process helps schools to learn to value all the students in the school, thus creating motivation for learning.

Community Governance

Some of the characteristics of community governance were perceived by Stewart and Stoker (1988) to include:
• "the government of difference, both responding to differences in needs and aspirations and creating differences. One learns from difference rather than uniformity;
• a capacity for local choice, which creates the potential for innovation, and the learning made possible by that innovation;
• the diffusion of power—change is more easily made on the smaller scale, and there are limits to political capacity at the centre;
• a concern for the community beyond the mere provision of service;
• local and visible government—decisions can more easily evolve when made close to the community than when made in corridors and committees of central government;
• a renewed basis for accountability in local democracy."

Summary and Conclusions

The initial discussions of social exclusion that began in France in the 1970s were focused on disabled and seriously marginalized persons. However, the current debate has expanded this group considerably, and has become more concerned with features of modern life that, broadly speaking, threaten to exclude people from citizenship and deny them certain rights. This analytic framework fits well with other contemporary discussions of social exclusion, such as that developed by Sen (1992, 1999) using a capabilities model. By extension, social exclusion for children is best understood in terms of a rights-based approach stemming from the UN Convention on the Rights of the Child.

A rights-based approach raises a large number of questions, not only about the form of services and support that must be provided to prevent a denial of rights, but also in terms of how systems are evaluated. For instance, a utilitarian approach to education would promote education in ways that would raise the sum total of achievement in the education system, and thus would target resources on those best placed to make use of them. In contrast, a rights-based approach calls for maximizing the potential of each child, irrespective of his or her potential contribution to the overall economy. Thus, policies aimed to combat social exclusion should change the focus of evaluation criteria from one based on averages to one relying, in addition, on the distribution of access and achievements. Such an approach would go beyond human capital formation to include the psychological and social resources underpinning social and cultural capital, to add up to what has been described as identity capital—the key protector against adult social exclusion in modern society.

Much work remains to be done to elaborate on all of these different factors, but it is clear from the data presented that a start has been made, and that focusing on the causes of social exclusion in childhood is a powerful approach. There is wide recognition of the complexities of the processes that can lead to social exclusion, the need to find holistic and preventive solutions, and the involvement of disability issues in the wider debate. Statistics and indicators in this area are rather new, but they have been well-received, certainly provide another dimension to the discussion, and are essential for policy formulation. The case study I have cited from the UK shows the creative energy and innovative approaches that need to be put into communities to help to prevent exclusion.

Much is known about the nature of the causes of the difficulties and their extent; much less is known about the effectiveness of the approaches taken and the extent to which they provide the equal capabilities identified by Sen as needed to overcome social exclusion. Developing evaluation models to provide data about the effectiveness of the approaches that are being implemented is of the essence, and will be an important next step in coming research programs.

Notes

1. The views expressed in this chapter are those of the author and invited experts and cannot be taken to represent official policy of the OECD.

2. This chapter has been prepared by Peter Evans at the Organisation for Economic Co-operation and Development, Centre for Educational Research and Innovation (OECD/CERI) from papers commissioned by OECD/CERI from a number of national experts. The author would like to thank Professor John Bynner and Professor Stephan Klasen for their agreement to reproduce substantial portions of their own texts in the first part of this chapter; and to Professor Stewart Ranson, Professor Suzanne Bronheim, Professor Phyllis Magrab, and Professor Raymond Crowel for agreeing to reproduce substantial sections of their case studies on the UK and the United States.

3. The three others related to participation are the ability to "go out with family and friends" (62% see that as a necessity), being "useful to others" (70%) and having a "social life" (42%). Unfortunately, a more direct question on the ability to participate in economic, social, and public life on equal terms was not asked in the survey (Golding 1995).

4. Not all of the Articles in the Convention are stated in ways that make them legally enforceable claims, and the Convention as a whole is only enforceable in most countries if it has been translated into appropriate national legislation. This chapter is not concerned with this aspect, and uses the Convention only to highlight areas where the spirit of the Articles is not adhered to.

5. For example, equal opportunities in access to leisure activities could be interpreted as merely providing for nondiscrimination of access. Equal capabilities would, in addition, also call for efforts to ensure that all groups

of the population effectively feel able to participate, and might necessitate specific interventions to open such facilities to children with particular disadvantages.

6. The special concern about physically and mentally disabled children is understandable, in view of the fact that disabled children still face many barriers in developing and developed countries. At the same time, there are good reasons to extend this concern to nondisabled children who are otherwise disadvantaged.

7. This does not, of course, mean that educational policies should be geared exclusively towards meeting these rights. It merely means that, in an assessment of the benefits and costs of alternative educational policies, these rights are and should be an important consideration.

8. At the same time, establishing the empirical linkages may be very important in order to generate societal consensus around policies combating social exclusion, particularly if it can be shown that social exclusion hurts everyone and not just those suffering from it. The complete reliance on this approach is quite tricky, as it might get bogged down in empirical issues, rather than focusing on important policy questions.

9. The work described here is based on a fuller account of the working of Education Action Zones in the UK (Ranson 1999).

10. The Department for Education and Employment of the UK government, now the Department for Education and Skills (DfES).

References

Bailey, D. B., Jr. (1997). "Evaluating the Effectiveness of Curriculum Alternatives for Infants and Pre-Schoolers at High Risk." In *The Effectiveness of Early Intervention,* ed. M. J. Guralnick. Baltimore: Paul H. Brookes.

Becker, G. S. (1975). *Human Capital.* Washington, D.C.: National Bureau of Economic Research.

Berghman, J. (1995). "Social Exclusion in Europe: Policy Context and Analytical Framework." In *Beyond the Threshold: The Measurement and Analysis of Social Exclusion.* ed. G. Room. Bristol, UK: Policy Press.

Bergman, L. R., and D. Magnusson. (1991). "Stability and Change in Patterns of Extrinsic Adjustment Problems." In *Problems and Methods in Longitudinal Research: Stability and Change,* ed. D. Magnusson, L. R. Bergman, G. Rudinger, B. Trestad. Cambridge: Cambridge University Press.

Birch, H. G., and J. D. Gussow. (1970). *Disadvantaged Children: Health, Nutrition and School Failure.* New York: Harcourt Brace and World.

Blair, C., and C. T. Ramey. (1997). "Early Intervention for Low Birth Weight Infants and the Path to Second Generation Research." In *The Effectiveness of Early Intervention,* ed. M. J. Guralnick. Baltimore: Paul H. Brookes.

Bronheim, S., P. Magrab, and R. Crowel. (1999). "Social Exclusion in the United States: Policy Implications for Community Solutions." Paris: Organisation for Economic Co-operation and Development. Available at: www.oecd.org/cer/obj5/docs.

Brooks-Gunn, J., E. Phelps, and G. H. Elder. (1991). "Studying Lives Through Time: Secondary Data Analyses in Developmental Psychology." *Developmental Psychology* 27: 899–910.

Bynner, J. (1996). "The Use of Longitudinal Data in the Study of Social Exclusion." Paris: Organisation for Economic Co-operation and Development. Processed.

———. (1999). *Risks and Outcomes of Social Exclusion Insights from Longitudinal Data.* Paris: Organisation for Economic Co-operation and Development. Available at: www.oecd.org/cer/obj5/docs.

Bynner, J., E. Ferri, and P. Shepherd, eds. (1997). *Twenty Something in the 1990s: Getting On, Getting By, Getting Nowhere.* Gower, UK: Ashgate.

Bynner, J., and J. Steedman. (1995). *Difficulties with Basic Skills.* London: London Basic Skills Agency.

Caspi, A., G. H. Elder, and E. S. Herber. (1990). *Childhood Person-*

ality and the Prediction of Life's Course Patterns. Cambridge: Cambridge University Press.

Caspi, A., A. R. Harkness, T. E. Moffitt, and P. A. Silver. (1996). "Intellectual Performance: Continuity and Change." In *Child to Adult*, ed. P. A. Silver and W. R. Stanton. Oxford: Oxford University Press.

Chase-Lansdale, P. L., A. J. Cherlin, and K. E. Kiernan. (1995). "The Long-Term Effects of Parental Divorce on the Mental Health of Young Adults: A Developmental Perspective." *Child Development* 66: 1614–34.

Chase-Lansdale, P. L, J. Brooks-Gunn, F. Mott, and D. A. Phillips. (1991). "Children of the National Longitudinal Survey of Youth: A Unique Research Opportunity." *Developmental Psychology* 7: 918–31.

Côte, E. (1996). "Sociological Perspectives on Identity Formation: The Culture Identity Link and Identity Capital." *Journal of Adolescence* 19: 491–96.

Douglas, J. W. B. (1964). *The Home and the School.* London: MacGibbon Kee.

Douglas, J. W. B., J. M. Ross, and H. R. Simpson. (1968). *All Our Futures*. London: Peter Davies.

Duffy, K. (1995). *Social Exclusion and Human Dignity in Europe*. Strasbourg: Council of Europe.

Duncan, G. D., and J. Brooks-Gunn, eds. (1997). *Consequences of Growing Up Poor*. New York: Russell Sage Foundation Press.

Ebata, A. T., A. C. Petersen, and J. J. Conger. (1990). "The Development of Psychopathology in Adolescence." In *Risk and Protective Factors in the Development of Psychopathology*, ed. J. Rolf, A. S. Masten, D. Cicchetti, K. H. Nuechterlein, and S. Weintraub. Cambridge: Cambridge University Press.

Ebersold, S. (1999). *Exclusion and Disability*. Paris: Organisation for Economic Co-operation and Development. Available at: www.oecd.org/els/edu/ceri/conf220299.

Elliot, J., and M. Richards. (1991). "Parental Divorce and the Life Chances of Children." *Family Law* 481–484.

Evans, P. (2001). "Equity Indicators Based on the Provision of Supplemental Resources for Disabled and Disadvantaged Students." In *In Pursuit of Equity in Education*, ed. W. Hutmacker, D. Cochrane, and N. Bottani. Boston: Kluwer Academic.

Farrington, D. (1987). "Early Precursors of Frequent Offending." In *From Childhood to Citizens*, vol. 3, ed. J. Q. Wilson and G. C. Loury. New York: Springer Verlag.

Farrington, D., R. Loeb, and W. B. Van Kannen. (1990). "Long Term Criminal Outcomes of Hyperactivity, Impulsivity, Attention Deficit and Conduct Problems in Childhood." In *Straight and Devious Pathways from Childhood to Adulthood,* ed. L. Robins and M. Rutter. Cambridge: Cambridge University Press.

Feinstein, L. (1998). "Pre-School Educational Inequality? British Children in the 1970 Cohort." Discussion Paper 404. London: Centre for Economic Performance, London School of Economics.

Fergusson, D. M., L. J. Horwood, F. T. Shannon, and J. M. Lawton. (1989). "The Christchurch Developmental Study: A Review of Epidemiological Findings." *Paediatric and Perinatal Epidemiology* 3: 302–25.

Ferri, E. (1976). *Growing Up in a One-Parent Family.* Slough, UK: National Foundation for Educational Research.

————, ed. (1993). *Life at 33: The Fifth Follow-up of the National Child Development Study.* London: National Children's Bureau.

Gardner, H. (1993). *Multiple Intelligence: The Theory in Practice.* New York: Basic Books.

Garmetzy, N. (1985). "Risk and Protective Factors in the Development of Psychopathology." In *Recent Research in Developmental Psychopathology,* ed. J. E. Stevenson. Cambridge: Cambridge University Press.

————. (1993). "Developmental Psychopathology: Some Historical and Current Perspectives." In *Longitudinal Research on Individual Development,* ed. D. Magnusson and P. Casaer. Cambridge: Cambridge University Press.

Golding, P. (1995). "Public Attitudes to Social Exclusion: Some Problems of Measurement and Analysis." In *Beyond the Threshold: The Measurement and Analysis of Social Exclusion,* ed. G. Room. Bristol, UK: Policy Press.

Goleman, D. (1996). *Emotional Intelligence: Why It Can Matter More Than IQ.* London: Bloomsbury.

Graham, J. (1998). "Promoting a Less Criminal Society: What Works in Preventing Criminality." In *Reducing Offending: An Assessment of Research Evidence on Ways of Dealing with Offending Behaviour,* ed. P. Goldblatt and C. Lewis. Home Office Research Study 187. London: Home Office.

Graham, J., and B. Bowling. (1995). *Young People and Crime.* Home Office Research Study 145. London: Home Office.

Gregg, P., S. Harkness, S. Machin, and J. Thomas. (1998). *Child Development and the Family Income.* York, UK: Joseph Rowntree Foundation.

Gregg, P., and S. Machin. (1997). "Blighted Lives: Disadvantaged

Children and Adult Unemployment." *Centrepiece* 2: 14–18.

Guralnick, M. J, and B. Neville. (1997). "Designing Early Intervention Programmes to Promote Social Competence." In *The Effectiveness of Early Intervention*, ed. M. J. Guralnick. Baltimore: Paul H. Brookes.

Hobcraft, J. (1998). "Intergenerational and Life Course Transmission of Social Exclusion: Influences of Childhood Poverty, Family Disruption and Contact with the Police." CASEpaper 15. London: CASE Publications.

Kiernan, K. E. (1995). "Transition to Parenthood: Young Mothers, Young Fathers—Associated Factors and Later Life Experiences." Welfare State Programme, WSP–113. London: STICERD, London School of Economics

————. (1997). "The Legacy of Parental Divorce: Social, Economic and Demographic Experiences in Adulthood." CASEpaper 1. London: CASE Publications.

Klasen, S. (2002). "Social Exclusion, Children, and Education: Conceptual and Measurement Issues." *International Journal of Theory and Research In Education. Special Issue: Human Rights, Inclusion and Education.*

Macbeath, A. (1999). *Schools Must Speak for Themselves: The Case for School Self-Evaluation.* London: Routledge.

McLeod, J. D., and N. J. Shanahan. (1990). "Poverty, Parenting and Children's Mental Health." *American Sociological Review* 58: 351–66.

Moffitt, E. E., and H. L. Harrington. (1996). "Delinquency: The Natural History of Antisocial Behavior." In *Child to Adult*, ed. P. A. Silva and W. R. Stanton. Oxford: Oxford University Press.

Organisation for Economic Co-operation and Development. (1995). *Children and Families at Risk.* Paris: Author.

————. (1996). *Successful Services for Our Children and Families at Risk.* Paris: Author.

————. (1998). *Co-ordinating Services for Our Children Youth at Risk: A World View.* Paris: Author.

————. (1999). *Inclusive Education at Work.* Paris: Author.

————. (2000). *Special Needs Education: Statistics and Indicators.* Paris: Author.

Osborn, A. F., and J. E. Millbank. (1987). *The Effects of Early Education.* Oxford: Clarendon Press.

Parsons, S., and J. Bynner. (1998). *Influences on Adult Basic Skills.* London: London Basic Skills Agency.

Perkins, D. (1995). *Outsmarting IQ: The Emerging Science of Learning Intelligence.* New York: Free Press.

Pilling, D. (1990). *Escape from Disadvantage.* London: Falmer Press.

Quinton, D., and M. Rutter. (1988). *Parenting Breakdown: The Making and Breaking of Intergenerational Links.* Aldershot, UK: Ashgate.

Ranson, S. (1999). *The New Learning for Inclusion and Capability: Towards Community Governance in the Education Action Zones.* Paris: Organisation for Economic Co-operation and Development.

Robins, L., and M. Rutter. (1990). *Straight and Devious Pathways from Childhood to Adulthood.* Cambridge: Cambridge University Press.

Roeser, R. W., J. S. Eccles, and C. Freedman-Doan.(1999). "Academic Functioning and Mental Health in Adolescence: Patterns, Progressions and Routes from Childhood." *Journal of Research in Adolescence* 14:135–74.

Room, G. (1995). *Beyond the Threshold: The Measurement and Analysis of Social Exclusion.* Bristol, UK: Policy Press.

Rutter, M. (1988). *Studies of Psycho-Social Risk: The Power of Longitudinal Data.* Cambridge: Cambridge University Press.

———. (1990). "Psychosocial Resilience and Protective Mechanisms." In *Risk and Protective Factors in the Development of Psychopathology,* ed. J. Rolf, A. S. Masten, D. Cicchetti, K. H. Nuechterlein, and S. Weintraub. Cambridge: Cambridge University Press.

Rutter, M., B. Maughan, J. Meyer, A. Pickles, J. Silberg, E. Simonoff, and E. Taylor. (1997). "Heterogeneity of Anti-Social Behavior: Causes, Continuities, and Consequences." In *Motivation and Delinquency,* ed. R. A. Deinstbier and D. W. Osgood. Nebraska Symposium on Motivation, vol. 44. Lincoln: University of Nebraska Press.

Rutter, M., H. Giller, and A. Hagell. (1998). *Anti-Social Behavior by Young People: The Main Messages from the Major New Review of the Research.* Cambridge: Cambridge University Press.

Schweinhart, L. J., H. V. Barnes, and D. P. Weikart. (1993). *Significant Benefits: The High/Scope Perry Preschool Study through Age 27.* High/Scope Perry Preschool Series, no. 10. Ypsilanti, Mich.: High/Scope Educational Research Foundation.

Sen, A. (1992). *Poverty Reexamined.* Cambridge, Mass.: Harvard University Press.

———. (1999). *Development as Freedom.* New York: Knopf.

Silva, P. A. (1996). "Health and Development in the Early Years." In *Child to Adult,* ed. P. A. Silva and W. R. Stanton. Oxford: Oxford University Press.

Silva, P. A., and W. R. Stanton, eds. (1996). *Child to Adult*. Oxford: Oxford University Press.

Stattin, H., and D. Magnusson. (1989). "The Role of Early Aggressive Behaviour in the Frequency, Seriousness and Types of Later Crime." *Journal of Consulting and Clinical Psychology* 57: 710–18.

Timms, D. W. G. (1991). *Individual Characteristics, Parental Ideology and Mental Health in Adolescents*. Project Metropolitan, Research Report no. 34. Stockholm: University of Stockholm.

———. (1995). *Mental Health, Mental Illness and Family Background*. Project Metropolitan, Research Report no. 42. Stockholm: University of Stockholm.

Stewart, J., and G. Stoker. (1998). *From Local Administration to Community Government*. Fabian Research Series no. 351. London: Fabian Society.

UNICEF. (1989). *The Convention on the Rights of the Child*. New York: Author.

Wadsworth, M. (1991). *The Imprint of Time: Childhood History and Adult Life*. Oxford: Clarendon Press.

Werner, E. E. (1989). "Vulnerability and Resiliency: A Longitudinal Perspective." In *Children at Risk: Assessment, Longitudinal Research and Intervention,* ed. M. Brambring, F. Loesel, and H. Skowronek. Berlin: Walter de Gruyter.

Alternative Concepts for the Measurement of Children's Poverty: Review, Assessment, and a New Approach[1]

Robert Haveman and Andrew Bershadker

Introduction

Although nearly all societies strive to reduce poverty, no standard measure of poverty exists among the researchers, scholars, and policymakers who study and fight this social ill. Some social scientists and policymakers stress sociological aspects of well-being. Individuals living in squalid housing are deemed "housing poor." People with health deficits are "health poor." Individuals deprived of social contacts are described as being socially isolated, and hence poor in this dimension. Some advocate combining these and other measures into a multidimensional poverty concept. The goal would be to weight and aggregate these measures, obtaining an "index of poverty." In this context, individuals who fail "to reach 'minimally acceptable' levels of different monetary and nonmonetary attributes necessary for a subsistence standard of living" are defined as being poor.[2] Such an aggregation can greatly complicate policy design and discussion. Indeed, each dimension implies both a distinct target population and a distinct set of anti-poverty policies.

Moreover, to be useful, each separate component requires broad acceptance of numerous definitions and standards. What aspects of economic well-being are to be measured? Is there a cut-off level of well-being that separates the poor from the non-poor? Should we, (or even) can we, differentiate between exogenous constraints that force an individual below some level, and endogenous choices that an individual has made to put him or herself below that level?

These questions are particularly challenging when the relevant concept is "social poverty" or "social exclusion." Even defining such a concept is difficult. The European Union has stated:

> The concept of social exclusion is understood as a multidimensional phenomenon, where exclusion conceptually is characterized as the process which prevents people from a full participation in the society, i.e., from being socially integrated. Social exclusion is also considered as a relative phenomenon, meaning that the low income population of a given country and its characteristics are always compared to the characteristics of the rest of the population of that country.[3]

But such a statement begs a number of questions. We must define what "society" is. Is it the individual's immediate community, some larger circle of contacts, some form of the "majority," or something else entirely? We must define what "exclusion" is. If a person has many professional contacts, but lacks personal ones, is that person "socially excluded"? Is the relevant measure the quantity of contact, quality of contact, or some combination? How do we measure the quality of a social contact?

If the definitions of "society" and "exclusion" are resolved, then what aspects of inclusion are to be taken as relevant in determining whether a member of society is insufficiently included? For example, is a person who receives community support (welfare) to be thought of as included, or as excluded? Perhaps the answer to this question will depend on certain personal attributes such as a disability, substance abuse, or mental retardation. If so, which conditions are relevant? Furthermore, once this has been resolved, what measure of a given dimension of societal involvement is to be used as the norm? Is it the mean level of a particular indicator of social involvement, the median, or some proportion of these overall measures? Is an individual who has chosen to limit his or her social contacts better (or worse) off than one whom, despite his or her efforts, remains socially isolated? Finally, how do we account—or do we even try to account—for the subjective aspects of social exclusion? Two individuals, identical in every observable way, may feel quite differently about their social situations.

In this chapter, we approach the question of social exclusion, and in particular, children's social exclusion, from a somewhat different direction. We ask what fraction of the population of children live in families lacking the ability to connect with society in a specific, perhaps controversial, dimension. In recent years, the "message" sent to U.S. citizens generally, and especially to the economically and socially disadvantaged, has been that of self-reliance and economic independence (see discussion in "Why Another Concept of 'Resources Poverty?'," below). In particular, people have been urged to rely more on their own efforts and less on assistance from the public sector. The implicit corollary to this message is that those who are self-reliant will be welcomed as full, equal members of society.

This message has a substantive basis. Clearly, individuals who have the capability to work and contribute as functioning members of society—to be self-reliant—are more connected to that society; they certainly feel more connected. Given the currently dominant social message of self-reliance, we attempt to identify those families—and more specifically, the children in those families—who do not possess the skills and abilities to comply. We suggest that these non-self-reliant families and children are the truly destitute; that they experience a greater degree of social exclusion than the population of income poor.

Alternative Concepts of "Resources Poverty"

Economists tend to prefer a concept of hardship that reflects "economic position," or economic resources. However, economists hold widely varying perspectives on how available economic resources should be defined, in order to identify those people whose economic position lies below some minimally acceptable level. Some rely on the cash income of a family, and compare this value to a minimum-income standard taken to represent "needs" (also known as a poverty line). This economic concept underlies the official U.S. poverty measure (referred to below as "official poverty"), and its proposed revision based on the National Research Council (NRC) Panel Report (Citro and Michael 1995).[4]

However, even accepting income as the base concept leaves a number of important questions unanswered. For example, if income is taken to be the best indicator of economic status, is the appropriate measure annual income, an average of several year's income, or lifetime income? Should we examine pre-tax, pre-transfer income (or labor market earnings) or income after accounting for taxes and/or transfers? Should in-kind transfers be counted or excluded? Others adopting an economic concept of poverty look to the level of consumption as an indicator of the level of living.[5] Still others rely on families' own assessment of their economic well-being, and move from this assessment to a judgment regarding who is and how many are poor.

In addition to requiring a precise definition of economic position or well-being, a poverty measure must specify a minimum level of well-being (or "needs") in terms that are commensurate with a definition of "resources."[6] Ideally, such a needs measure would impose no social norm or judgment on people's preferences among goods or services (e.g., necessities vs. luxuries), or between work and leisure. Moreover, it would allow for differentiation according to household size and composition, and it would enable intertemporal variability in access to these resources and (in principle, at least) one's ability to "enjoy" the fruits of the resources (e.g., one's health status).

Each definition of "resources" embodies a judgment regarding why some families have a low economic position, while others do not. Statistical indicators of poverty derived from all of these resources concepts (and definitions of need) identify aspects of "hardship" that reflect a particular social objective. Use of them as a test of policy, therefore, requires the general acceptance of that objective. The many concepts of economic resources that can serve as the basis for poverty measures complicate policy design, as each concept implies both a different target poverty population and a different set of policies. When these poverty measures are used to indicate the prevalence and composition of children's poverty, the status of the family in which children live is attributed to the children themselves. Hence, a poor child is one that lives in a family whose resources (somehow defined) lie below its needs.

In the following sections, we discuss the judgments underlying these different definitions. It should be noted that judgments about whether the poverty concept is *absolute* or *relative* underlie all these poverty measures. The indicator is absolute if the definition of "needs" is fixed, so that the poverty threshold does not change with the standard of living of the society. A relative, income-based poverty measure uses a poverty line that is in some way related to the society's general standard of living.[7]

The Official U.S. Measure of Poverty

The official U.S. poverty measure (including its recently proposed revisions) is used to track the level and composition of poverty in the United States, and serves as the basis for measuring poverty for subgroups of the population, including children and the elderly. This measure has several distinct characteristics. First, it is a measure of income poverty; the purpose is to identify those families that do not have sufficient cash income to meet what is judged to be their annual needs. As such, it compares two numbers for each living unit—the level of its annual cash income, and the level of income that a unit of its size and composition requires to secure a minimum level of consumption. By relying solely on annual cash income as the indicator of resources, this measure ignores many potential sources of family well-being (e.g., social inclusion or "security") that may be weakly tied to cash income. Second, it is an absolute measure of poverty. Cash income is compared to income requirements, and that is that. As a result, even if the income of every non-poor individual in the society should increase, the prevalence of poverty in the society would not be affected.

The official U.S. poverty measure—whether or not a household has sufficient income from *either government support or its own efforts* to boost it above some minimum income threshold—has a particular philosophical basis. The implied social objective is that, together, the community's efforts and those of the individual should insure that some minimal level of cash income is attained. Hence, responsibility for the poverty status of individual families (and for the prevalence of poverty in the nation) lies with *both* individual *and* social choices, together with the structure of markets and political arrangements.

Implicit in this definition of poverty, then, is the presumption that, although people may experience hardship in many dimensions (e.g., education, housing, food, social contacts, security, and environmental amenities) or appear to others to be destitute in these dimensions, only a sufficiently low level of money income matters. This position rests on the following assumptions:

- money can buy those things whose absence makes people feel destitute;

- money income is a good proxy for welfare (or utility); and

- a particular year's income is an acceptable indicator of longer-term income.[8]

The most fundamental criticisms of the official measure focus on the basic social objective upon which it rests. Perhaps actual cash income is not the most salient indicator of well-being or position—perhaps public in-kind assistance should also be included, or public cash transfers should be excluded; perhaps some aspect of social functioning or noneconomic living arrangements should be incorporated in the measure. Similarly, in assessing poverty trends over time, perhaps the general trend in the overall level of living should be taken into account. Other poverty indicators may reflect these alternative judgments.

Aside from taking exception to the social objective that underlies this measure, most criticisms of it focus on the adequacy of the annual cash income measure of "command over resources." While the current cash income numerator may reflect the extent to which the family has cash income to meet its immediate needs, this indicates little about the level of consumption spending potentially available to the family. For many families, annual income fluctuates substantially over time. Unemployment, layoffs, a decision to undertake mid-career training or change jobs, health considerations, and (especially) income flows from farming and self-employment, may all cause the money income of a household to change substantially from one year to the next. As a result, the consumption spending of the family in any given year may differ substantially from the family's reported income in that year (see Mayer and Jencks 1992; Slesnick 1993).[9]

Even as an indicator of a family's ability to meet its immediate needs, the current income measure is flawed. It reflects neither the recipient value of in-kind transfers (e.g., Food Stamps and Medicaid, both of which are major programs in the United States) nor the taxes for which the family is liable.[10] Similarly, whereas current cash income—and hence the official poverty measure— reflects financial flows in the form of interest and dividends from the assets held by individuals, the assets themselves are not counted, nor is the value of leisure (or voluntary nonwork) time reflected in the measure.[11]

The U.S. official poverty measure is also silent on the differences in the implicit value that families place on income from various sources. Income from public transfers, market work, and returns on financial assets are treated as being equivalent in contributing to the family's well-being. As an absolute measure of poverty, the U.S. official measure also implicitly assumes that it is the circumstances of those at the bottom of the distribution that matter, and not income inequality per se. A growing gap between those with the least money income and the rest of society need not affect the official poverty rate.[12]

Similarly, the arbitrary nature of the denominator of the poverty ratio—the minimum income needs indicator—has also been criticized.[13] Given its conceptual basis and the crude empirical evidence on which the dollar cutoffs rest, the U.S. official poverty lines are essentially arbitrary constructs. Adjustments in the poverty line to account for different family sizes and structures also rest on weak conceptual and empirical foundations.

Finally, the data base on which the official U.S. poverty measure rests, the annual March Current Population Survey, undertaken by the U.S. Bureau of the Census, has been faulted for failing to accurately capture true cash income. In particular, the survey may suffer from serious underreporting of income components deriving from public transfers, assets, and illegal activities (see Rector, O'Beirne, and McLaughlin 1990).[14]

Relative Income Poverty Measures

Use of a relative standard for measuring resource poverty rests on the belief that poverty is not absolute, but rather is largely a matter of *economic and social distance*. A relative poverty measure stresses how the resources of a family (relative to its needs) allow it to function, relative to the rest of society. The use of a relative measure, it is argued, allows us to take into consideration changes in the overall economy (in terms of wages and prices), and changes in standard of living expectations (in terms of consumption, for example). As Fuchs states: "Today's comfort or convenience is yesterday's luxury and tomorrow's necessity. In a dynamic society it could hardly be otherwise."[15]

One prominent relative poverty definition considers those with incomes less than one-half of median income to be in poverty, hence reflecting the view that poverty is only meaningful when compared to overall income or spending levels.[16] The choice of a standard equal to one-half of median income is admittedly arbitrary. When first offered in the 1960s, this measure approximated the level of the Orshansky poverty line measure for a family of four.[17] However, today the U.S. official needs standard stands at approximately one-third of median income (Burtless and Smeeding 2001).[18]

This measure, of course, has other weaknesses. Critics of a relative measure point out its weakness in assessing the efficacy of anti-poverty efforts. The nature of the measure ensures that the poverty threshold will rise most rapidly in periods of economic growth, when those at the bottom of the distribution experience real growth in earnings and consumption. Hence, even though poor families may perceive themselves as better off during a prosperous period, the poverty rate may not fall, thus overstating the poverty problem. As Ruggles (1990) has stated: "poverty cannot decline under a relative poverty measure without some change in the shape of the income distribution as a whole."[19]

Consumption-Based Poverty Measures

A primary criticism of income poverty measures is that the annual cash income concept on which they rest is a poor indicator of the permanent income (or lifetime resources) of the family unit. Using such a measure, a wealthy family with a well-educated head and substantial assets, but a year of low income, would be classified as "poor." One proposal designed to avoid this problem involves the use of measured family consumption to determine poverty status, based on the argument that family consumption is a superior proxy for the family's permanent income, or family command over resources. Slesnick (1993) argues that poverty measures that rely on annual money income are "severely biased indicators of the level of poverty in the postwar United States.... Households in the lower tail of the income distribution are disproportionately represented by those with temporary reductions in income, and typically exhibit high ratios of consumption to income in an effort to maintain their standard of living."[20] It is this classification of *temporarily* low-income families as *permanently* needy that Slesnick believes artificially drives up the poverty rate. Slesnick's consumption-based poverty indicator uses household real consumption expenditure per equivalent adult (taken to be the quotient of real household consumption, a household-specific cost of living index, and an equivalence scale) as the indicator of resources. Slesnick's equivalence scales are designed to reflect total household budget needs, rather than just food needs. The consumption measure is combined with a poverty threshold designed to be "conceptually consistent" with the official poverty standard.[21]

The resulting consumption poverty measure suggests a much lower poverty rate than the official definition. Slesnick attributes this result to the over-representation of families experiencing a transitory income reduction among any year's income poor population. Because consumption decisions are based on permanent income (and are uncorrelated with transitory income), these temporarily income-poor households will have high ratios of consumption to income, and hence are not classified as poor in a consumption-based measure.[22]

Slesnick's consumption poverty measure has been criticized on several grounds. One particularly salient criticism concerns the nature of the equivalence scales that Slesnick employs. While some poverty indicators, including other consumption-based indicators (see Cutler and Katz, 1991), have shown a growing poverty rate over the last two decades, the Slesnick measure suggests that poverty in the United States has been secularly decreasing over that period. Triest (1998) attributes this result to the equivalence scales that Slesnick employs, equivalence scales that, he says, "take on values outside the range which many observers would consider reasonable."[23]

In addition to these criticisms specific to the Slesnick consumption poverty measure, there are other concerns associated with the use of a consumption-based measure. One impediment to utilizing a consumption-based poverty measure is the difficulty of obtaining complete and accurate family expenditure data. Although difficult in its own right, measuring a family's income is far easier than accurately calculating the amount a household spends in a year. Furthermore, consumption may not fully reflect a family's true well-being; it is possible that simple frugality may be mistaken for poverty.

Finally, like measures of income poverty, consumption-based poverty measures may not adequately reflect one's real position in society. Like income poverty measures, this position assumes that consumption is a good proxy for individual well-being, and superior in this dimension to current income.

Subjective Measures of Poverty

One additional poverty indicator should be mentioned—poverty measured by the subjective responses of individuals to questions inquiring into their perception of their economic position or well-being, relative to some norm.[24] Like the official U.S. measure, these subjective measures are based on an "access to resources" concept. However, because the subjective thresholds applied by people are likely to change as the incomes of the respondents change, this measure tends to be a relative, rather than an absolute, poverty indicator.

Typically, subjective poverty measures are based on surveys of households that ask the respondent to stipulate the minimum level of income or consumption that they consider to be "just sufficient" to allow them to achieve a minimally adequate lifestyle. One approach assumes that people have in mind some level of living that they consider "minimally adequate" (the minimum income necessary to "get along"). If they respond that their own level of living exceeds that minimum, one could by observing their actual income obtain both a monetary poverty line (by inference) and a poverty rate.[25]

Patricia Ruggles (1990) has pointed out the appeal of subjective measures: "After all, 'poverty' is a socially determined state, and in the end official thresholds come down to what some collection of politicians and program administrators consider an adequate level of resources to support a life in a particular community. It seems in many ways more appropriate to ask the members of that community directly what they consider a minimally adequate income level" (pp. 21–22). This characteristic suggests that, at least in this "threshold setting" dimension, subjective poverty measures may be more accurate indicators of the extent of social exclusion in a society.

Of course, these measures are not without their drawbacks. Subjective measures are implicitly based on individual opinions of what "minimally adequate" or "enough to get by" are. As such, a subjective poverty measure requires us to assume that individual perceptions of these notions reflect the same level of real welfare for all respondents. As Hagenaars (1986) indicated, this approach has merit only if "people associate a certain common, interpersonally comparable feeling of welfare with a certain verbal description." Clearly, those accustomed to having a car, a diet high in meats, and their own washer and dryer are more likely to consider those items "necessary," relative to those with alternative tastes or customs.

The more formal variant of this subjective approach relies on the normed "welfare function of income" (see note 25). It, too, depends greatly on the specific functional form and parameters that are used, and on the variables (e.g., family size, education, one- vs two-earner families, or social reference group) assumed to be determinants of the level of the function. There is no firm basis for these choices, which implies an unattractive arbitrariness to the measure. Moreover, the choices that are made are embedded deep in a computational algorithm, making the dependence of the poverty measure on these choices opaque.

A number of subjective measures have been developed and tested, mainly in Europe. Despite minor differences in terminology and question phrasing among these measures, they have yielded highly diverse results. Three different methods found three different poverty thresholds, ranging from 85 percent to 229 percent of the official 1992 threshold. This wide variation with only small changes in question wording is likely attributable to differences in how respondents interpret the question.

The effectiveness of subjective measures is also limited by the nature of the data collection method. Most estimates are based on small sample sizes, yielding large standard errors. While standard errors are reduced with increasing sample size, most estimates show wide variation around the mean, impeding the setting of a reliable and generally accepted poverty threshold (Citro and Michael, p. 135).

Why Another Concept of "Resources Poverty"?

Each of the several resources-based poverty indicators we have discussed reflects a particular social objective—that all households should have sufficient resources to enable them to attain a minimum acceptable level of living. A quite different social objective would argue that those people in society who have the least adequate economic position or well-being (or, possibly, the most socially excluded) are those who do not have the capability to make it "on their own," to be self-reliant. Two reasons—one conceptual and the other practical—suggest that a poverty indicator that incorporates this capability consideration may better capture social exclusion than do resources-based measures.

The *conceptual reason* is the more basic. A measure of poverty that reflects people's "permanent capabilities" reduces the emphasis on individual decisions that they make (in particular, the decision to work and earn). Moreover, while having insufficient resources (income or consumption) to cover basic needs is a matter worthy of public concern and action, being resource poor is often transitory. Identifying those people who are incapable of generating sufficient resources to meet their basic needs may provide a more meaningful measure of long-term poverty and social exclusion.

This capability-based, self-reliant position has its foundations in the writings of Amartya Sen, among others.[26] In his words, "[T]he basic failure that poverty implies is one of having minimally adequate capabilities," (p. 111) and, hence, that "poverty is better seen in terms of capability failure than in terms of the failure to meet the "basic needs" of specified commodities" (p. 109). He calls for "reorienting poverty analysis from *low incomes* to *insufficient basic capabilities*," (italics in the original) arguing that "the reorientation from an income-centered to a capability-centered view gives us a better understanding of what is involved in the challenge of poverty" (p. 151). In essence, being incapable of independently securing sufficient income to meet basic needs may reflect a more debilitating and vulnerable situation—and a situation reflecting more social exclusion—than being short of cash income in a particular year, living currently in substandard housing, or temporarily living at a consumption level below a minimally acceptable standard.

There is also a policy-related reason for developing a measure of poverty that focuses on the inability of an individual or family to be self-reliant. In recent years, there has been renewed civic discussion and debate regarding appropriate norms and standards for individual responsibility and behavior, and hence the appropriate role of the state. A prominent viewpoint in this debate emphasizes the merits of individual independence (relative to reliance on government programs), the possible negative effects of government programs on individual behavior, and the desirability of a smaller economic and social policy role for government.[27] Through its emphasis on individual self-reliance, this point of view implicitly rejects the proposition that cash income or measured consumption should be sufficient to cover basic needs.

Advocates of a self-reliance viewpoint argue that the substitution of welfare and other public transfers for income generated by people's own efforts is a cause of the U.S. resource (or income) poverty problem. Public transfers are viewed as inducing inefficient behaviors, generating dependence on public support, and fostering the creation of a dysfunctional social class that is at the core of many of the nation's problems.[28] To those who emphasize self-reliance, then, income-based measures have little relevance as indicators of the nation's poverty problem.

It is in this context that a poverty concept based on the inability to be self-reliant becomes relevant. If policy is to reflect the view that people must employ their own capabilities to secure economic independence, it becomes important to identify the size and composition of the group of citizens who do not possess the required skills and resources. Given such a social goal, a self-reliant poverty measure could enable the United States to gauge its progress in attaining this objective.

Indeed, having a self-reliant poverty measure forces the question of collective responsibility toward those incapable of being economically independent. At one extreme might be the position that the public sector's only responsibility is to make clear that self-reliance *is* the norm. In such a world, voluntary private charity might or might not provide for families that were unable to be self-reliant, and the problem of poverty would vanish as a public issue. An alternative position would be to consider how best to increase the abilities of people who are not economically independent to become self-reliant. Public concern with poverty is then recast: How can public policy efficiently reduce the population that is unable to be self-reliant? What instruments are available, and which are the most cost-effective?

When such a measure is applied to the question of children's poverty, the presumption is clear: Children are poor if they are being raised in a family that lacks the capability to generate sufficient income through its own efforts to meet the family's basic needs.

A Measure of Self-Reliant Poverty [29]

One capability-based poverty measure—a self-reliant poverty measure—is based on the concept of a family's Net Earnings Capacity (NEC), which reflects a family's ability to achieve economic independence (i.e., to attain a minimum level of living) through the use of its own capabilities.[30]

The NEC of a family[31] is obtained by first estimating what each adult in the family, given his/her capabilities and characteristics, would be able to earn in the labor market if he or she was to work to capacity (taken to be full-time, full-year market employment) and then adding these estimates. This value is called the family's Gross Earnings Capacity (GEC). Adjustments are then made to the GEC for constraints on working at capacity due to health problems or disability and the expenses (primarily childcare costs) that would be required if all of a family's working-age adults did work at capacity to yield NEC. Finally, the family's NEC is compared to a "minimum living conditions needs standard" (the official poverty line for the family). If the NEC is above the poverty line, the family's ability to earn exceeds a necessary minimum level of consumption, and the family is considered "able to be self-reliant." Families whose NEC level falls below the official poverty line are considered "unable to be self-reliant," and are classified as being in self-reliant poverty.

Measuring self-reliant poverty requires several implicit conventions, norms, and assumptions, and the poverty indicator based on this concept has merit only insofar as they are accepted as appropriate. (A more complete description of the estimation procedure is presented in the Appendix.) To summarize:

• The NEC concept is an appropriate indicator of the capability of a family to generate an income stream that could be used for meeting needs.

• The norm of full-time, full-year work is an accepted, socially determined norm representing the full use of human capital.

• The adjustments made to GEC for health problems and disability accurately measure the effect of the factors that keep individuals from fully using their earnings capacity.

• The adjustment made to GEC reflecting the required costs of making full use of human capital (primarily childcare costs) accurately reflects these unavoidable work-related costs.[32]

While the capability basis of this self-reliance poverty indicator has important and attractive features, the measure itself has drawbacks, including the following:

• The estimate of NEC reflects the application of one set of complex statistical techniques to survey data, and equally defensible procedures might lead to somewhat different results.

• Attribution of poverty status to any particular family requires prediction from statistical estimates rather than values measured in survey data (such as income), and hence is inappropriate for the purpose of, for instance, public benefit determination.

• Only those capabilities that are reflected in market wages are captured in the measure; the potential services of other valuable, though nonmarketed capabilities are neglected. Also, any shortcomings of labor market wages in reflecting the social value of marketed services are not captured in the NEC measure.[33]

Moreover, as a measure of social exclusion, the self-reliance poverty indicator focuses on the ability of a person or family to connect to the labor market, neglecting many other ties that people may have to their communities, their neighbors, or the larger society.

By focusing on the measurement of poverty, we accept the economic status of a family as the appropriate unit of observation. This convention implicitly assumes that family structure is exogenous to the level of available economic resources, and underlies all efforts to track the level of poverty in a society over time. In this chapter, we attribute the economic status of a family to each child in that family.[34]

The Prevalence of Self-Reliant Children's Poverty, 1975–97

In this section, we present estimates of the trend in self-reliant poverty of children in the United States over the past two and one-half decades, as an illustration of the norms and procedures outlined above and in the Appendix. A comparison of the trend in children's self-reliant poverty with the official children's poverty trend provides evidence of the nation's progress in reducing "capability poverty" relative to income poverty.

The Overall Trends in Self-Reliant and Official Poverty

Table 1 presents the trends in the prevalence of self-reliant and official children's poverty from 1975 to 1997, for the population of children less than 6 years of age.[35] The table shows that both measures of children's poverty show an upward trend over the period, but that self-reliant poverty has done so in a much more monotonic fashion. The self-reliant measure exhibits much less cyclicality than the official measure, and the absolute and percentage increases in the self-reliant measure are greater than those for the official measure.[36] In fact, Table 1 shows that the prevalence of children's self-reliant poverty more than doubled, from

Table 1: Percentage of Children under Six in Self-Reliant Poverty, by Characteristic of Household Head

	Average Poverty Rate			Growth Rate (%)
	1975–77 (%)	1995–97 (%)		
All	8.74	18.93		3.94
Race of Head				
White	4.24	10.45		4.62
Black	26.05	40.71		2.26
Hispanic	19.31	32.10		2.57
Other	5.64	15.66		5.23
Sex of Head				
Male	3.23	9.28		5.41
Female	39.86	34.00		-0.79
Education of Head				
Less than High School	21.55	44.75		3.72
High School Graduate	6.50	21.86		6.26
Some College	2.55	14.20		8.96
College Graduate	0.17	0.91		8.80
Families with Children				
All	8.74	18.93		3.94
Couples	3.09	7.03		4.19
Single Fathers	15.95	37.53		4.37
Single Mothers	39.86	54.30		1.56
White	28.75	43.51		2.09
Black	46.85	60.33		1.27
Hispanic	54.96	64.64		0.82
Other	38.99	52.41		1.49
Single Mothers on Welfare	48.26	68.35		1.76
Single Mothers not on Welfare	27.49	44.22		2.41

Note: Growth rates are calculated using the average poverty rates shown and assume twenty years of growth.

8.7 percent to 18.9 percent (or almost 4% annually), while official poverty rose from 16.2 percent to 21.0 percent (only 1.3% annually).[37] Another way of stating the increase in self-reliant poverty is to note that over 2.8 million more U.S. children lived in families that were incapable of generating sufficient income to meet the socially accepted minimum level of living in the mid-1990s than in the mid-1970s.[38]

The primary reason for these different patterns is clear. While the self-reliant poverty rate reflects the *potential* of a child's family to generate income, the official poverty rate reveals income *realizations*. The rapid increase in the self-reliant poverty rate indicates a decline in the potential of families with the least human capital to generate income. The much slower upward drift of the official poverty rate indicates a less rapid decline in family-realized income among those at the bottom of the income distribution.

Trends in Self-Reliant Poverty Rates among Groups

The overall trends in children's poverty described in Figure 1 (page 230) hide a variety of changes in the prevalence of children living in self-reliant poor families within subgroups of the U.S. population. These patterns are indicated in Table 1 for groups distinguished by various characteristics of the head of the family, including race, gender, education, and family structure. Across the groups indicated in the table, the annual growth in the rate of children's self-reliant poverty ranged from -0.8 percent per year (for those living in families headed by a female) to 9.0 percent per year (for those with some college).

While the rate of self-reliant children's poverty grew by 4.6 percent annually over the 1975–97 period for whites, annual growth was much lower for blacks (2.3% per year) and Hispanics (2.6% per year). Similarly, while the growth of self-reliant children's poverty was 5.4 percent per year for families headed by males, the self-reliant children's poverty rate for families headed by women actually *fell* by nearly 1 percent per year.[39] The growth in self-reliant children's poverty was also faster for families headed by more educated people than it was for those with little schooling.

Table 1a lists the primary subgroups in Table 1 with the highest self-reliant children's poverty *growth rates* over the 1975–97 period.[40] From these comparisons, it is clear that many of the population subgroups experiencing the most rapid growth in self-reliant children's poverty since 1975 are groups generally viewed as possessing substantial human capital, and hence economically secure—families headed by men, whites, individuals with schooling beyond high school, and married couple families. Indeed, all of the groups with high rates of growth of children's poverty (except high school graduates and single fathers) have self-reliant poverty rates below the 1995–97 national average of 18.9 percent.[41]

A more surprising pattern concerns the groups that have experienced the lowest growth in self-reliant children's poverty over the period. The growth rates for these groups (shown in table 1b) ranged from -0.8 percent per year to 2.6 percent per year—well below the overall rate of 3.9 percent per year. Although nearly all of these groups have relatively little human capital and the highest poverty rates,[42] they have recorded the lowest annual percentage increases in self-reliant children's poverty over the past twenty-five years.

In sum, children living in families with the greatest human capital (lowest levels of self-reliant poverty) have experienced the largest *relative* increases in self-reliant poverty over the past twenty-five years. Children living in families with less human capital and earnings capacity have experienced relatively low rates growth of self-reliant poverty.[43]

Composition of the Population of Children Living in Self-Reliant Poor Families

This evidence on levels and trends in aggregate rates of children's poverty helps define the characteristics of those children who live in families that are poor by the self-reliant poverty definition. In this section, we describe briefly the characteristics

Table 1a: Self-Reliant Children's Poverty Growth Rates, 1975–1997

Characteristic of Family Head	Average Annual Growth (%)	Self-Reliant Children's Poverty Rate in 1995–97 (%)
Male-headed Families	5.4	9.2
Married Couples with Children	4.2	7.0
Single Fathers	4.4	37.5
Whites	4.6	10.5
College Graduates	8.8	0.9
Some College	9.0	14.2
High School Graduates	6.3	21.9

Table 1b: Groups with the Lowest Growth in Self-Reliant Poverty, 1975–1997

Characteristic of Family Head	Average Annual Growth (%)	Self-Reliant Children's Poverty Rate in 1995–97 (%)
Female family head	-0.8	34.0
Hispanic single mother	0.8	64.6
Black single mother	1.3	60.3
White single mother	2.1	43.5
Black	2.3	40.7
Hispanic	2.6	32.1

of these self-reliant poor children, and the changes in these characteristics over time. We compare these patterns with those of children living in families that are poor by the official definition.

Table 2 shows the composition of the population of children aged less than 6 who live in self-reliant poor families, and changes in this composition over the twenty-three-year period. That is, it shows the share of children in self-reliant poor families that have a particular demographic characteristic. It also indicates the proportion of each group in self-reliant poverty, relative to that group's proportion in official poverty.[44]

Family Racial Composition, Self-Reliant Poor Children

We first consider the racial composition of the population of children living in self-reliant poor families. In the mid-1970s, children living in minority-headed families comprised approximately 64 percent of self-reliant poor children, and their share of the self-reliant poor population grew over time; by the end of the 1995–97 period, minorities accounted for more than 65 percent of self-reliant poor children. Among the minority groups, the share attributed to blacks fell from 44 to 32 percent—an annual rate of change of nearly -1.6 percent. The share of Hispanics among self-reliant poor children grew by 2.3 percent per year over the period, increasing from 19 to 29 percent from 1975–77 to 1995–97.

The ratios of self-reliant children's poverty rates to the official rates indicate that the shares of self-reliant poverty comprised by the children in the various racial groups have converged with their respective shares of the officially poor population. At the beginning of the period, the share of the self-reliant children's poor population comprised by whites stood at 79 percent of their share of the officially poor population. Similarly, blacks' share stood at 121 percent. By the end of the period, the comparative share for whites was nearly 100 percent (indicating equal percentages of the two populations), while the ratio of blacks' self-reliant share to official share had fallen to 111 percent. The most interesting fact is the change in the ratio for Hispanics, which fell from 1.20

Table 2: Composition of Population of Children under Six in Self-Reliant Poverty, by Characteristic of Household Head

	Composition of Self-Reliant Poor Population					
	1975–77			*1995–97*		
	Share of Population (%)	Relative to Official Share (%)		Share of Population (%)	Relative to Official Share (%)	Growth Rate of Share (%)
Race of Head						
White	36.23	0.79		34.88	0.97	-0.19
Black	43.90	1.21		31.97	1.11	-1.57
Hispanic	18.52	1.20		29.17	0.97	2.30
Other	1.36	0.57		3.98	0.76	5.53
Sex of Head						
Male	31.34	0.71		29.86	0.99	-0.24
Female	68.66	1.23		70.14	1.00	0.11
Education of Head						
Less than High School	66.83	1.13		41.16	0.95	-2.39
High School Graduate	28.06	0.91		37.69	1.05	1.49
Some College	4.74	0.64		20.02	1.15	7.47
College Graduate	0.37	0.14		1.13	0.32	5.74
Families with Children	100.00	1.00		100.00	1.00	0.00
Percent Comprised by:						
Couples	29.67	0.69		27.21	0.81	-0.43
Single Fathers	1.67	1.86		9.33	1.62	8.99
Single Mothers	68.66	1.23		63.46	1.05	-0.39
Characteristics of Single Mothers						
White	31.04	0.85		31.58	0.96	0.08
Black	52.62	1.05		42.18	1.03	-1.10
Hispanic	15.10	1.21		23.07	1.01	2.14
Other	1.23	1.08		3.17	0.92	4.84
Single Mothers on Welfare	72.14	0.97		52.18	0.89	-1.61
Single Mothers not on Welfare	27.86	1.10		47.82	1.17	2.74

Notes: "Share of Population" indicates the percentage of self-reliant poor children in a family whose head has the given characteristic. Conditional shares are given for subcategories; thus children of "White Single Mothers" comprise 31 percent of the 69 percent of self-reliant poor children in Single Mother families. "Relative to Official Share" is the ratio of the group's self-reliant share to its official share. Growth rates are calculated using the average poverty rates shown, and assume twenty years of growth.

213

(indicating a 20% larger share of the self-reliant poor than the officially poor population) to 0.97 (indicating a 3% smaller share).

Family Gender Composition, Self-Reliant Poor Children

Throughout the period, self-reliant poor children were far more heavily concentrated in female-headed families than was the population of officially poor children. Approximately 69 percent of the self-reliant poor lived in female-headed families at the beginning of the period, about 23 percent more than the percentage of officially poor families (approximately 56%). By the end of the period, over 70 percent of self-reliant poor children lived in female-headed families. From the beginning to the end of the period, the share of young children living in female-headed families shown in the two poverty indicators converged, and by 1995–97, the share of children living in female-headed families was equal for the two measures.[45]

Family Educational Composition, Self-Reliant Poor Children

The share of children in the self-reliant poor population living in a family headed by someone with less than a high school degree was very high at the beginning of the period: nearly 70 percent. However, as the number of working-age family heads without a high school degree decreased over time, the share of children in self-reliant poverty living in such families fell to approximately 41 percent. Conversely, as the average level of education in the United States rose, the percentage of self-reliant poor children living in families headed by a person with a higher level of schooling rose. By the end of the period, approximately 21 percent of self-reliant poor children lived in families headed by individuals with more than a high school degree, up from approximately 5 percent in 1975–77. The growth rates of the self-reliant poverty population shares for the two highest schooling groups were 7.5 and 5.7 percent, while those for the two lowest schooling groups were -2.4 and 1.5 percent.

Family Structure Composition, Self-Reliant Poor Children

Among children living in families headed by a self-reliant poor single mother, the composition of the population shifted from families headed by white or black single mothers to families headed by Hispanic or other single mothers. At the beginning of the period, children living in self-reliant poor families headed by a black single mother comprised 53 percent of children living with poor single mothers. Over time, this percentage decreased to approximately 42 percent. Correspondingly, the share of children in Hispanic-headed self-reliant poor single-mother families rose from 15 percent to 23 percent.[46]

In sum, at the beginning of the period children living in self-reliant poor families were concentrated in those family types that are the most economically vulnerable (e.g., families headed by blacks and/or single mothers). However, this concentration eroded over time. For example, the shares of self-reliant poor children living in black families decreased from 44 to 32 percent, and in single-mother families from 69 to 63 percent.[47] Despite these declines, the share of the population of children living in self-reliant poor families is more heavily concentrated in these groups than is the share of children who are in the officially poor population—the ratios of self-reliant to official poverty shares for these groups are 1.11 and 1.05, respectively.

What Accounts for These Patterns?

Interesting questions center on the economic, demographic, and cultural factors that account for these self-reliant poverty prevalence and composition trends. For example, what might account for the more rapid growth of self-reliant children's poverty, compared to official children's poverty, over this period? How can we explain the slow growth (or decrease) in the self-reliant poverty rate for children living in family types commonly thought of as being the most vulnerable—racial minorities, female-headed families (both single females and with children), or families headed by a person with low schooling—relative to the high growth rates recorded for less vulnerable groups: whites, married couples with children, and those with relatively high levels of schooling?

Clearly, the underlying determinants of these patterns are numerous, and interact in complex and difficult-to-understand ways. Indeed, any change that affects: a) the structure of work opportunities available in the economy (the demand side of the labor market); b) people's choices in response to these opportunities (the supply side of the labor market); c) the demographic structure of the population; or d) public policy measures, is likely to have a differential effect on trends in the prevalence of children living in self-reliant and official poverty.

In the following paragraphs, we indicate the likely effects of some of the more prominent economic and demographic changes that occurred over the 1975–1997 period, upon the patterns of self-reliant and official poverty that we have presented.[48] These changes include:

- decline in the real value of public cash income transfers
- increase in labor force participation of women
- increase in male joblessness[49]
- increase in female wage rates
- decrease in male wage rates
- decrease in racial wage disparities
- increase in wage inequality within age/race/schooling groups
- increases in the black and Hispanic population shares (relative to whites)
- increase in prevalence of divorce and out-of-wedlock childbearing, and the "atomization" of the family unit[50]

We now examine the trends in overall children's self-reliant and official poverty, the relative trends in child poverty between male- and female-headed families, and the relative trends in child poverty between white- and black/Hispanic-headed families.

Increasing Overall Children's Poverty Rates, Especially Self-Reliant Children's Poverty

Turning first to the overall patterns of growth over time for the self-reliant and official children's poverty measures, we examine those economic and demographic trends that may have contributed to the large increase in self-reliant poverty (3.9% per year) relative to official poverty (1.3% per year).

First, we consider the decline in public transfer income. Such income is included in the concept of economic resources used to define official poverty, but not self-reliant poverty. Hence, the decreasing value of cash transfers (primarily welfare benefits) has directly contributed to the increase in the official poverty rate, while having no effect on the prevalence of self-reliant poverty. Because the latter poverty rate has risen more rapidly than the former, other factors must have been sufficient to override this effect.

Second, we note the trends in labor force participation and employment, particularly among women. The large rise in female employment over the past quarter century has contributed to sustaining the incomes of families containing women, hence constraining the growth of official poverty. In contrast, employment rates do not affect Earnings Capacity (EC) since EC depends on the level of human capital, not its utilization. Hence, growing female employment has contributed to the relatively slower growth of official poverty, relative to that of self-reliant poverty. In contrast, male employment rates have been declining. This trend tends to raise official poverty, but have no effect on self-reliant poverty.

Third, while real female wage rates have tended to increase over time, male wage rates have eroded. Wage rates, as opposed to the utilization of capacity, affect both self-reliant and official poverty; hence, changes in wage rates (either male or female) tend to have the same directional effect on poverty, irrespective of measure. The net effect of this relative wage rate change on the differential trends in the growth of poverty is, therefore, unclear.[51]

Fourth, the substantial increase in "within-group" wage inequality over the period has pulled those at the bottom of the subgroup wage distribution further from their respective group-mean wage. Because wage rates are reflected in the definition of economic resources for both poverty definitions, this development has served to increase both the official and the self-reliant poverty rates. However, the self-reliant measure "weights" all of the potential work hours of the adults in a family, while the official measure reflects the wage rate paid only for actual hours worked. Hence, this factor has contributed to a more rapid rise in the rate of self-reliant poverty relative to official poverty, accounting for some of the divergence in trends between the two measures.

Finally, irrespective of whether economic position is measured by income or the capability to earn income, families headed by members of racial minorities or single mothers are concentrated at the bottom of the distribution. Since the mid-1970s, the prevalence of families with both characteristics has increased substantially. Although demographic changes have contributed to the growth in both self-reliant and official poverty measures over this period, the differential effect of these changes on the two poverty rates is unclear.

Decreasing Female-Headed Children's Poverty, Increasing Male-Headed Children's Poverty

Although both self-reliant and official poverty rates for children living in female-headed families exceed those for children living in families headed by a male, the poverty rates of children in male-headed families have risen, while those of children in female-headed families have decreased. What could have caused these relative movements in poverty rates?

Clearly, the decline in the real value of income transfers has increased the poverty rates of children in families headed by women, to a much greater extent than those of children in male-headed families. As a result, this factor cannot explain the relative growth in poverty for children in male-headed families observed over this period.

Other factors, however, help to explain the disparate growth patterns in poverty rates between male-headed and female-headed families. These include the rapid increase in the *labor force participation and employment rate of women* (which has lowered the official poverty rate for those living in female-headed families, but has had no effect on the rate of self-reliant poverty for such families); the *increase in female wage rates and the decrease in male wage rates* (resulting in a decrease in both self-reliant and official female-headed poverty rates, and an increase in male-headed poverty rates); and the *increase in male joblessness* (increasing official poverty for those living in male-headed families, but having no effect on the rate of self-reliant poverty for these families). It seems likely that the relative (and absolute) declines in both male wage rates and male labor supply have accounted for this "gender twist" in poverty rates, irrespective of the poverty measure used.

Rising White, Relative to Black and Hispanic, Children's Poverty

The steady reduction in racial wage and earnings gaps has been a persistent trend in the U.S. economy since the mid-1970s. This pattern accounts for the low relative growth in poverty rates among blacks and Hispanics relative to whites, irrespective of the definition of poverty used. Joblessness among low-skilled workers has also increased somewhat more for whites than for minority groups. This has contributed to the relative movements in official poverty trends for these groups.

Self-Reliant and Income Poverty: Which Better Reflects "Social Exclusion"?

Both self-reliant and official indicators of poverty may be considered proxies for measures of the extent to which children live in families that are excluded from their societies. Indeed, each of these indicators presumes that the children identified as poor have a number of attributes implying that they are "distant" from the norm of the population in a variety of important dimensions, and hence experience social exclusion.[52]

An interesting exercise might be to follow the lead of the European Union (EU), and inquire into the relationship between people's poverty situations and indicators of their social exclusion.[53] In its analysis, the EU links the income poverty status of families to indicators of social exclusion, including "their socio-demographic characteristics, their activity status and a number of variables reflecting their means, perceptions and satisfaction with respect to their standard of living and quality of life." These social exclusion indicators include such things as:

- Poor labor market performance (e.g., nonemployment, nonparticipation, low occupation) of parents;
- Dysfunctional family structure (e.g., single parent, many children, disabled siblings);
- Non-standard family size (e.g., very large family);
- Low education of parents;
- Non-majority race or ethnic group;
- Involvement with community or public programs; and
- Poor health of parents.

In its analysis, the EU calculates an indicator reflecting the concentration of families in the low-income group that have various characteristics thought to be related to social exclusion, relative to the concentration of families in the entire population with these characteristics. For example, if 60 percent of low-income families had a head who was not employed, while 20 percent of all families in the society had a head who was not employed, this indicator of the social exclusion of the low-income group would be 3.0. This ratio, together with others, is taken to form a picture of the social exclusion of the poor.

In the context of the present study, it is possible to adapt this procedure so as to compare the extent to which the self-reliant and official poverty measures are linked to various dimensions of social exclusion. For example, if 50 percent of children in self-reliant poor families have a particular social-exclusion-related characteristic, while only 40 percent of children living in officially poor families have this characteristic, one could make the case that, at least in this dimension, self-reliant poverty is a superior indicator of social exclusion.

Table 3 presents this calculation for a few social exclusion dimensions, comparing self-reliant poverty with official poverty. In particular, we assume that living in a single-father or single-mother family; being a member of a racial minority and living in a single mother family; being a member of a racial minority; or being a single mother not participating in the social welfare system[54] imply *more* social exclusion. This calculation suggests that the self-reliant measure is a superior indicator of social exclusion relative to the official (income) poverty measure for family structure, race, and connection to public support system dimensions. However, the two poverty measures are similar indicators of social exclusion for the education dimension. Thus, at least in these family structure, race, and connection to public support system dimensions, children living in self-reliant poor families are more likely to feel distant from social norms, out of the "mainstream," and stigmatized. They would know that even if their families played by the rules (e.g., worked at their full capacity), they would be viewed by others as not "making it," and in that sense would be (or feel) socially excluded.

Conclusion

We have reviewed the concept and measurement of children's poverty, described and assessed a number of approaches to measuring children's poverty, and suggested a capability-based concept and measure of this social indicator. We have then applied this self-reliant poverty measure to the children living in U.S. families headed by a working-age person over the 1975–97 period. We have also compared trends in children's poverty prevalence and composition to the official measure of poverty. How many U.S. children live in families that are unable to earn enough to escape poverty? Has the prevalence of such self-reliant poverty changed over time? What are the characteristics of the children living in such low-capability families? How do these patterns for self-reliant poor children compare with those for officially poor children? Are the characteristics of the families of children in self-

Table 3: Linkages of Self-Reliant and Official Children's Poverty to Indicators of Social Exclusion, 1995–97 (Percentage of Children under 6 Years Old and under 18 Years Old Living in Poor Families)

	Children Under 6				Children Under 18		
	Share in				Share in		
	Official Poverty (%)	Self-Reliant Poverty (%)	Ratio of Self-Reliant to Official		Official Poverty (%)	Self-Reliant Poverty (%)	Ratio of Self-Reliant to Official
Mother-only family	60.5	63.5	1.05		61.3	66.0	1.08
Black Hispanic Single mother	63.8	65.3	1.02		63.6	63.0	0.99
Single mother, not socially assisted	41.4	47.8	1.15		45.0	51.5	1.14
Father-only family	5.8	9.3	1.64		4.6	7.7	1.67
Black	28.8	32.0	1.11		29.9	32.9	1.10
Hispanic	30.0	29.2	0.97		28.3	27.2	0.96
Head with high school degree or less	79.1	78.8	1.00		78.4	78.2	1.00

reliant poverty more closely linked to indicators of social exclusion than are the characteristics of children in official (income) poverty?

Several conclusions stand out. First, while both the official and self-reliant children's poverty rates have increased over the period 1975–97, self-reliant children's poverty has grown more rapidly and more steadily. The official poverty rate grew by 1.3 percent per year over this period, while the self-reliant poverty rate rose by nearly 4 percent per year.

Second, the highest self-reliant children's poverty rates are concentrated among the population groups that are generally recognized as among the nation's most vulnerable: blacks, Hispanics, single-parent families with children, and those with low levels of schooling. Over most of the period since the mid-1970s, the concentration of children in these groups who are poor by the self-reliant criterion has exceeded their concentration in official poverty. To the extent that these characteristics are also measures of social exclusion, the population of children in self-reliant poverty would seem to be more outside the social mainstream than is the population of children in official poverty.

Third, in spite of the rapid growth of self-reliant poverty, groups commonly thought of as being the most vulnerable—families headed by a member of a racial minority, a female, or a person with low education—have recorded decreases or relatively low increases in poverty relative to those recorded for less vulnerable groups. The converse of this pattern is also true: Since the mid-1970s, groups generally viewed as relatively secure economically— families headed by whites and those with relatively high levels of schooling, and married-couple families with children—experienced above-average growth in self-reliant poverty rates, and growth rates substantially greater than those for groups with low earnings capacity.

The large and rapidly growing number of children living in families who are unable to be self-reliant is discouraging for a society that prides itself on providing opportunities for individuals to prosper and thrive by working hard and playing by the rules. A growing population of U.S. children would remain below the minimally acceptable level of living defined by the nation's official poverty line, even if their families were to fully use their capabilities. The message advocated by some—that it is necessary for workers and families to rely on their own resources—seems to have come at the same time that increases in wage and earnings inequalities have made this goal less attainable for those with few skills and little human capital.

APPENDIX
The Estimation of Self-Reliant Poverty: Data and Empirical Procedures

To estimate self-reliant poverty, we rely on a multistep estimation procedure. We first obtain predicted values of the earnings of each working-age adult, were he or she to work full-time, full-year (FTFY), and call these values individual Earnings Capacity (EC). We then adjust these values for health and disability constraints on employability, and randomly shock them to simulate the effect of unmeasured variables. These values are aggregated into own-family units; this aggregate family earnings value plus property income yields each family's Gross Earnings Capacity (GEC). The GEC is then adjusted for required childcare costs, to obtain the Net Earnings Capacity (NEC) of the family. Children in families with a NEC below the relevant official poverty line are identified as being in self-reliant poverty. This Appendix describes this procedure in more detail.

The first step is to predict the earnings capacity for each prime-aged individual in our sample. The data used in this analysis are drawn from the repeated cross sections of the U.S. population contained in the March Current Population Surveys (CPS) for 1976 to 1998.[55] From these surveys, we select a sample of 18–64 year old, non-institutionalized, non-student, non-self-employed civilians on which to estimate the model.[56] We estimate a two-equation model of full-time, full-year labor force participation and earnings, drawing on Heckman (1979). Such a specification is appropriate, since individuals can select into the full-time, full-year labor force.

Exhibit 1 lists the variables used in the model, gives a description of each, and indicates (*) which variables form exclusion restrictions. Such variables are assumed to affect the FTFY labor force participation decision, but not the earnings of the individual. We assume that nonlabor income, participation in a health-related income support program, the state unemployment rate, veteran status (for men) and the maximum Aid for Families with Dependent Children (AFDC) benefit for a family of four (for women) affect the labor force participation decision but—conditional on FTFY work—do not affect earnings.

The first stage is a probit regression of FTFY labor force participation on the vector of explanatory variables assumed to influence such participation.[57] We fit four such probits for each year, one for each race/gender group (whites/non-whites, males/females). (The coefficient estimates, standard errors, sample sizes, and log-likelihoods for each probit are available from the authors upon request.)

The second stage is a set of selectivity corrected OLS regressions of the log of earnings on those variables in Exhibit 1 assumed to influence earnings. To correct for self-selection into the FTFY labor force, we append the inverse Mills ratio, derived from the coefficients in the first stage estimation, to the set of regressors. (The regression results, with corrected standard errors, for the four race/gender groups in the twenty-eight years of our study, along with sample sizes, R-squared statistics and the corrected standard error of the regression, are available from the authors upon request.)

Using the coefficient estimates and each individual's characteristics, we predict FTFY log earnings for each prime-aged adult in our sample.[58] Note that since we desire estimates of earnings capacity for each individual, unconditional on self-selecting into the FTFY labor force, we make unconditional predictions of earnings capacity. That is, in making our predictions, we set each individual's inverse Mill's ratio equal to the mean inverse Mill's ratio for workers. This ensures that the mean of the predicted log earnings distribution (among FTFY workers) equals the mean of

Exhibit 1: Variable Definitions

<u>Variable</u>	<u>Description</u>
Age	Age of the individual.
Age Squared	Age of the individual, squared.
Education	Years of schooling completed by the individual.
Education Squared	Years of schooling completed by the individual, squared.
Age * Education	Age of the individual times years of schooling.
Northeast, South, West	Region-specific dummy variables. North Central is omitted.
City, Suburb	SMSA status dummies. Rural is omitted.
Married, Spouse Present	Dummy variable indicating the presence of a legal spouse in the household.
Have Children under 18	Dummy variable indicating the presence of unmarried children under the age of 18 in the family.
Number of Children under 18	Number of unmarried children under the age of 18 in the family.
Have Children under 6	Dummy variable indicating the presence of children under the age of 6 in the family.
Number of Children under 6	Number of unmarried children under the age of 6 in the family.
Non-Labor Income (000s)*	Total family income from sources exogenous to the labor market decisions of the individual (in thousands of dollars).
Health Program*	Dummy variable indicating the individual's participation in a health-related income support program.
Unemployment Rate*	Unemployment rate in the individual's state of residence.
Veteran*	Dummy variable indicating veteran status (men only).
Maximum Welfare Benefit*	Maximum welfare benefit for a family of four in the individual's state of residence (women only).
Hispanic	Dummy variable indicating Hispanic ethnicity (non-whites only).

Notes: Starred variables indicate exclusion restrictions. These variables are included only in the first stage FTFY labor force participation equation. All other variables are included in both stages. For women, Have Children under 18 and Married, Spouse Present are interacted, obtaining an expanded set of dummy variables: Single, No Children; Single, With Children; Married, No Children; and Married, With Children. Non-labor income is the family's non-wage income, less total family social security, supplemental security, public assistance, alimony, and child support, less individual unemployment compensation, worker's compensation, veteran's payments, and retirement income.

the actual log earnings distribution (among FTFY workers), while assigning the same earnings capacity value to individuals with identical characteristics, regardless of their selection into or out of the FTFY labor force.

To account for unobserved human capital and labor demand characteristics and "luck" in earnings determination process, we apply a random shock to each individual's earnings capacity prediction. Specifically, we add to each FTFY log earnings prediction the standard error from the individual's race/gender earnings equation times a normal (0,1) random variable. In making this adjustment, we assume that the distribution of FTFY earnings within a race/gender cell is normal with a standard deviation equal to the standard error of the race/gender earnings regression.

The final adjustment to the individual EC prediction is one for constraints on work due to illness and disability. We calculate an adjustment factor, Э, equal to (50-WC)/50, where WC is the number of weeks the individual did not work due to those reasons. If, in addition, the individual reported receiving income from a health-related income support program[59] or working part-time because of illness, disability or unemployment, we multiply WC by 0.5, implying that these exogenous factors constrained capacity work to 20 hours per week. This individual, case-by-case adjustment is made for each year. Hence, for any given year, aggregate earnings capacity for the entire working-age population will reflect the overall magnitude of these year-specific constraints. If the incidence of these constraints is constant over time, the intertemporal pattern of aggregate modified earnings capacity will parallel that of the unmodified aggregate, but be a smaller value. If the incidence of these constraints across population groups is constant over time, our modified value enables reliable comparisons of trends in earnings capacities among population groups.

To summarize, the predicted value of an individual's earnings capacity is described by the following equation:

$$EC_i^* = \exp(X_i Ǝ + \Phi^* m_j) * Э_{i.},$$

where X_i are the explanatory variables from the second-stage estimation, $Ǝ$ is the vector of estimated coefficients, Φ is the standard error of the regression corresponding to the individual's race/gender group, m_i is a randomly distributed N(0,1) variable and ∍ is the adjustment factor noted above.

To obtain the GEC of a family, we add all the EC_i^*s for the prime-aged adults in a family, and add property income (interest, dividends, rental income, alimony and child support). To obtain the NEC, we adjust for those unavoidable costs incurred in moving to FTFY work. We focus on childcare expenses as the most prominent component of these costs.

We draw upon documents from the U.S. Census Bureau and the U.S. General Accounting Office (GAO)[60] as the basis for our childcare estimates. The GAO surveyed childcare providers in four sites across the United States (two urban and two rural) in 1996. The study presents a range of weekly childcare costs of $79 to $154 for children aged 0 to 5, and $32 to $81 for children aged 6 to 11. We use estimates from the middle of the GAO's range: $90 per child per week for children aged 0 to 5 and $50 per child per week for children aged 6 to 11.

Using information on regional and SMSA status differences in childcare costs obtained from the Census Bureau's Current Population Report, we created the following matrix of adjustment factors to apply to the GAO estimates:

	Northeast	Midwest	South	West
City	1.124	1.033	1.017	1.086
Suburb	1.104	1.013	0.997	1.066
Rural	0.944	0.852	0.836	0.905

We multiply the GAO childcare estimates by the appropriate adjustment factor, according to each family's region and SMSA status.

We also use information contained in the Current Population Report to adjust the childcare cost estimates over time. Data on average childcare costs from 1986 to 1993 reveals an average annual growth rate of approximately 3.1 percent. We use that growth rate to project our childcare costs backward from 1996 through 1975, obtaining weekly per-child costs, by region and SMSA status, for children aged 0 to 5 and 6 to 11. We assume that childcare costs are incurred 50 weeks per year. These per-child per-year costs are multiplied by the number of children in the family aged 0 to 5 and 6 to 11 as appropriate, and subtracted from the family GEC to obtain the family NEC.

To obtain the self-reliant poverty population, we calculated the ratio of each family's NEC to the relevant official, family-size specific poverty line;[61] those families with a ratio less than unity are identified as self-reliant poor.

Note that the adjustments for health, disability, unemployment, and childcare differ from the preliminary estimates in Haveman and Bershadker (1998). In that study, the health, disability, and unemployment adjustment did not take into account participation in a health-related income support program. Additionally, childcare costs were set at $1,546 per child per year for children aged 6 to 11, and $3,865 per child per year for children aged 0 to 5 (in 1995 dollars). Adjustments were made only for inflation and not for regional variation, SMSA status, or real growth over time. (Annual estimates of the prevalence of self-reliant and official poverty for various population subgroups by characteristic of the head of family, as well as the composition of the two poverty populations, again by characteristic of the household head, are available from the authors.)

Figure 1: Self-Reliant and Official Poverty Rates for
Children Under Six in Prime-Age Headed Families, 1975 to 1997
Poverty Rate
30
25
20
15
10
5
0
1975
1977
1979
1981
1983
1985
1987
1989
1991
1993
1995
1997
Year
SR Poverty Rate
Official Poverty Rate

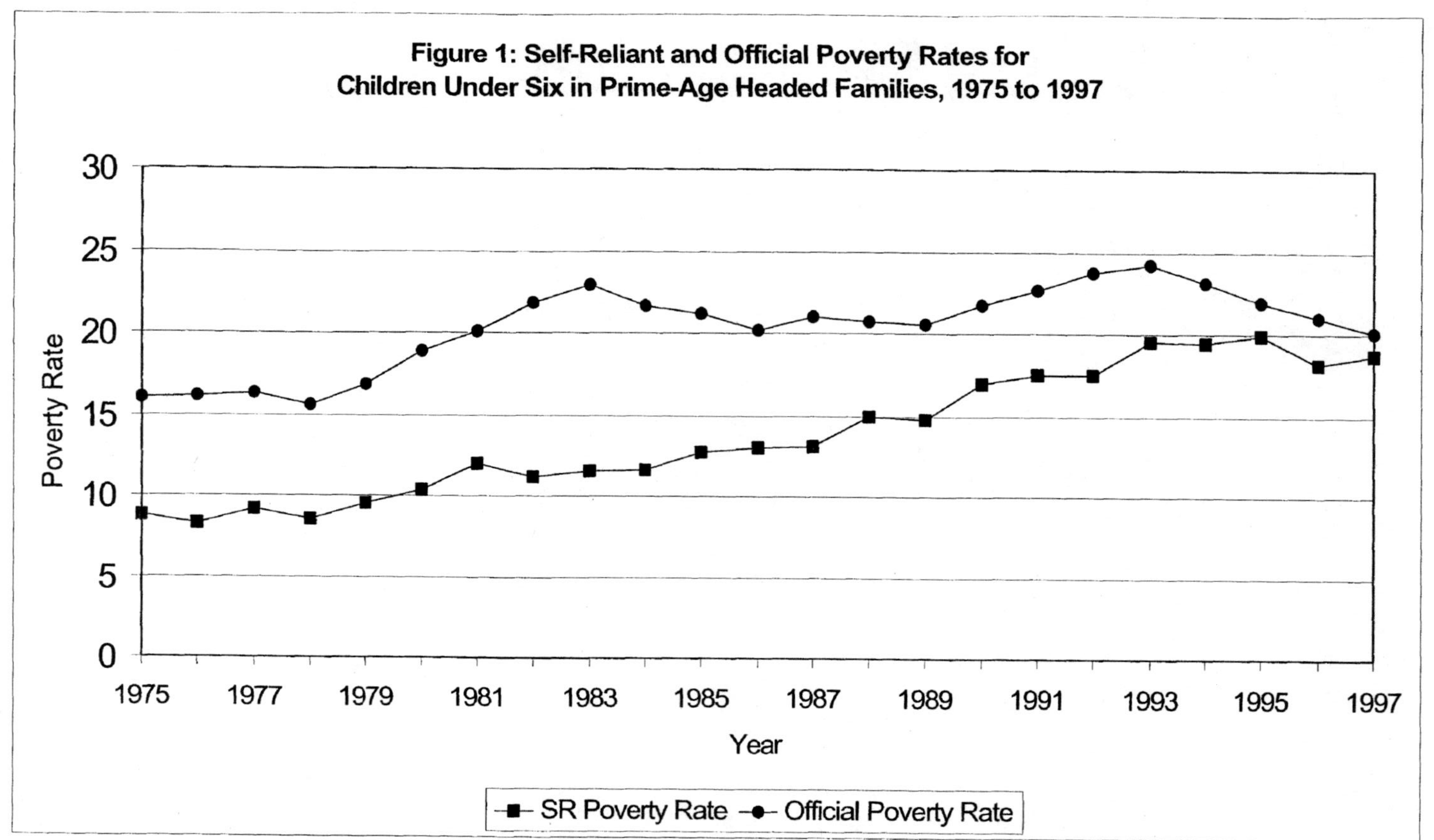

230

Notes

1. This research was supported by a grant to the Institute for Research on Poverty from the Office of the Assistant Secretary for Planning and Evaluation of the U.S. Department of Health and Human Services, the Jerome Levy Institute of Bard College, and the Graduate School of the University of Wisconsin–Madison. The authors thank Dawn Duren for skilled typing. The views represented here do not necessarily reflect those of the U.S. Treasury Department.

2. See Bourguinon and Chakravarty (1998). Others who have advocated such a multidimensional view of poverty include Kolm (1977), Atkinson and Bourguinon (1982), and Tsui (1995). Federman et al. (1996) empirically explore a variety of dimensions of hardship for those in the U.S. who are income poor.

3. This quotation is from the Eurostat news release describing the contents and findings of Eurostat (2000).

4. The official definition of poverty has played a very special role in the development of U.S. social policy. Tobin (1970) has argued that one of the most important contributions of the War on Poverty era was the establishment of an official, national poverty line. Indeed, because of the official adoption of this measure, the nation made a commitment to annually chart the nation's progress toward poverty reduction by publishing and publicizing a statistical poverty index. Because of this measure, Tobin argued, "no politician will be able to . . . ignore the repeated solemn acknowledgments of society's obligation to its poorer members." This measure has been the official U.S. poverty standard since the early 1960s (see Fisher 1992), and poverty rates are published annually in the U.S. Bureau of the Census publication, *Poverty in the United States*, Series P60.

5. See Mayer and Jencks (1992, 1994), Slesnick (1993), and Cutler and Katz (1991).

6. Sen (1983) considered the needs standard (or poverty line) to have "some absolute justification of its own," it being a level below which "one cannot participate adequately in communal activities, or be free of pubic shame from failure to satisfy conventions" (p. 167).

7. See Kilpatrick (1973), who defines a completely relative poverty measure as having a poverty threshold that has an elasticity of 1 with respect to the general standard of living, while an absolute poverty line employs a threshold that has an elasticity of 0.

8. This presumption is viewed by many as overly narrow. Clearly, the sociological perspectives discussed in the introduction take a broader approach.

9. This pattern is especially true for those households in the tails of the distribution of annual income in a particular year. For example, in 1994, consumer units in the Labor Department's annual Consumer Expenditure Survey reported average pretax income of approximately $6,800, but average consumption expenditures of approximately $14,000.

10. The failure to account for the effect of taxes is particularly troublesome in the U.S. context. The Earned Income Tax Credit (EITC) has expanded into a major form of income support for the low-income working population. Total national "expenditures" on the credit exceed $30 billion, and low-income families (of three persons) can receive up to $3,800 per year in an EITC refund. However, because the refundable payments are viewed as negative taxes, they are not reflected in the definition of income used in the official poverty measure.

11. This is less the case for the NRC-proposed revision to the official poverty measure, as it attempts to account for some in-kind benefits in assessing the relationship of resources to needs.

12. Relative poverty measures have become the accepted measure of poverty in Europe, especially in the European Union. However, in recent years interest in the development of an absolute poverty measure for EU members has increased, and currently efforts are underway to develop such a measure. See Bradshaw (2001).

13. See Ruggles (1990).

14. Moreover, annual cash income may be inaccurately reported to the survey interviewer. The respondent—an adult in the family, and often a nonworking adult—may not know the true income of family members, such as adult children living at home, or may not wish to reveal to the interviewer income that derives from questionable sources.

15. Ruggles (1990, p. 94).

16. Because the official measure is adjusted only for price level changes over time, it will decline in relation to a relative measure if there is real growth in family income.

17. Ruggles (1990, p. 19).

18. Eurostat, the statistical agency for the European Union, uses a one-half of median income standard in its first analysis of poverty in the community. More recently, Eurostat has moved toward adoption of 60 percent of the median as the threshold. See Bradshaw (2001).

19. Ruggles (1990, p. 19). Lampman (1972) has emphasized this weakness of the relative standard as an indicator of the nation's progress in reducing poverty. "While income poverty is a relative matter, I do not think we should engage in frequent changes of the poverty lines, other than to adjust for price change. As I see it, the elimination of income poverty is usefully thought of as a one-time operation in pursuit of a goal unique to this generation."

20. Slesnick (1993, p. 2).

21. The poverty threshold is simply the total expenditure required by the reference household to purchase the Economy Food Plan, divided by the appropriate cost of living index and equivalence scale. In other words, those who consume above the level required to purchase the Economy Food Plan are classified as non-poor, while those who consume less are considered poor.

22. Slesnick refers to this as "the consumption-smoothing hypothesis." He supports this hypothesis by comparing the traits and characteristics of the "income poor" and the "consumption poor." The consumption poor (or, "permanent income poor") have substantially lower rates of home ownership, fewer physical assets in the form of consumer durables, higher food and necessities budget shares, and less dissaving (indicating less access to credit) than do the income poor.

23. The equivalence scales used by Slesnick are adapted from those developed by Jorgenson and Slesnick (1987). They adjust for family size by using the age of the household head as a proxy for family size, assuming that more older children and adults would be present in households with older heads; the actual number of children in the household is not considered. While this may be a good proxy in some instances, it contains substantial measurement error, and is likely to be especially inaccurate in tracking poverty trends over time due to intertemporal changes in the age of the household head, family size, and the number of children present (Triest 1998). Triest also finds the adjustment for gender of household head to be "very crude": a female-headed household is estimated to need only 62 percent of what an identically situated male-headed household would need. Even though it is likely that this adjustment is meant to account for the presumption that more children are present in female-headed households, Triest finds the adjustment "excessively large." Triest also notes that the adjustments made for regional differences are of "counterintuitive magnitudes." For example, the measures indicate that, to attain equivalent well-being, southern U.S.

households require more than 1.5 times the expenditure needed by similarly situated households in the western part of the United States.

24. This general approach to poverty measurement has been called the "Leyden School" approach. Bernard van Praag is the central figure in this area; see Hagenaars (1986) and van Praag, Hagenaars, and van Weeren (1982). See also Ruggles, (1990, p. 21). Comparison of subjective poverty prevalence and composition between the United States and the Netherlands may be found in de Vos and Garner (1991).

25. This "minimum income" approach to poverty measurement is employed in Goedhart et al. (1977). An alternative approach involves construction of an indicator of well-being that is comparable across people (based on income levels that individuals subjectively state to be "excellent," "good," etc.), and then identifying as "poor" individuals whose indicator of well-being is less than a particular level (e.g., "sufficient"). This indicator of well-being has been conceptualized in a "welfare function of income," which is hypothesized to be described as a lognormal distribution function. This original concept is developed in van Praag (1968) and was used to derive a poverty measure in Hagenaars (1985).

26. Sen's position is most clearly articulated in his 1995 book, *Inequality Reexamined.* Development of the philosophical and value basis for this viewpoint is found throughout his many writings on inequality and poverty, especially his 1979 Tanner Lecture at Stanford University (Sen 1980), Hennipman Lectures at the University of Amsterdam in 1982, and *On Economic Inequality* (Sen 1997).

27. Evidence that being "self-reliant" or "economically independent" has taken on increased weight in U.S. social policy is the Temporary Assistance for Needy Families (TANF) provision in the 1996 welfare reform legislation, which eliminated entitlement to public transfer benefits by single-parent households, and imposed firm limits on the period that eligible families could receive support. The message to single parents, irrespective of their skills, training or home demands, was that they had to learn to "get by on their own." Similarly, advocates of the privatization of the Social Security retirement program envision that some portion of the contributions made on behalf of working-age individuals will be assigned directly to them, with the requirement that they manage these financial resources themselves (with constraints), and then rely on the accumulated assets in these private accounts in their retirement years. Proposals for medical savings accounts as a replacement for Medicare benefits, tighter eligibility criteria for disabled children's receipt

of Supplemental Security Income benefits, the shift from defined benefit to defined contribution pension plans, and the emphasis on loans rather than grants to cover the rising costs of higher education, are other manifestations of this emphasis on self-reliance as a substitute for public support.

28. One of the earliest of the proponents of this view was Charles Murray. His influential book, *Losing Ground* (1984) was the first in a large stream of writings, speeches, and political candidacies that argued that government policy—especially welfare and other income support measures—was causal to the problem of income poverty. A corollary is that government should require self-reliance, rather than providing assistance to the poor.

29. This definition and measure of poverty is discussed in more detail in Haveman and Bershadker (2001). The discussion in this section draws from that study.

30. A related measure of family capability is Becker's (1965) concept of "full income," which includes both income realized through market work and the value of leisure time. Adjusting this measure to reflect differences in the size and composition of the consumption unit yields full income (or potential real consumption) per equivalent consumer unit. Such a comprehensive concept of economic position reflects the level of consumption a family could attain from the full use of their resources. A poverty measure that rests on the full income concept would indicate whether or not a family had the capability to support a level of real consumption in excess of needs: that is, to be self-reliant.

31. Since the emphasis is on self-reliance, the measure applies only to those families headed by an individual aged 18 to 65; that is, those individuals whom society expects to be independent.

32. We made an effort to adjust for the unavoidable costs associated with the full utilization of family capabilities in the labor market, concentrating on required childcare costs. Some may argue that at least one parent in families with young children (or the only parent in the case of single parents) should remain out of the labor force to care for these young children. Under this norm, the EC of such parents would be set at zero. While this alternative norm would undoubtedly change the NEC of families with children, the family's self-reliant poverty status would be affected only to the extent that the *difference* between the estimated EC for the stay-at-home parent and the estimated childcare expense was large enough to move the family from a position above its poverty line

to one below it. To the extent that the percentage of families so affected is constant over time, such an alternative would affect only the level and not the trend of self-reliant poverty. Furthermore, note that our method of childcare accounting in no way presumes that parents with young children *should* work; it only predicts a NEC value for that family *if* they work full-time, full-year. Our adjustments for childcare costs fail to account for within-region variations in quality-constant expenses, and the ability of some families to engage relatives in childcare at costs below our estimates. Moreover, we have ignored a variety of other required expenses, such as transportation and clothing costs associated with full-capacity work. We believe that our methods reasonably capture the bulk of expenses incurred should all adults in a family engage in full-time, full-year work.

33. We have abstracted from labor demand constraints on market earnings in two ways. First, we ignore general equilibrium considerations. We make no adjustments for changes in the structure of wages if all prime-aged adults were to work full-time, full-year. We simply ask, given the *observed* structure of full-time, full-year earnings, how much each individual would expect to earn if he or she independently moved to full-time, full-year work. As such, EC is a statistical indicator reflecting this value. Notice, however, that our measure does account for changes in the structure of full-time, full-year earnings arising from recessions and expansions. Our EC indicator measures the annual rental value of an individual's human capital, as reflected in the individual-specific regressors in the annual earnings equations. If, for a given set of regressors, full-time, full-year earnings, and hence earnings capacities, are depressed in a recession (or inflated in an expansion), our self-reliant poverty measure will register an increase (or decrease) in that dimension of poverty. Second, our measure abstracts from the effects of cyclical labor demand conditions on the *ability to find* employment. Again, we measure each individual's full-time, full-year earnings, assuming each individual finds a full-time, full-year job. As such, adjusting for changes in the distribution of wages, but not for changes in relative employment, is appropriate. To the extent possible, we account for long-term exogenous constraints on earnings potential imposed by health and disability problems by taking individuals' statements that annual hours of not working because of these conditions accurately reflect the impact of these constraints. We acknowledge that these adjustments are imperfect proxies of the true values of the health/disability effects on the annual

rental value of individual human capital stocks. Results published in Haveman and Bershadker (1998) adjust EC for the ability to find a job by incorporating each individual's report of hours unemployed into the health and disability adjustment factor. Consideration of similar work suggested further accounting for unemployment by imputing an estimate of hours unemployed to individuals not in the labor force. Such an estimate would be relatively higher during recessions and lower during expansions. We believe such an adjustment would move our measure further from a true measure of EC based on intrinsic individual characteristics. The point is to "tag" each adult with an EC value equal to what that individual would earn if he or she did, in fact, have a full-time, full-year job.

34. This approach, using actual income as the indicator of economic resources rather than individual EC, is adopted in Duncan, Boisjoly, and Smeeding (1996) and Haveman and Knight (2000). In this approach, family structure can be treated as endogenous to the level of economic resources or capabilities.

35. We define "prevalence" as the percentage of children who live in families that are designated as poor. As such, this is also known as the "head-count" poverty measure. See Sen (1992) for a discussion of this and other poverty indicators. Note that the official children's poverty rates apply only to children from families headed by prime-aged adults, and hence differ from official U.S. Census publications that include head-count poverty rates for all families. Similar estimates for children aged less than 18 years are available from the authors, upon request.

36. Given that the official poverty rate rests on the flow of cyclically sensitive actual current income, this greater cyclicality is not surprising. The primary factors that account for the difference in levels between the non-self-reliant and official poverty measures are: 1) the counting of transfer income in the official measure but not in the non-self-reliant measure; 2) the prevalence of less than full-time, full-year work among families, which is reflected in the official measure; and 3) the adjustment for childcare costs in the non-self-reliant poverty measure, but not the official poverty measure.

37. Jencks and Mayer (1996) calculate a children's poverty rate that rests on an alternative implicit equivalence scale, a family income measure that includes both the income of nonrelatives in the living unit and the value of public in-kind benefits, and an alternative price index. The official children's poverty rate rose from by approximately 4 percentage

points from 1969 to 1989, while their recalculated children's poverty rate fell by 1.3 percentage points.

38. Detailed estimates on which this and subsequent tables are based are available from the authors upon request. The self-reliant poverty rates and growth patterns shown here adopt a somewhat different set of assumptions than preliminary estimates of overall poverty in Haveman and Bershadker (1998), due to revisions in the health/disability and childcare adjustments, and elimination of the unemployment adjustment that was included in those estimates. See also notes 30 and 31.

39. Female-headed families include families headed by a single mother and couples with children "headed" by a female as indicated in our survey data. Similarly, male-headed families include single men with children and couples with children "headed" by a male, as indicated in our data.

40. Those categories with annual self-reliant children's poverty growth rates in excess of the overall national growth rate (3.9% per year) are shown. The "other" racial group has been omitted due to small sample size. We note that the tabulations show present growth rate comparisons, rather than changes in the number of individuals in poverty. A low annual growth rate for a large group or a group with a high poverty rate (e.g., single mothers) may represent a larger increase in the number of poor individuals than a larger annual growth rate for a small group or a group with a low poverty rate.

41. Notice that self-reliant poverty has increased within each education group. We believe this is due to changing demographics and increased within-group wage inequality. In particular, if education is correlated with EC, then as the size of the population of individuals with higher levels of education rises, the percentage of individuals with a given education level below a particular EC threshold will also rise.

42. Indeed, children living in Hispanic and black single mother families have self-reliant (and official) poverty rates that are approximately three times the national average.

43. A similar, though less pronounced, inverse relationship between the growth rate and the level of poverty is also found for the official poverty measure.

44. For example, in 1975–77, the share of children living in black self-reliant poor families was 111 percent of that group's share of official poverty. A ratio of 1.00 would indicate a particular group's share of self-reliant poverty equaled its share of official poverty.

45. Cash welfare income is included in the resource measure used in the official poverty measure, while only earnings potential is included in the self-reliant measure. The decline in welfare benefit generosity over the period probably accounts for the relative increase in the share of children in female-headed families in official poverty, leading to convergence in this aspect of the composition of children's poverty.

46. Among children living with self-reliant poor single mothers, 72 percent were receiving welfare payments in 1975–77; by 1995–97 this percentage fell to 52 percent of this group. This is largely due to changes in welfare law over the period.

47. Those living in families headed by an Hispanic person are an exception to this pattern. Consistent with the rapid growth in the population of this group since the mid-1970s, the share of the self-reliant poor population comprised of persons living in such families increased by nearly 3 percent per year.

48. See Haveman (2000) for a discussion of several of these trends, and references to studies that have documented them.

49. See Juhn (1992).

50. Over the 1975–97 period, average family size has decreased substantially, as families have had fewer children and as family members who lived with others in prior years have established their own living units.

51. Because average male work hours exceed average female work hours, the decrease in male wages is likely to have increased official poverty over the period by more than the increase in female wages has reduced it. Other factors must have been sufficient to override this effect, in causing the more rapid growth in self-reliant poverty.

52. While we have used indicators of the extent of social exclusion of the families in which children live, we recognize that children themselves may be socially excluded, apart from the status of their families. This distinction is emphasized in Phipps and Curtis (2001).

53. See Eurostat (2000).

54. The ambiguity of the direction of the relationship of this indicator to social exclusion should be noted. Phipps and Curtis (2001), for example, classify dependence on social assistance as a dimension of social exclusion. Our procedure reflects a judgment that recipients of income support benefits are "connected" to public programs and the provision of the services that they offer.

55. The March Current Population Survey is an annual survey of

over 60,000 U.S. families, containing detailed information on the income and labor market activities and outcomes of the adults in the families. Interviewers also obtain information on family size and composition. The Survey uses a stratified random sample, so that using the appropriate weighting factors (provided by the U.S. Bureau of the Census) yields a picture of the economic status and labor market activities of the entire U.S. population.

56. We exclude the self-employed, since their earnings represent a return to both human and physical capital that cannot be disentangled using CPS data.

57. We define FTFY labor force participation as 2,000 or more hours of work in a year.

58. We predict FTFY earnings for students and the self-employed, even though these individuals were excluded from the estimation.

59. An individual is considered to be in a health-related income support program if he or she 1) receives Social Security income, is between 19 and 22, is not a single parent and is not a student; 2) receives Social Security income, is between 23 and 59, and is not a single parent; 3) receives Supplemental Security income; or 4) receives workers' compensation.

60. U.S. Bureau of the Census (1995), and U.S. General Accounting Office (1997).

61. The poverty thresholds were constructed by (1) deflating the year-specific versions of the poverty thresholds to 1967 using the CPI-U (the inflation index the Census Bureau has used to inflate the poverty line) and (2) reinflating the deflated version to the appropriate year using the CPI-U-X1. The first year available for the CPI-U-X1 index is 1967. We started with the current version of the poverty thresholds because in 1981 the Census Bureau stopped the differential treatment of female-headed households and farm residences, and extended the poverty matrix to families of nine or more persons. CPI-U-X1 was used because CPI-U exaggerates the true rise in living costs in the 1970s, due to the inordinate weight given to the cost of newly-purchased homes (U.S. Congressional Budget Office 1988, pp. 6–9).

References

Atkinson, A., and F. Bourguinon. (1982). "The Comparison of Multidimensional Distributions of Economic Status." *Review of Economic Studies* 49: 183–201.

Becker, G. S. (1965). "A Theory of the Allocation of Time." *Economic Journal* 75: 493–517.

Bourguinon, F., and S. R. Chakravarty. (1998). "The Measurement of Multidimensional Poverty." Document 98–12. Paris: DELTA.

Burtless, G., and T. Smeeding. (2001) "The Level, Trend and Composition of Poverty." In *Understanding Poverty*, ed. S. Danziger and R. Haveman. Cambridge, Mass.: Harvard University Press.

Citro, C. F., and R. T. Michael, eds. (1995). *Measuring Poverty: A New Approach*. Washington, D.C.: National Academy Press.

Cutler, D. M., and L. F. Katz. (1991). "Macroeconomic Performance and the Disadvantaged." Brookings Papers on Economic Activity 2. Washington, D.C.: Brookings Institution Press.

Danziger, S., M. Corcoran, S. Danziger, C. Heflin, A. Kalil, J. Levine, D. Rosen, K. Seefeldt, K. Siefert, and R. Tolman. (2001). "Barriers to the Employment of Welfare Recipients." In *Prosperity for All: The Economic Boom and African Americans*, ed. R. Cherry and W. M. Rodgers III. New York: Russell Sage Foundation Press.

de Vos, K., and T. I. Garner. (1991). "An Evaluation of Subjective Poverty Definitions: Comparing Results from the U.S. and the Netherlands." *Review of Income and Wealth* 37(3): 267–85.

Duncan, G. J., J. Boisjoly, and T. Smeeding. (1996). "Economic Mobility of Young Workers in the 1970s and 1980s." *Demography* 33(4): 497–509.

Eurostat. (2000). "Social Exclusion in the EU Member States." *Population and Social Conditions* CA-NK-00-001-EN-I. Available at: www.europa.eu.int/comm/eurostat/Public/datashop.

Federman, M., T. I. Garner, K. Short, W. B. Cutter IV, J. Kiely, D. Levine, D. McGough, and M. McMillen. (1996). "What Does it Mean to be Poor in America?" *Monthly Labor Review*, December 1–17.

Fisher, G. M. (1992). "The Development and History of the Poverty Thresholds." *Social Security Bulletin* 55(4): 3–14.

Garfinkel, I., and R. Haveman. (1977). *Earnings Capacity, Poverty and Inequality*. New York: Academic Press.

Haagenaars, A. J. M. (1986). *The Perception of Poverty.* Amsterdam: North Holland.

Haveman, R. (1987). *Poverty, Policy and Poverty Research.* Madison: University of Wisconsin Press.

—————. (2000). "Poverty and the Distribution of Economic Well-Being since the 1960s." In *Economic Events, Ideas, and Policies,* ed. G. L. Perry and J. Tobin. Washington, D.C.: Brookings Institution Press.

Haveman, R., and A. Bershadker. (1998). "Self-Reliance as a Poverty Criterion: Trends in Earnings-Capacity Poverty, 1975–1992." *American Economic Review* 88(2): 342–47.

—————. (1998). "The 'Inability to be Self-Reliant' as an Indicator of Poverty: Trends for the U.S., 1975–1995." DP 1171-98. Madison: University of Wisconsin Institute for Research on Poverty.

Haveman, R., and L. Buron. (1992). "Who Are the Truly Poor? Patterns of Official and Net Earnings Capacity Poverty, 1973–1988." In *Poverty and Prosperity in the USA in the Late Twentieth Century,* ed. D. Papadimitriou and E. Wolff. New York: St. Martin's Press.

Haveman, R., and B. Knight. (2000). "Youth Labor Market Opportunities, Living Arrangements, and Economic Independence: A Cohort Analysis from the Early 1970s to the Late 1980s." DP 1201-99. Madison: University of Wisconsin Institute for Research on Poverty.

Haveman, R., and M. Mullikin. (2001). "Alternative Measures of National Poverty: Perspectives and Assessment." In *Ethics, Poverty, Inequality and Reform in Social Security,* ed. Erik Schokkaert. London: Ashgate.

Heckman, J. A. (1979). "Sample Selection Bias as a Specification Error." *Econometrica* 47(1): 153–61.

Jencks, C., and S. E. Mayer. (1996). "Do Official Poverty Rates Provide Useful Information about Trends in Children's Economic Welfare?" IPR Working Paper no. 96-1. Evanston, Ill.: Institute for Policy Research at Northwestern University.

Jorgenson, D. W., and D. T. Slesnick. (1987). "Aggregate Consumer Behavior and Household Equivalence Scales." *Journal of Business and Economic Statistics* 5(2): 219–32.

Juhn, C. (1992). "Decline of Male Labor Market Participation: The Role of Declining Labor Market Opportunities." *Quarterly Journal of Economics* 57(1): 79–122.

Kolm, S. (1977). "Multidimensional Egalitarianisms." *Quarterly Journal of Economics* 91: 1–13.

Lillard, L. A., and R. Willis. 1978. "Dynamic Aspects of Earnings

Mobility." *Econometrica* 46 (5): 985–1012.

Mayer, S. E., and C. Jencks. (1992). "Recent Trends in Economic Inequality in the United States: Income vs. Expenditures vs. Material Well-Being." In *Poverty and Prosperity in the USA in the Late Twentieth Century*, ed. D. Papadimitriou and E. Wolff. New York: St. Martin's Press.

———. (1994). "Has Poverty Really Increased Among Children Since 1970?" Working Paper 94–14. Evanston, Ill.: Institute for Policy Research at Northwestern University.

Murray, Charles. (1984). *Losing Ground: American Social Policy, 1950–1980*. New York: Basic Books.

Rector, R. K., W.O. Beirne, and M. McLauchlin. (1990). *How Poor are America's Poor?* Washington, D.C.: Heritage Foundation.

Ruggles, P. (1990). *Drawing the Line: Alternative Poverty Measures and Their Implications for Public Policy*. Washington, D.C.: Urban Institute Press.

Sen, A. (1980). "Equality of What?" In *Tanner Lectures on Human Values*, ed. S. M. McMurrin. Cambridge: Cambridge University Press.

———. (1992). *Inequality Reexamined*. Cambridge, Mass.: Harvard University Press.

———. (1997). *On Economic Inequality*. Oxford: Clarendon Press.

Slesnick, D. T. (1993). "Gaining Ground: Poverty in the Postwar United States." *Journal of Political Economy* 101(1): 1–38.

Triest, R. K. (1998). "Has Poverty Gotten Worse?" *Journal of Economic Perspectives* 12(1): 97–114.

Tsui, K. Y. (1995). "Multidimensional Generalizations of the Relative and Absolute Indices: The Atkinson-Kolm-Sen Approach." *Journal of Economic Theory* 67: 251–25.

U.S. Bureau of the Census. (1995). "What Does it Cost to Mind Our Preschoolers?" *Current Population Reports*. Series P70-52. Washington, D.C.: Government Printing Office.

U.S. Congressional Budget Office.(1988). "Trends in Family Income: 1970–1986." Washington, D.C.: Government Printing Office.

U.S. General Accounting Office. (1996). "Alternative Poverty Measures." GAO/GGD-96–183R. Washington, D.C.: Government Printing Office.

———. (1997). "Implications of Increased Work Participation for Child Care." GAO/HHES-97–75. Washington, D.C.: Government Printing Office.

van Praag, B., M. S. Aldi, J. M. Haagenaars, and H. van Weeren. (1982). "Poverty in Europe." *Review of Income and Wealth* 28(3): 345–59.

Waite, L. J., A. Leibowitz, and C. Witsberger. (1991). "What Parents Pay For: Child Care Characteristics, Quality and Costs." *Journal of Social Issues* 47(2): 33–48.

Social Exclusion of Children in the United States: Identifying Potential Indicators

J. Lawrence Aber, Elizabeth Thompson Gershoff, and Jeanne Brooks-Gunn[1]

If developments in Europe over the last decade are any indication, the concept of social exclusion has the potential to reframe policy research and policy development, and perhaps the entire policy discourse, on problems facing children and families. The concept of social exclusion could extend policy discussions from an exclusive focus on income poverty to a more nuanced appreciation of the factors that exclude children and families from opportunities and experiences. Unlike the concept of poverty and disadvantage, social exclusion remains relevant to societies with robust economies and low poverty rates (such as many Scandinavian countries). Children can be and are excluded from basic activities that define membership in a culture or society, even when they are not poor. Social exclusion may also prove increasingly relevant—perhaps for different reasons—to societies that still experience high poverty rates, such as the United States and the UK.

Using the concepts of strategic frame analysis (Gilliam and Bales 2001), "social exclusion" is likely to produce very different conclusions about causes of and solutions to children's problems than "poverty." Whereas the U.S. public is likely to attribute the responsibility for poverty to individual children and their families, the concept of exclusion can reframe the attribution to social and structural responsibility, and thus also social and structural solutions. In the U.S. context, new policy concepts take on power and influence not only by reframing old problems to promote new insights and new policy responses, but also by allowing policy researchers and policymakers to measure and monitor the new concept across places and over time, and to evaluate the impact of new policy actions on trends over time.

For these reasons, this chapter focuses on our nation's current ability to measure and monitor the social exclusion of children through a system of indicators. We hope to contribute to the larger literature on the development and use of indicators of children's well-being both in this country (Hauser, Brown, and Prosser 1997) and internationally (Ben-Arieh et al. 2000). Although informed by European efforts to measure and monitor social exclusion (Mikulic et al. 1999), this chapter is different in two respects. First, it defines social exclusion more broadly (as will be described in more detail below) than do Mikulic et al. (1999). Second, where possible, it points to U.S. data sources by which "social exclusion" might be operationalized.

In this chapter, we will briefly describe several current conceptual definitions of social exclusion of children, noting that most now consider social exclusion to be a dynamic, multidimensional concept. We will present for U.S. audiences descriptions of eight potential domains of exclusion, and identify numerous specific measures of social exclusion in each domain. Throughout, we identify national data sources when they exist in the United States; European sources as exemplars, where U.S. sources do not exist; and critical features of social exclusion for which we have been unable to identify any data sources. In the final sections of the chapter, we explore potential uses of indicators of social exclusion of children, and outline a research agenda for the further development of such indicators.

Defining Social Exclusion of Children

In thinking about the definition of social exclusion of children, it is important to consider the question, "excluded from *what?*" In general, social exclusion involves exclusion of any person from situations and activities considered to be normal or desirable (Burchardt, Le Grand, and Piachaud 1999; Percy-Smith 2000), such as having:

- economic security;
- adequate housing;

- crime-free neighborhoods;
- adequate employment;
- after-school activities for youths;
- political influence (including voting);
- an active and involved community;
- available friends and social support;
- available local services (infrastructure); and
- educational opportunities.

Social exclusion also is conceptualized as relevant to several life domains, including those related to production, consumption, wealth, political life, and social life (Burchardt, Le Grand, and Piachaud 1999). The term "social exclusion" implies that the goal is for all children and families to be *in*cluded. So what exactly would "inclusion" look like? Chanan (2000) has delineated inclusion as entailing:

- living in a household in which at least one person is employed;
- having maximum opportunity for local community involvement without being dependent on it;
- living in a household that participates in local and national voting;
- living in a household that keeps informed about national and international news;
- living in a household that enjoys culture and entertainment;
- being a part of a social network;
- having the choice and means to live in a different locale;
- living in a neighborhood with easy meeting places and transportation; and
- living without fear of crime and harassment.

In current conceptions of social exclusion, the majority of its components are tied to the socioeconomic and cultural status of adults. By extension, the majority of factors that constitute (or predict) exclusion in the lives of children are out of the control of children and rarely alterable by them. This fact is reflected in the list of identified predictors of social exclusion: characteristics of the individual (e.g., health, education level); events in an individual's life (e.g., job loss); characteristics of the area an individual lives in (e.g., physical condition, level of unemployment); and social, civil, and political institutions of society (e.g., racial discrimination, welfare policies) (Burchardt, Le Grand, and Piachaud 1999). As children age into adolescence and young adulthood, their own characteristics and abilities help to shape their experience with social exclusion; yet, for the most part, when we speak of the social exclusion of children, we refer most often to the social exclusion of their parents (and sometimes of their schools and communities).

Although children have little effect on whether they or their families are socially excluded, the experience of social exclusion can have a significant impact on how children interact with their peers and perceive themselves relative to their peers. Children and adolescents are keenly aware of the consequences of social in-equality (Brooks-Gunn and Duncan 1997; Duncan, Brooks-Gunn, and Klebanov 1994).

Children may feel excluded relative to their peers when their parents cannot find jobs that pay above minimum wage; in such cases, although parents may be able to provide basic housing, food, and clothing, they will not be able to buy their child the latest video game, clothes, or shoes. The child's lack of these goods will restrict the child's ability to share common experiences with peers or to "fit in" with the current styles of dress. Children who are unable to share in these aspects of a common youth culture may, in a very real way, feel excluded from their peers and may feel stigmatized, discriminated against, and alienated (Klasen 1998). Whether and how children internalize the experience of exclusion is a key determinant of long- and short-term outcomes of exclusion for children.

Potential Indicators for the Measurement of Social Exclusion of Children

Social exclusion is not merely a "you're in" or "you're out" phenomenon; rather, social exclusion is a dynamic experience with multiple, interconnected levels (Percy-Smith 2000). Whether a child or family is excluded may change over time, as will the subjective experience of that exclusion. Because social exclusion involves such dynamic and interconnected aspects, longitudinal data are required to understand its effects (Burchardt, Le Grand, and Piachaud 1999). Unfortunately, most national studies that measure the indicators of interest are primarily cross-sectional and/or domain-specific. Thus, it will be important for researchers to optimize use of the longitudinal, multidomain data available in the few ongoing, in-depth longitudinal studies (e.g., Panel Study of Income Dynamics, National Longitudinal Study of Youth, Early Childhood Longitudinal Study; Brooks-Gunn et al. 2000; Brooks-Gunn et al. 1995).

We started generating possible indicators of the social exclusion of children by first consulting the list of social exclusion indicators developed by Eurostat and the Organization for Economic Co-operation and Development (OECD) for use in the European Union (Mikulic et al. 1999; see Exhibit 1). We supplemented these potential indicators with others, reported in several sources, that utilized nationally representative data for the United States. Those sources included Federal Interagency Forum on Child and Family Statistics (2000); U.S. Department of Health and Human Services (2000); Annie E. Casey Foundation (2000); and data collected by J. F. Zaff (2000). As much as possible, we identified indicators that adhered to recent recommendations for indicators of social exclusion (Mikulic et al. 1999), namely that the indicators:

1. be easily understood by the public and congruent with their concerns;

2. be relatively easy to quantify;

3. follow international conventions;

4. allow comparisons over time;

5. be able to be operationalized at the local area level;

6. emphasize both objective and subjective indicators;

7. characterize living conditions of both poor and non-poor;

8. be experienced by majority of the population;

9. allow international comparisons; and

10. allow easy connections between non-monetary and monetary indicators.

We derived eight domains that would encompass these indicators of children's social exclusion: *basic living, family economic participation, housing, health, education, public space, social participation, and subjective experience of exclusion.* Before detailing the domains and indicators of exclusion, we must call attention to several factors that, although they are not considered part of social exclusion, do place children who experience them at significant risk of exclusion (Packham 1999; Social Exclusion Unit 1998; Sparkes 1999). These are being of a minority ethnic group, being disabled, being in a single-parent family, and being a child in foster care. To date, such factors have not been included as aspects of social exclusion per se. Yet—given their strong links with other exclusion factors— we may want to consider, in the future, an additional domain that encompasses these risks. At this point, we have included childhood disability under the Health domain and participation in special education services for disabled children in the Education domain.

For each of the domains that follow, we have sorted the potential indicators into subdomains, based on those that we consider necessary components of exclusion/inclusion, those that are normative for this society, and those that are desirable for members of this society but not absolutely required for inclusion. Examples from the basic living domain include food security as *necessary,* affording new clothes as *normative,* and having a color television as *desirable* (see Exhibit 2).

Suggested indicators, and a list of U.S. nationally representative surveys that include these indicators, are provided in each domain's respective exhibit. The full name of each survey and the agency or institute that conducts it are provided in Exhibit 10. A few indicators have been proposed by the Eurostat group on measuring social exclusion (Mikulic et al. 1999) from variables used in the European Community Household Panel. However, we have not yet identified these variables in any U.S. survey. Finally, we note at the outset that these indicators are suggestive and by no means exhaustive.

Basic Living

The *basic living* category is an index of a family's consumption of the goods and services that are viewed by the majority culture as necessary for participation in the essential activities of the society (see Exhibit 2). The most basic and necessary among these are indicators having to do with families' ability to afford food, clothing, and transportation. As normative indicators, we have included the quality of food consumed and whether a family can afford new clothes. The desirable subdomain of indicators in this category refer to purchases and activities which, although not essential to basic survival, are viewed by a majority of the culture to be necessary for inclusion in mainstream society (e.g., a television, a telephone, an automobile, a computer; going out to a restaurant occasionally; inviting friends to one's home for a meal).

Family Economic Participation

The *family economic participation* domain captures those indicators that have heretofore been considered crucial determinants of family disadvantage, namely income and human capital indicators (see Exhibit 3). It is central to the notion of social exclusion that children living in families without an adult participating in the labor market are, by definition, excluded (Percy-Smith 2000); however, having a job does not guarantee inclusion (Campbell 2000), and thus we can view parents' participation in the labor market as a necessary, although not sufficient, condition for children's social inclusion. A family's low income, particularly if it falls below the U.S. poverty line, is a necessary component of exclusion that relates to all other components. There are several indices of families' financial hardship in the normative subdomain of economic participation, such as whether the family receives public assistance or whether the family has experienced significant financial difficulty. Also included are aspects of the human capital of the adults in the family, particularly their education level, job training, and job prestige, which will determine whether a family is excluded by affecting whether a child's parents are able to obtain the stability and financial remuneration of employment. Although not necessary for inclusion, having financial assets is considered a desirable buffer against financial hardship (Aber et al. 1997).

Housing

A family's housing situation may lead to social exclusion if it constrains opportunities and impairs control over family members' daily lives (Hawtin and Kettle 2000). Simply obtaining an adequate residence is a challenge in many neighborhoods that lack a range of affordable housing options. This is especially true for ethnic minorities who are faced with housing discrimination as well as economic discrimination in access to home mortgages (Massey 1999; Wilson 1987). At the extreme of housing difficulty and those needs that must be met for inclusion there is homelessness, which puts children and families at a distinct disadvantage (Whitman, Accardo, and Sprankel 1992). Families without a permanent residence have difficulty obtaining employment, education, regular health care, and social networks. Low-income families who are able procure housing, but who must spend more than 50 percent of their take-home income on it, face substantial difficulty in financing their food, clothing, and utility needs. Among normative indicators, children whose families can only afford housing that is in physical disrepair or crowded (e.g., less than one room per person) are at risk for both physical and mental health problems. Finally, it is desirable that families feel invested, both socially and economically, in their homes and neighborhoods. Families who feel insecure in their housing, either because they experience financial troubles that precipitate frequent moving, live in public housing, or do not feel safe in their homes or neighborhoods, will be less likely to establish roots in their communities; such children and their families may feel socially excluded. It is important to note that merely having, or even owning, housing does not ensure inclusion: families must have a home in which they feel safe and in which they are willing and able to invest, in order to feel included in the community and society (Hawtin and Kettle 2000). (See Exhibit 4 for examples of indicators.)

Health

Socially excluded families may be unable to maintain proper health for a variety of reasons (see Exhibit 5). Having low income can restrict a family's ability to procure adequate physical, dental, and mental health care (Moran and Simpkin 2000). If a family lives in a neighborhood with few health care options—or, for poor children, affordable options such as public health clinics—children may not receive adequate care (pre- or postnatal) to ensure their optimal development (Brooks-Gunn et al. 1998). Although low income is a primary risk for poor child health, inequalities in children's health may also arise from inadequacies in housing, education, safe learning environments, or safe neighborhoods (Moran and Simpkin 2000). Deteriorating housing and neighborhoods pose physical risks for children (e.g., exposure to lead paint and other toxins; development of asthma; risk of injury from broken glass and busy streets). In turn, poor health may reinforce exclusion by limiting participation in education, work, and social activities (Moran and Simpkin 2000). Beyond health care and physical risks, a family's ability (and inclination) to provide healthy foods for their children will also affect children's development; U.S. children from wealthier families and in more affluent neighborhoods are more likely both to eat fruit and/or to exercise (Currie 2001). Unfortunately, social inclusion does not guarantee healthy eating: with the rise of corporations providing cheap soft drinks and snack products, inclusion in society may also mean adopting the mainstream culture's poor eating habits (Moran and Simpkin 2000).

We consider all of the health indicators to be either necessary or normative, as they are all key components of children's well-being. Having health insurance and receiving regular medical and dental care are essential to inclusion, as are living in areas free from lead exposure and poor air quality. Normative indicators include a healthy birth, access to mental health services, and not having a disability that prevents easy participation in daily activities. A final component of health and exclusion, specific to adolescents, is avoidance of teenage parenthood. Teenage parenthood is viewed as both a cause and consequence of social exclusion (Social Exclusion Unit 1999). Social exclusion may precipitate teenage pregnancy by restricting access to family planning services. Teenage parents are more likely than their peers be unemployed and to live in poverty. Moreover, they are likely to be trapped by their lack of education, as well as the lack of available and affordable childcare (Brooks-Gunn and Chase-Lansdale 1995; Social Exclusion Unit 1999).

Education

Because children spend a majority of their time in schools, schools are viewed as primary socializers of children, and thus children excluded from schools are viewed as a threat to society (Packham 1999). The term "passive exclusion" denotes a child's removal from mainstream education, due to such circumstances as the child's disruptive behavior or the child's disability. Undoubtedly, many children benefit from more individual attention in special education classes, yet exclusion of disruptive and difficult children from mainstream education may reinforce social exclusion (Klasen 1998). Typically, "active exclusion" from education involves the child abandoning school through repeated truancy or dropping out altogether. Necessary indicators of exclusion (see Exhibit 6) include children under 18 years of age not being enrolled in school, whether they have been held back in school, and whether they receive special education services. Suspensions, expulsions, and truancy are normative signs of exclusion in the education domain; access to quality childcare and education are desirable indicators.

A variety of factors contribute to children's low educational attainment or poor school performance. Demographic factors of children and families, such as income level, family size, parent's marital status, level of parental involvement in school, and whether a child is in foster care, are several key predictors of educational achievement (Sparkes 1999). At the policy level, educational spending per pupil is positively associated with educational attainment, even after controlling for poverty levels (Sparkes 1999). Thus, economic policies that link funding of schools to the local tax base ensure that economic disadvantage translates into educational disadvantage (Klasen 1998). Furthermore, policies that place pressures on schools to maintain high test scores may also lead schools to exclude problematic students quickly before attempting to help them (Sparkes 1999).

Children who perceive that they are being stigmatized, stereotyped, dehumanized, or alienated are at high risk of excluding themselves from schools through truancy or by dropping out. Thus, because of their risk for stigmatization, children from lower socioeconomic backgrounds, children from certain ethnic groups, and/or children in state care are more prone to truancy and lower levels of educational attainment than those in other groups (Walton 2000). Furthermore, students who have poor relationships with teachers, who feel left out of decision-making, or who feel that they are being treated unfairly are also more likely to be truants or drop-outs (Sparkes 1999). Self-exclusion from education in turn leads to participation in local and street-based youth networks and disengagement from opportunities provided by education and job training (Johnston et al. 2000).

Education is clearly a factor in the perpetuation of social exclusion across successive generations (Phillips et al. 1998). The quality of education a child receives, and the level of education he or she attains, are strong predictors of whether that child will become a socially excluded adult: children with low levels of educational attainment, numeracy, or literacy are at higher risk for low rates of employment, and low earnings and high social exclusion, as adults (Sparkes 1999; Walton 2000). Thus, educational quality is a desirable indicator: schools that do not provide a "quality" education (e.g., education that promotes functional literacy, numeracy, social skills, and job readiness) play a significant role in perpetuating social exclusion throughout childhood and into adulthood.

Public Space

Social exclusion at the neighborhood level is manifested in deprived communities by disinvestment by private and public institutions (Brooks-Gunn, Duncan, and Aber 1997; Sanderson 2000). Paul A. Jargowsky (1997) has identified three aspects of neighborhoods that help determine whether a population is socially excluded (or, in his terms, part of the "underclass"): (1) economic, institutional, and social processes that contribute to the poverty level of the community; (2) concentration of poverty in certain neighborhoods; and (3) concentrations of the excluded causing certain behavioral responses in those who live there. As with the health domain, we have only identified necessary and normative indicators for the public space domain (see Exhibit 7 for sample indicators).

Where a child's family lives determines his or her access to places, activities, resources, services, amenities, public transportation, and information (Pitts and Hope 1997; Sanderson 2000); thus, parents in socially excluded neighborhoods face difficulties meeting the daily needs of their children. Many excluded neighborhoods experience the withdrawal of public services for families, which in turn undermines social capital and contributes to social exclusion (Berlin, Brooks-Gunn, and Aber 2001; Leventhal, Brooks-Gunn, and Kamerman 1997; Pitts and Hope 1997); even when services exist in such "poverty pockets," they are overcrowded and overloaded (Van Kempen 1997). The concentration of disadvantages in excluded neighborhoods makes both living in and escaping such disadvantages more difficult (Wilson 1987). By the last years of the twentieth century, the number of people living in neighborhoods with high concentrations of poverty had increased steeply (Jargowsky 1997). Such poverty pockets are particularly disadvantageous to children, as they are characterized by a lack of social contacts, few social clubs and cultural events, few opportunities for socialization into steady work and family life, and exposure to illegal means of survival (Van Kempen 1997).

Although poor-quality neighborhoods can have direct effects on the physical and mental health of children and families, such neighborhoods precipitate social patterns and behavior that can only be explained by the specific characteristics and social structure of the local environment in which they evolve (Leventhal and Brooks-Gunn 2000; Van Kempen 1997). One manifestation of such patterns is increased rates of violent and criminal behavior in disadvantaged neighborhoods. Children exposed to violence, either as observers or victims, are at high risk for behavioral and emotional problems brought on by increased levels of depression, suicidal ideation, and post-traumatic stress disorder (Horn and Trickett 1998; Mazza and Reynolds 1999; Stiffman et al. 1999).

It is important to note that neighborhood-level social exclusion from, and inequalities in, access to services are not restricted to urban, disadvantaged communities, and may in some ways be more acute in rural areas. Low population density in rural areas requires that families travel to services, but public transportation in rural neighborhoods is rare, and thus low-income rural families without their own transportation receive fewer services than those in urban areas (Sanderson 2000).

Social Participation

Several factors determine whether children will be able to participate socially: the economic security of their families; whether the society supports positive relationships between children and their communities; whether children belong to social networks; and whether children are able to participate in social, economic, political, and cultural processes to their maximum potential (Beck, van der Maeson, and Walker 1997). The social quality of a community and society is characterized by the extent to which citizens are able to participate in, and contribute to, the social and economic life of their communities in ways that enhance their own well-being (Beck, van der Maeson, and Walker 1997). The quality of children's social interactions is determined by the resources available to children, whether children are able to use those resources, and whether those who use the resources are able to get what they want from them (Berman and Phillips 2001). We include as necessary indicators those related to children's relationships with significant others in their lives, as well as the extent to which children engage in delinquent and/or antisocial behaviors. We consider children's participation in organized activities to be normative and consider children's participation in volunteer and civic-related activities to be desirable. (See Exhibit 8 for sample indicators.)

The social networks of the excluded are something of a paradox. Although socially excluded communities are functionally excluded from mainstream social networks related to employment and financial services (Van Kempen 1997), these communities often develop informal social networks that help families manage their lives (e.g., by providing connections to informal work or informal credit arrangements) (Johnston et al. 2000). Such informal networks, and the strategies developed by inhabitants to deal with their difficult conditions, may become an important part of their cultural capital (Van Kempen 1997). The lack of formal, organized social networks in some communities means that families in poor neighborhoods do not have others who can share the burden of raising children and providing guidance, support, and social control for them (Wilson 1996). Thus, sparse infrastructure means that the burden of socialization falls solely on individual families who are already incapacitated by the additional burden of coping with the stress of poverty (McLoyd 1990).

Children can become positively involved in their communities in a variety of ways (Flanagan and Faison 2001). They can perform volunteer work, hold part-time jobs, participate in religious organizations, and keep up to date on current events through newspapers and television. They can work on political campaigns and write to public officials. Unfortunately, most research to date has focused on the extent to which children become negatively involved in their communities, specifically by committing delinquent, criminal, or violent acts. A social exclusion approach to such behaviors emphasizes them as reactions to exclusion from mainstream networks and activities.

Subjective Experience of Social Exclusion

Recent writings on social exclusion have increasingly focused on the individual's experience of social exclusion as an important component (Percy-Smith 2000). The proposed social exclusion indicators from Eurostat (Mikulic et al. 1999) specifically include measures of an individual's satisfaction with his or her life situation. Extending this to children, we might ask children how satisfied they are with their housing situation, school, and leisure time. Additionally, measuring children's overall happiness, self-satisfaction, self-concept, and locus of control would provide insight into how the experience of social exclusion lowers children's perceptions of themselves and children's beliefs about how much they control their present lives and their futures. Exhibit 9 is a preliminary attempt to suggest indicators of this domain, which for now we consider to be desirable, rather than necessary or normative.

Values and Indicator Choices

Values [2]

Many of the indicators we have suggested implicitly or explicitly represent values regarding what (we think) is normal or appropriate for children and families. Examples of such values include having working parents, not receiving public assistance, and having a home in which to live. Just as indicators of children's well-being are based on value judgements about the states and experiences that constitute a happy and healthy environment, indicators of social exclusion hinge upon value judgements about the absence of such states and experiences. Values are thus inherent in the task of developing indicators, yet they must be acknowledged and perhaps challenged. Why do we believe that it is better for a child to have a working parent? Is it out of our concern for the child's present well-being because the child will be better provided with food and other necessities; out of our concern for our own potential financial costs, because the child will be less likely to be dependent on public assistance; or out of our concern for the child's future contribution to society, because the child will have an appropriate work model? Or are all three true to varying degrees? We have done our best to select available indicators that we, in agreement with other researchers, value as necessary, normative, or desirable for positive child development.

Individual- Versus Society-Level Indicators

As stated above, the concept of social exclusion has the potential to shape and redirect public policies related to children and their families. However, this is most likely to be true for indicators under direct societal-level control rather than those highly determined by individual-level control. Policymakers and the public will be hesitant, if realistically so, to try to change individual-level indicators, such as completion of a high school education. Although society can take the important step of guaranteeing that families have livable incomes, it cannot control how parents allocate those funds (e.g., do they buy nutritious foods or fast foods?). Indeed, many such choices about how to spend limited money are difficult ones that parents should not have to make (e.g., should they pay the rent or buy medicine?).

Policymakers intent on reducing the exclusion of children must be simultaneously concerned with the inclusion of their parents, rather than blaming the children for the parents' proverbial "sins." The fact is that deprivation and exclusion in their lives are entirely linked with the exclusion of their parents.

Relations among Domains

As mentioned above, we have organized the indicators into eight distinct domains. Although such an organization is comprehensive, it may also be unwieldy, particularly if our goal is to capture the attention and energies of policymakers who will be more concerned with practical than with theoretical linkages.

Several participants at the conference on Social Exclusion and Children suggested alternative ways to categorize our indicators, which we describe briefly here.

Robert Haveman, of the University of Wisconsin-Madison, suggested dividing the indicators into supply-side and demand-side indicators. On the supply side, he would place those indicators that embody what society needs to do in order to increase the inclusion of children and families. Examples of supply-side indicators would be the prevalence of child mental-health services or the availability of affordable housing. Demand-side indicators would focus on individual-based sources of exclusion; these would include both involuntary sources of exclusion, such as a physical disability or mental illness, and voluntary sources of exclusion, such as truancy from school. Such a conceptualization makes clear where societal effort toward reducing exclusion should be directed, although society would have an easier time resolving exclusion on the supply than the demand end.

John Hills, of the Center for Analysis of Social Exclusion at the London School of Economics, argued that the current eight domains should be reduced to two: one focused on children's material needs and one focused on indicators related to children's future flourishing. This latter category, Hills suggests, would encompass social interaction, the development of self-determination, and barriers to flourishing (e.g., those derived from safety or health concerns). Such a dichotomy is consistent with the approach taken by group of international collaborators working on indicators: namely that indicators of children's current "well-being" be distinguished from indicators of their future "well-becoming" (Ben-Arieh et al. 2000). Although we find such an approach intriguing, it contrasts with our view that indicators of social exclusion should be distinct from indicators of well-being, for inclusion in and of itself is not our primary concern—but rather the physical, mental, and social benefits made possible by inclusion.

Constance Flanagan, of Pennsylvania State University, also suggests organizing the indicators along two dimensions that overlap with those described by Hills, namely those indicators related to the nurturing and protection of children, and those indicators concerned with children's rights and abilities to engage in self-determination and societal participation. Such an organization would value participation equally with the meeting of children's basic needs, which may indeed get to the heart of what "inclusion" should mean.

How Can Indicators of the Social Exclusion of Children Be Used and Improved?

We have demonstrated that a wide range of measures is available for use by policymakers, opinion leaders, and other interested parties to operationalize a multidimensional and dynamic conception of the social exclusion of children in the U.S. In this section, we wish to stimulate discussion about the potential uses of such measures and about research needed to improve both the measures and their use.

One important activity is an examination of the validity of measures of social exclusion. If proponents of the concept of social exclusion are correct in their assertion—that "social exclusion" identifies both social-political-cultural processes and a population of children whose life chances are compromised, in a way that neither "poverty" nor "disadvantage" do—then studies of the convergent, discriminant, predictive, and construct validity of measures of social exclusion are needed. Validity studies might address such questions as:

• How much of the variation in the social exclusion of children is explained by traditional measures of poverty and disadvantage?

• What important processes and outcomes are predicted by measures of social exclusion of children that are not predicted by measures of poverty and disadvantage?

• What subgroups of children or communities are identified as in need of public attention and action by measures of social exclusion that are not identified by measures of poverty and disadvantage?

An example of a research initiative that would address some of these questions would be one that determines whether and how the levels/trends/dynamics of social exclusion of children differ from the levels/trends/dynamics of child poverty and/or racial-residential segregation. Well-designed validity studies could also provide answers to two other key questions: 1) Is there a subset of measures of social exclusion that can capture the critical variation required? 2) Are there relations among the indicators, the knowledge of which could improve their use in policy formulation, implementation, and evaluation?

There are over 100 individual measures outlined in Exhibits 1 through 8, derived from 26 distinct data sources and representing 8 domains of the social exclusion of children (an average of 13 measures per domain, ranging from 7 to 17 measures per domain). This organization of data does not inhibit the study of national trends in the component variables, but it does preclude analysis of the relations among the various components of social exclusion. Since social exclusion is conceptualized as a multidimensional, dynamic concept, the ideal indicator system would permit the examination of relations among all the important components over time. This is not cost efficient, or even feasible, without a reduced set of variables and measures. For these reasons, we encourage policy researchers to conduct studies on the intercorrelations of dimensions of social exclusion over time, in the service of identifying a reduced set of critical indicators that can be used as part of a national (or local) measurement and monitoring system.

A reduced set of variables and measures collected on the same samples of children over time would enable policy researchers to understand the causal relations among the indicators in the service of identifying "leading" and "lagging" indicators of social exclusion. In the economic domain, this distinction is critical to the nature and timing of public decisions about the economy. Some workers in the "social indicators" movement have the same aspirations in the social domain, namely to identify negative trends before they fully develop so as to prompt and guide early action.

A reduced number of core or critical variables would increase the possibility of collecting a comprehensive set of data at the local, state, and national levels. Unless indicators of the social exclusion of children can be disaggregated to the state and local levels, the probability of informing and influencing state and local decision making is reduced. For instance, it would be very valuable to identify states and locales that are comparable in child poverty and disadvantage indices but which vary in other indices of children's social exclusion. Presumably, much could be learned about the political and civic cultures, policies, and services of states and communities in which children are socially *in*cluded despite poverty and disadvantage.

The Most Important Uses of Indicators of the Social Exclusion of Children

In our opinion, the two most important uses of a system of indicators of social exclusion of children are to provide new insights into and new applications for policy interventions; and to monitor and guide the progress of programs and policies designed to reduce the social exclusion of children at the local, state, and national levels. The concept of social exclusion directs attention to "exclusion *from* what," as noted above, as well as to "exclusion *by* what." Specifically, what are the forces, processes, institutions, and groups that cause or lead children to be socially excluded? Can there be any doubt that the historical combination of racial discrimination and residential segregation continues to lead the social exclusion of millions of African-American children? With current rapid growth in the proportion of U.S. children who are Latino/a and Asian, how will U.S. social institutions and processes adapt to the language and culture changes required to include immigrants' children in the American dream?

A refined system of indicators of the social exclusion of children that has been shown to be valid, and that can be used at the local, state, and national levels, can contribute to a new policy discourse. The questions "exclusion *from* what?" and "exclusion *by* what?" could help rebalance the United States' concentration on individualistic explanations for poverty, disadvantage, and exclusion by directing attention to social-structural explanations. Both new policy proposals and new ideas about how to monitor and evaluate the influence of policies on the social exclusion of children could be advanced by using the right kind of social indicator system.

Notes

1. The authors wish to thank Sheila B. Kamerman for organizing the conference, and their funders, the Annie E. Casey Foundation and the Ford Foundation (Aber and Gershoff) and the NICHD Research Network on Child and Family Well-Being (Brooks-Gunn), for their support.

2. We thank Maria Cancian, a discussant at the conference on Social Exclusion and Children, for suggesting that we consider the role of values in our choice of indicators.

Exhibit 1: European Union Indicators of Social Exclusion Used by Eurostat

Indicator	Indicators on Means	Indicators on Perception	Indicators on Confidence
Basic Needs and Consumption	1. Access to telephone(s) 2. Access to a color television 3. Access to automobile(s) 4. Access to a video recorder 5. Access to a microwave 6. Access to a dishwasher	7. Household ability to afford an adequate diet 8. Household ability to afford new clothes 9. Household ability to afford to keep home warm 10. Household ability to invite friends or family for drinks/dinner 11. Household ability to afford a week's holiday away from home	
Housing	12. Accommodation rented from a public, municipal, or non-profit agency 13. Shortage of space (<1 room per person) 14. Presence of shower or bath in the dwelling 15. Presence of a place to sit outside (garden or balcony)	16. Shortage of space (subjective) 17. Inconvenience from humidity 18. Inconvenience due to rot in windows and frames 19. Perceived risk of crime or vandalism in the area	20. Satisfaction with the housing situation
Education	21. Highest level of completed education		
Labor Market	22. Living in a non-working household 23. Living in a household where unemployment benefits are a source of income 24. Personal position in the labor market (ILO definition)		25. Satisfaction with the housing situation
Health	26. Coverage by medical insurance 27. Hospitalization in past 12 months	28. Health status (self-reported) 29. Limitations in daily activities due to a chronic health problem, illness, or disability	

Indicator	Indicators on Means	Indicators on Perception	Indicators on Confidence
Family Ties and Social Relations		30. Frequency of contacts with family or friends 31. Frequency of contacts with neighbors	
Social Participation	32. Membership in a club or association		33. Satisfaction with the amount of leisure time
Indicators of the Household Financial Situation/ Financial Stress		34. Household ability to make ends meet 35. Household ability to pay scheduled utility bills 36. Household ability to save regularly	37. Satisfaction with the financial situation

Exhibit 2: Indicators of Social Exclusion: Basic Living Domain
(See Exhibit 10 for Key to Abbreviations)

Social Exclusion Indicator	Potential Data Sources
Necessary Subdomain	
Household suffers from food insecurity	CPS-FSS, NHANES, ECLS, NSAF
Household cannot afford to adequately heat home	(ECHP)
Household cannot afford any clothes	(ECHP)
Household cannot afford telephone	CPS
Household cannot afford automobile (and lives more than 15 minute's walk from public transportation)	(ECHP)
Normative Subdomain	
Quality of diet is poor	CSFII
Household cannot afford new clothes	(ECHP)

Desirable Subdomain	
Household's nutrition is poor (lack of fruits, vegetables, milk products, meat)	Ad Health
Household does not have a computer	CPS
Household cannot afford to invite friends for dinner/drink	(ECHP)
Household cannot afford a week's vacation away from home	(ECHP)
Household cannot afford color television	(ECHP)
Household cannot afford VCR	(ECHP)
Household cannot afford microwave	(ECHP)
Household cannot afford dishwasher	(ECHP)

Exhibit 3: Indicators of Social Exclusion: Economic Participation Domain

Social Exclusion Indicator	Potential Data Sources
Necessary Subdomain	
Child does not have a parent in the workforce	CPS, ECLS, NLSY, PSID
Child does not have a parent earning income (through either employment or assistance [e.g., SSI])	CPS, ECLS, NLSY, PSID
Family income is below poverty line (per income: needs)	CPS, Green Book
Normative Subdomain	
Family receives cash and near-cash transfers	CPS, PSID
Family receives in-kind benefits (food stamps, Medicaid)	CPS, PSID
Main source of family income is benefits	(ECHP)

Household has difficulty making ends meet	ECLS, PSID
Household was unable to pay utility bills in last 12 months	NSAF
Child's parent(s) has/have not completed high school	CPS, ECLS, NLSY, PSID
Parents' jobs have low occupational prestige	PSID, NLSY, ECLS
Child's parent(s) has/have not completed job training	PSID, NLSY, ECLS
Desirable Subdomain	
Family does not have monetary assets (savings, stocks, etc)	PSID
Household is unable to save	(ECHP)

Exhibit 4: Indicators of Social Exclusion: Housing Domain

Social Exclusion Indicator	Potential Sources
Necessary Subdomain	
Family does not have a permanent residence (is homeless)	??
Family's housing is physically inadequate (lacks plumbing; has unvented rooms, water leakage, cracks, rats)	AHS, NHANES
Family's housing is crowded (<1 room: person)	AHS
Family's housing cost burden exceeds 50%	AHS
Normative Subdomain	
Family's housing has no place to sit outside	(ECHP)
Family's housing has damp floors, walls	(ECHP)

Family's housing has rot in windows, floors	(ECHP)
Family does not feel safe and secure in home	??
Family has residential instability (several moves per year)	CPS, NHANES, ECLS, PSID
Family lives in public housing	(ECHP)
Desirable Subdomain	
Family is unable to get mortgage to buy a home	??
Family does not own a home	CPS, PSID, ECLS
Family is faced with limited supply of homes in neighborhood	??
Family is not committed to investing in the home	??

Exhibit 5: Indicators of Social Exclusion: Health Domain

Social Exclusion Indicator	Potential Sources
Necessary Subdomain	
Child is not covered by health insurance (private or public)	CPS, ECLS
Child has not had physical exam by doctor/nurse in last year	Ad Health, NHANES, ECLS
Child has not had dental exam by dentist/hygienist in last year	Ad Health, NHANES, ECLS
Child's mother did not receive prenatal care	NHANES
Child has not had recommended immunizations	NIS, NHANES
Child has had lead exposure	NHANES
Quality of child's air (re: ozone, carbon monoxide, particulates, lead, nitrogen dioxide, sulfur dioxide) is poor	AIRS

Normative Subdomain	
Child did not have healthy birth (5 min apgar > 8, bw > 2500 g, gestational age of 37+ weeks, prenatal care)	NHANES
Child born with low birth weight	NVSS, ECLS, PSID, NLSY
Child has no access to mental health services	Ad Health
Child has physical limitation that restricts activity	Ad Health, NHIS, NHANES
Child has emotional or physical problem causing him/her to miss school or an activity	Ad Health
Child has permanent health condition (heart problems, asthma, physical disability, diabetes, migraines)	Ad Health, NLSY, NHANES, NSAF
Adolescent has no access to drug or alcohol treatment	Ad Health
Adolescent has no access to family planning services	Ad Health

Exhibit 6: Indicators of Social Exclusion: Education Domain

Social Exclusion Indicator	Potential Sources
Necessary Subdomain	
Child is not enrolled in school	NSAF
Child is under 18 years old but neither in school nor working	CPS
Child is under 18 years old and has dropped out of school	CPS
Child has repeated a grade	Ad Health, NLSY, ECLS
Child receives special education for mental retardation or learning disability	Ad Health, NLSY, ECLS
Normative Subdomain	
Child is eligible for, but not enrolled in, subsidized childcare	??
Child is suspended from school	Ad Health, NELS, NLSY, NSAF
Child has been excluded from mainstream schools for behavior problems	ECLS
Child is a truant from school	NLSY, NSAF
Desirable Subdomain	
Family has no access to quality childcare	NHES
Family has no access to quality public schools	??

Social Exclusion Indicator	Potential Sources
Necessary Subdomain	
Neighborhood does not have access to public transportation	??
Family's neighborhood does not have access to health services, grocery stores, schools, and commercial goods and services (particularly financial services)	??
Child has exposure to observed violence (aggravated assault, rape, robbery, homicide)	NCVS, ECLS, NLSY
Child is subject to victimization (aggravated assault, rape, robbery, homicide)	NCVS, YRBSS
Family's neighborhood has inadequate infrastructure (walking distance to parks, variety in types of housing)	CPS
Normative Subdomain	
Family lives in neighborhood with high poverty level	CPS, ECLS, PSID
Family lives in neighborhood with high crime and vandalism	CPS
Family lives in neighborhood with social disorganization	CPS, PSID

Exhibit 8: Indicators of Social Exclusion: Social Participation Domain

Social Exclusion Indicator	Potential Sources
Necessary Subdomain	
Child does not have positive relationship with parents	Ad Health, NELS, NLSY
Child does not have relationships with people at school	Ad Heath, NELS
Child does not have relationships with friends	Ad Health, MTF, NLSY
Child engages in delinquent behaviors (painting graffiti, lying, stealing, running away, robbery, selling drugs)	Ad Health, MTF, NELS, NLSY, NSAF, PSID, SPD, NHANES
Child engages in physical fights	Ad Health, MTF, NHANES, YRBSS
Child has committed violent crime (aggravated assault, rape, robbery)	NCVS
Child carries a weapon	Ad Health, MTF, YRBSS
Child has been arrested, spent time in juvenile detention	NELS, SPD, NACJD
Child belongs to a gang	NELS, SPD, NLSY
Normative Subdomain	
Child does not have people to turn to when he/she has problems	Ad Health, NELS, NLSY, NHANES
Child does not attend religious services	HSB, MTF, NELS, NSC, SPD, ECLS, NLSY
Child does not participate in extracurricular activities	Ad Health, HSB, MTF, NELS, NSAF, NSC, PSID
Child does not participate in organized sports	Ad Health, NELS, NSAF, NSC, PSID
Desirable Subdomain	
Child does not participate in community or volunteer work	MTF, NELS, NLSY, NHES
Child does not read newspaper/watch local and national news	MTF
Child does not participate in politics (works on campaign, demonstrates, writes to officials)	MTF
Child does not hold part-time job	NELS, SPD

Exhibit 9: Indicators of Social Exclusion: Subjective Experience of Exclusion Domain

Social Exclusion Indicator	Potential Sources
Desirable Subdomain	
Child's satisfaction with housing situation	(ECHP)
Child's satisfaction with school	(ECHP)
Child's satisfaction with leisure time	(ECHP)
Child's overall happiness	MTF, NLSY
Child's self-satisfaction	Ad Health, HSB, MTF, NLSY
Child's locus of control	NELS
Child's self-concept	NELS, NSAF, NSC, PSID

Exhibit 10: Key to Abbreviations for Potential Sources

Abbreviation	Survey Title	Agency/Organization Conducting Survey
Ad Health	National Longitudinal Study of Adolescent Health	Carolina Population Center, University of North Carolina, Chapel Hill
AFCARS	Adoption and Foster Care Analysis and Reporting System	US: Administration on Children and Families
AHS	Annual Housing Survey and American Housing Survey	US: HUD
AIRS	Aerometric Information Retrieval System	USEPA: Office of Air and Radiation
CPS	Current Population Survey	US Census Bureau
CPS-FSS	Current Population Survey: Food Security Supplement	US Census Bureau
CSFII	Continuing Survey of Food Intakes by Individuals	USDA, Center for Nutrition Policy and Promotion
(ECHP)	European Community Household Panel	EU: Eurostat
ECLS	Early Childhood Longitudinal Survey (Kindergarten and Birth Cohorts)	USDoE: National Center for Education Statistics
Green Book	The Green Book	US Congress, House Ways and Means Committee
HSB	High School and Beyond	USDoE: National Center for Education Statistics
MTF	Monitoring the Future	Institute for Social Research, University of Michigan
NACJD	National Archive of Criminal Justice Data	University of Michigan (with FBI data)
NAEP	National Assessment of Educational Progress	USDoE: National Center for Education Statistics
NHANES	National Health and Nutrition Examination Survey	CDC: National Center for Health Statistics
NCVS	National Crime Victimization Survey	USDoJ: Bureau of Justice Statistics
NELS	National Education Longitudinal Study	USDoE: National Center for Education Statistics
NHES	National Household Education Survey	USDoE: National Center for Education Statistics
NHIS	National Health Interview Survey	CDC: National Center for Health Statistics
NIS	National Immunization Survey	CDC: National Center for Health Statistics and National Immunization Program
NLSY	National Longitudinal Study of Youth	USDoL: Bureau of Labor Statistics
NSAF	National Survey of America's Families	Urban Institute
NSC	National Survey of Children	Foundation for Child Development/Child Trends, Inc.
NVSS	National Vital Statistics System	CDC: National Center for Health Statistics
PSID	Panel Study of Income Dynamics: Child Development Supplement	Institute for Social Research, University of Michigan
SPD	Survey of Program Dynamics	US Census Bureau
YRBSS	Youth Risk Behavior Surveillance System	CDC: National Center for Chronic Disease Prevention and Health Promotion

References

Aber, J. L., N. G. Bennett, D. C. Conley, and J. Li. (1997). "The Effects of Poverty on Child Health and Development." *Annual Review of Public Health* 18: 463–83.

Annie E. Casey Foundation. (2000). *Kids Count Data Book 2000*. Baltimore: Author.

Beck, W., L. van der Maeson, and A. Walker, eds. (1997). *The Social Quality of Europe*. The Hague: Kluwer Law International.

Ben-Arieh, A., N. H. Kaufman, A. B. Andrews, R. George, B. J. Lee, and J. L. Aber. (2000). *Measuring and Monitoring Children's Well Being*. Vienna: European Centre for Social Welfare Policy and Research.

Berlin, L. J., J. Brooks-Gunn, and J. L. Aber. (2001). "Promoting Early Childhood Development through Comprehensive Community Initiatives." *Children's Services: Social Policy, Research and Practice* 4: 1–24.

Berman, Y., and D. Phillips. (2001). *Indicators of Social Quality for Children: Consultation Paper for the Meeting on Monitoring and Measuring Children's Well-Being*. Vienna: European Centre for Social Welfare Policy and Research.

Brooks-Gunn, J., L. J. Berlin, T. Leventhal, and A. Fuligni. (2000). "Depending on the Kindness of Strangers: Current National Data Initiatives and Developmental Research. *Child Development* 71: 257–67.

Brooks-Gunn, J., B. Brown, G. Duncan, and K. A. Moore. (1995). "Child Development in the Context of Family and Community Resources: An Agenda for National Data Collection." In *Integrating Federal Statistics on Children: Report of a Workshop*, ed. National Research Council Institute of Medicine. Washington, D.C.: National Academy Press.

Brooks-Gunn, J., and P. L. Chase-Lansdale. (1995). "Adolescent Parenthood." In *Status and Social Conditions of Parenting*, vol. 3 of *Handbook of Parenting*, ed. M. Bornstein. Mahwah, N.J.: Lawrence Erlbaum Associates.

Brooks-Gunn, J., and G. J. Duncan. (1997). "The Effects of Poverty on Children." *Future of Children* 7: 55–71.

Brooks-Gunn, J., G. J. Duncan, and J. L. Aber, eds. (1997). *Neighborhood Poverty*. New York: Russell Sage Foundation Press.

Brooks-Gunn, J., M. C. McCormick, P. K. Klebanov, and C. McCarton. (1998). "Health Care Use of 3-Year-Old Low Birthweight Premature Children: Effects of Family and Neighborhood Poverty." *Journal of Pediatrics* 132: 971–75.

Burchardt, T., J. Le Grand, and D. Piachaud. (1999). "Social Exclusion in Britain 1991–1995." *Social Policy and Administration* 33: 227–244.

Campbell, M. (2000). "Labour Market Exclusion and Inclusion." In *Policy Responses to Social Exclusion: Towards Inclusion?*, ed. J. Percy-Smith. Philadelphia: Open University Press.

Chanan, G. (2000). "Community Responses to Social Exclusion." In *Policy Responses to Social Exclusion: Towards Inclusion?*, ed. J. Percy-Smith. Philadelphia: Open University Press.

Currie, C. (2001). "Socioeconomic Circumstances among School-Aged Children in Europe and North America." In *Child Well-Being, Child Poverty and Child Policy in Modern Nations: What Do We Know?*, ed. L. Vleminckx and T. M. Smeeding. Bristol, UK: Policy Press.

Duncan, G. J., J. Brooks-Gunn, J., and P. K. Klebanov. (1994). "Economic Deprivation and Early Childhood Development." *Child Development* 65: 296–318.

Federal Interagency Forum on Child and Family Statistics. (2000). *America's Children: Key National Indicators of Well-Being, 2000.* Washington, D.C.: Government Printing Office.

Flanagan, C. A., and N. Faison. (2001). "Youth Civic Involvement: Implications of Research for Social Policy and Programs." *Social Policy Report* 15(1): 3–14.

Gilliam, F. D., and S. N. Bales. (2001). "Strategic Frame Analysis: Reframing America's Youth." *Society for Research in Child Development, Social Policy Report* 15(3): 3–14.

Hauser, R. M., B. V. Brown, and W. R. Prosser. (1997). *Indicators of Children's Well-Being.* New York: Russell Sage Foundation Press.

Hawtin, M., and J. Kettle. (2000). "Housing and Social Exclusion." In *Policy Responses to Social Exclusion: Towards Inclusion?*, ed. J. Percy-Smith. Philadelphia: Open University Press.

Horn, J. L., and P. K. Trickett. (1998). "Community Violence and Child Development: A Review of Research." In *Violence Against Children in the Family and the Community,* ed. P. K. Trickett and C. J. Schellenbach. Washington, D.C.: American Psychological Association.

Jargowsky, P. A. (1997). *Poverty and Place.* New York: Russell Sage Foundation Press.

Johnston, L., R. MacDonald, P. Mason, L. Ridley, and C. Webster. (2000). *Snakes and Ladders: Young People, Transitions and Social Exclusion.* Bristol, UK: Policy Press.

Klasen, S.(1998). *Social Exclusion and Children in OECD Countries: Some Conceptual Issues.* Paris: Organisation for Economic Co-operation and

Development.

Leventhal, T., and J. Brooks-Gunn. (2000). "The Neighborhoods They Live In: The Effects of Neighborhood Residence upon Child and Adolescent Outcomes." *Psychological Bulletin* 126: 309–37.

Leventhal, T., J. Brooks-Gunn, and S. Kamerman. (1997). "Communities as Place, Face, and Space: Provision of Services to Poor, Urban Children and Their Families." In *Policy Implications in Studying Neighborhoods,* vol. 2 of *Neighborhood Poverty,* ed. J. Brooks-Gunn, G. J. Duncan, and J. L. Aber. New York: Russell Sage Foundation Press.

Massey, D. S. (1999). "America's Apartheid and the Urban Underclass." In *Race and Ethnic Conflict: Contending Views on Prejudice, Discrimination, and Ethnoviolence,* 2nd edition, ed. F. L. Pincus and H. J. Ehrlich. Boulder, Colo.: Westview Press.

Mazza, J. J., and W. M. Reynolds. (1999). "Exposure to Violence in Young Inner-City Adolescents: Relationships with Suicidal Ideation, Depression, and PTSD Symptomatology." *Journal of Abnormal Child Psychology* 27: 203–13.

McLoyd, V. C. (1990). "The Impact of Economic Hardship on Black Families and Children: Psychological Distress, Parenting, and Socioemotional Development." *Child Development* 61: 311–46.

Mikulic, B., G. Linden, J. Pelsers, and J. Schiepers. (1999). *Social Reporting: Reconciliation of Sources and Dissemination of Data, Task 2b. The ECHP Non-monetary Variables as (Potential) Indicators of Poverty and Social Exclusion in the European Union.* Voorburg/Heelren, The Netherlands: Statistics Netherlands.

Moran, G., and M. Simpkin. (2000). "Social Exclusion and Health." In *Policy Responses to Social Exclusion: Towards Inclusion?,* ed. J. Percy-Smith. Philadelphia: Open University Press.

Packham, C. (1999). "School Exclusion: Alienation and the Dilemmas for Formal and Informal Educators." In *Welfare, Exclusion and Political Agency,* ed. J. Batsleer and B. Humphries. New York: Routledge.

Percy-Smith, J. (2000). "Introduction: The Contours of Social Exclusion." In *Policy Responses to Social Exclusion: Towards Inclusion?,* ed. J. Percy-Smith. Philadelphia: Open University Press.

Phillips, M., J. Brooks-Gunn, G. J. Duncan, P. K. Klebanov, and C. Jencks. (1998). "Family Background, Parenting Practices, and the Black-White Test Score Gap." In *The Black-White Test Score Gap,* ed. C. Jencks and M. Phillips. Washington, D.C.: Brookings Institution Press.

Pitts, J., and T. Hope. (1997). "The Local Politics of Inclusion: The

State and Community Safety." *Social Policy and Administration* 31: 37–58.

Sanderson, I. (2000). "Access to Services." In *Policy Responses to Social Exclusion: Towards Inclusion?*, ed. J. Percy-Smith. Philadelphia: Open University Press.

Social Exclusion Unit. (1998). *Truancy and School Exclusion.* London: Stationery Office. Available at: www.cabinet-office.gov.uk/seu/1998/trhome.

Social Exclusion Unit. (1999). *Teenage Pregnancy.* London: Stationery Office. Available at: www.cabinet-office.gov.uk/seu/1999/teenpreg.pdf.

Sparkes, J. (1999). *Schools, Education and Social Exclusion.* London: Centre for Analysis of Social Exclusion.

Stiffman, A. R., E. Hadley-Ives, D. Elze, S. Johnson, and P. Doré. (1999). "Impact of Environment on Adolescent Mental Health and Behavior: Structural Equation Modeling." *American Journal of Orthopsychiatry* 69: 73–86.

U.S. Department of Health and Human Services. (2000). *Trends in the Well-Being of America's Children and Youth: 2000.* Washington, D.C.: Government Printing Office.

Van Kempen, E. (1997). "Poverty Pockets and Life Chances: On the Role of Place in Shaping Social Inequality." *American Behavioral Scientist* 41: 430–49.

Walton, F. (2000). "Education and Training." In *Policy Responses to Social Exclusion: Towards Inclusion?*, ed. J. Percy-Smith. Philadelphia: Open University Press.

Whitman, B. Y., P. Accardo, and J. M. Sprankel. (1992). "Homeless Families and Their Children: Health, Developmental, and Educational Needs." In *Homelessness: A Prevention-Oriented Approach*, ed. R. I. Jahiel. Baltimore.: Johns Hopkins University Press.

Wilson, W. J. (1987). *The Truly Disadvantaged: The Inner City, the Underclass and Public Policy.* Chicago: University of Chicago Press.

———. (1996). *When Work Disappears: The World of the New Urban Poor.* New York: Knopf.

Zaff, J. F. (2000). "Indicators of Positive Development in Nationally Representative Surveys." Washington, D.C.: Child Trends. Unpublished manuscript.

Closing Note

The Editors

How can we or should we accept the conference challenge to think more broadly and systematically about a concept of disadvantage among children, beyond how to improve an absolute poverty line? What would be a richer concept? How can it be described if it cannot—initially—be measured?

The focus—as several have noted—should be on a relative measure: lacking what is required to participate in one's society (Townsend) or not having what the "custom of the country requires one to have" (Adam Smith). Social, as well as economic disadvantage, is relevant.

One possible strategy, we have noted, is to attempt to construct an answer, or at least an approach, by focusing sequentially on various domains and phenomena that may lead to "closing out." Choices could be made from::

- A jobless or workless household
- Poor skills
- Low income
- Poor health
- Involvement in crime
- Family breakdown
- Consumption patterns or living standards below local, regional, or national norms
- Disabilities
- Immigrant status

- Non-English speaking household
- Dropping out of school
- Being neither at school nor at work
- Lack of standard housing arrangements
- Lack of access to standard services

A list such as this enables one to ask—as was proposed—*who* is excluded *from what, by what,* and with *what results?* It would appear that one needs to look at institutions, participants, and processes; but perhaps (as suggested subsequent to the conference by Richard Nelson), the analytic process also must include attention to the pathways for normal *inclusion.* We might expand on this by posing the question (specifically regarding children): What does it mean for children in certain groups to be included, as well as to be excluded?

We believe that the good beginning represented by this conference should be followed up. A faculty group at Columbia University has begun to convene around some of the ideas raised here. Individual scholars could also identify research possibilities or room for conceptual papers. There is much to be done.

Appendix

The Authors

J. Lawrence Aber

Dr. J. Lawrence Aber is codirector of the Institute for Child and Family Policy and director (since 1994) of the National Center for Children and Poverty (NCCP). While a member of the psychology department at Barnard College and the Graduate Faculties at Columbia University (1982–1994), he directed the Barnard Center for Toddler Development, codirected the Columbia University Project on Children and War, and cofounded the Barnard-Columbia Center for Leadership in Urban Public Policy. Dr. Aber continues to consult with community-based programs for children, youth, and families; local, state, and federal agencies; and UNICEF on program and policy issues ranging from childcare and child abuse to youth violence and community development. He has published widely.

Andrew Bershadker

Dr. Andrew Bershadker received his Ph.D. from the University of Wisconsin-Madison in 1998, and is currently an economist in the U.S. Department of the Treasury's Office of Tax Analysis. His areas of interest include individual labor market outcomes; the economics of education, poverty, and community development; and the influence of tax policy in these areas. Other work, with Dr. Robert Haveman, has examined the accumulation and utilization of human capital, and new methods of identifying and measuring the size and composition of the human capital-deficient population.

Jeanne Brooks-Gunn

Dr. Jeanne Brooks-Gunn is the Virginia and Leonard Marx Professor of Child Development and Education at Teachers College, Columbia University. She is codirector of the Center for Children and Families at Teachers College, director of the Adolescent Study Program, and codirector of the Institute for Child and Family Policy. She is also a National Fellow at Harvard University's Inequality and Social Policy Program, a visiting scholar at the Office of Population Research at Princeton University, and a senior research affiliate for the Joint Center for Poverty Research at Northwestern University/University of Chicago. Dr. Brooks-Gunn's specialty is policy-oriented research, focusing on family and community influences upon the development of children and youth. Her research centers on designing and evaluating interventions aimed at enhancing the well-being of children who live with poverty and associated conditions. She is conducting the national evaluation of the Early Head Start program, and the middle childhood and adolescent follow-up to the Infant Health and Development Program.

Peter Evans

After receiving a degree in psychology and anthropology at the University of London, Dr. Peter Evans completed his Ph.D. in mental handicap at the University of Manchester. In 1976, he returned to the University of London to conduct courses for teachers of children with learning difficulties in the Department of Special Education, Institute of Education. In 1989 he moved to the Organisation for Economic Co-operation and Development (OECD) in Paris, where he is responsible for the work on disability and exclusion carried out at the Centre for Educational Research and Innovation. He has published some twenty books, as well as many articles and chapters, and has traveled extensively to study special education systems in both OECD and non-OECD countries.

Elizabeth Thompson Gershoff

Dr. Elizabeth Thompson Gershoff's research has focused on parent-directed and bidirectional contributions to the quality of parent-child interactions, as well as to ultimate child outcomes. Specifically, she has focused on the child outcomes associated with parents' attitudes about and use of corporal punishment. In her work at the National Center for Children in Poverty at Columbia University, Dr. Gershoff is interested in the ways in which parents can either buffer or exacerbate the effects of socioeconomic distress on children. Currently, she is also involved in a multinational effort to develop a protocol of indicators of children's well-being, and in a long-term evaluation of a violence-prevention program in New York City schools.

Janet C. Gornick

Dr. Janet C. Gornick is an associate professor of political science at Baruch College and the City University of New York Graduate Center. She holds a B.A. in psychology and social relations, a Masters in public administration, and a Ph.D. in political economy and government, all from Harvard University. She spent several years as a staff member at the Luxembourg Income Study (LIS) and continues as a staff member for their summer workshops. Most of her research is cross-national, and concerns the effects of family policies on child and family outcomes. Her core interest is in public programs that affect families' capacities to combine employment with caregiving, such as childcare, maternity, and parental leave, and the regulation of working time.

Robert H. Haveman

Dr. Robert H. Haveman is John Bascom Professor of Economics and Public Policy at the department of economics and the Robert M. La Follette Institute of Public Affairs, and research affiliate at the Institute for Research on Poverty, all at the University of Wisconsin-Madison. He received his B.A. from Calvin College in 1958, and his Ph.D. in economics from Vanderbilt University in 1963. Prior to 1970, he was professor of economics at Grinnell College, senior economist at the Joint Economic Committee, U.S. Congress, and research professor at the Brookings Institution. From 1970 to 1975, he was director of the Institute for Research on Poverty. In 1975–76, Dr. Haveman was a fellow at the Netherlands Institute for Advanced Study, and in 1984–85 he served as Tinbergen Professor at Erasmus University in Rotterdam. From 1988 to 1991, he was director of the Robert M. La Follette Institute of Public Affairs, and from 1993 to 1996 he served as chair of the department of economics. He was coeditor of the *American Economic Review* from 1985 to 1991. His primary fields of interest are public finance, the economics of poverty, and social policy (including disability policy).

Alfred J. Kahn

Dr. Alfred J. Kahn is professor emeritus, special lecturer, and codirector of the Cross-National Studies Research Program at the Columbia University School of Social Work (where he was a member of the faculty from 1947 to 1989). He taught social policy, social planning, the history of American social policy, and related courses. He was a long-term director of the doctoral program as well. He taught at the Smith College School of Social Work (summers, 1950–54) and was (part-time) Distinguished Visiting Professor, Fordham University Graduate School of Social Service, 1990–2000. Dr. Kahn's research has covered income transfers, social services, and comparative child and family policy. He is author, coauthor, and editor of more than 30 books and 250 articles, as well as study reports. He has consulted widely in the United States and abroad for state and local governments, international organizations, private agencies, the U.S. State Department, and United Nations agencies.

Sheila B. Kamerman

Dr. Sheila B. Kamerman is the Compton Foundation Centennial Professor for the Prevention of Children and Youth Problems at the Columbia University School of Social Work. She is the director of the Institute for Child and Family Policy and codirector of the Cross-National Studies Research Program. Her teaching areas are social policy, child and family policy, social services, and international social welfare. Her current research activities include a twenty-country comparative study of family change and family policies since World War II, a study of early childhood care and education policies and programs in the OECD countries, a study of parental leave policies in these countries, and a study of "best practices" in contracting for child and family social services. Dr. Kamerman has consulted widely for U.S. and international organizations. She is the author, coauthor, or coeditor of more than 30 books and monographs and nearly 200 articles and chapters.

John Micklewright

Dr. John Micklewright is head of research at UNICEF Innocenti Research Centre, Florence. He received his Ph.D. in economics from the London School of Economics in 1984, and then spent two years as Prize Research Fellow at Nuffield College, Oxford. From 1987 to 1996 he was lecturer, reader, and then professor of economics at Queen Mary and Westfield College, University of London, and from 1989 to 1996 professor of economics at the European University Institute, Florence. He has held visiting appointments in France, Austria, and Australia. His current research focuses on various aspects of child well-being in industrialized and transition countries. His many publications with collaborators cover comparative poverty analysis, income distribution, and the welfare of Europe's children.

Chiara Saraceno

Dr. Chiara Saraceno is professor of family sociology at the University of Turin, Italy, Faculty of Political Sciences. She was head of the department of social sciences from 1991 until 1998; at present she is head of the Inter-Department Center for Women's Studies. From 1969 to 1990 she taught at the University of Trento, where in 1989–90 she was also vice rector. She has written extensively on family change and family policies, on poverty and social policies, and on gender and women's issues. Her current research is on social policies and poverty; comparative family policies; the social and economic consequences of separation and divorce on women and men; and citizenship, gender, and the welfare state. She is chair of the Italian Poverty Commission at the Prime Minister's Office, and consultant to the Minister of Social Affairs on issues concerning poverty, social exclusion, and family policies. In this capacity, she has been and is a member of government commissions on the reform of the welfare state. She also represents the Ministry at the working party on social policy at the OECD. She was the Italian expert in the EC Observatory on Policies for Combating Social Exclusion from 1990 to 1994. She has published widely.

The Participants

Maria Cancian
Associate Professor of Public Affairs and Social Work
Robert M. La Follette Institute of Public Affairs
University of Wisconsin-Madison

Cyndi Chiao
Assistant to Ralph Smith
Annie E. Casey Foundation

Amanda Claremon
Program Associate
The Ford Foundation

Tom Corbett
Associate Professor, School of Social Work
Associate Director, Institute for Research on Poverty
University of Wisconsin-Madison

Sandra Danziger
Professor, School of Social Work
University of Michigan

Lucy Davidson
Associate Director of Science
Center for Child Well-Being
The Task Force for Child Survival and Development

Geraldine Downey
Associate Professor, Department of Psychology
Columbia University

Jeanne Fagnani
Director of Research, Centre National de la Recherche
Scientifique, University of Paris
Scientific Advisor, Caisse Nationale des Allocations Familiales

Constance A. Flanagan
Associate Professor, Agricultural and Extension Education
Faculty Affiliate, Population Research Institute
Faculty Affiliate, Institute for Policy Research and Evaluation
Pennsylvania State University

Nancy Folbre
Professor, Department of Economics
University of Massachusetts, Amherst

Christa Freiler
Children's Agenda Programme Coordinator
Laidlaw Foundation
Toronto, Canada

Ester Fuchs
Professor, Department of Political Science
Barnard College
Director, Center for Urban Research and Policy
Columbia University

Irwin Garfinkel
Professor, School of Social Work
Columbia University

Shirley Gatenio
Manager, Clearinghouse on International Developments in
Child, Youth, and Family Policies
Institute for Child and Family Policy
Columbia University

Sherry Glied
Associate Professor, School of Public Health
Columbia University

Naomi Goldstein
Director, Division of Child and Family Development,
Office of Planning, Research and Evaluation,
Administration for Children and Families
U.S. Department of Health and Human Services

Robert Granger
Senior Vice President
William T. Grant Foundation

Mark H. Greenberg
Senior Staff Attorney, Family Policy
Center for Law and Social Policy

Ron Haskins
Senior Fellow, Economic Studies
Codirector, Welfare Reform and Beyond
The Brookings Institution

John Hills
Professor and Director, Centre for Analysis of
Social Exclusion
London School of Economics

Christopher Jencks
Professor, John F. Kennedy School of Government
Harvard University

Judith Jones
Professor, School of Public Health
Columbia University

Jane Knitzer
Deputy Director, National Center for Children in Poverty
School of Public Health
Columbia University

Mary Clare Lennon
Associate Professor, School of Public Health
Columbia University

Robert Lieberman
Associate Professor, Department of Political Science
Columbia University

Susan Mayer
Associate Professor, Graduate School of Public Policy Studies
Deputy Director, Joint Center for Poverty Research
University of Chicago

Marcia K. Meyers
Associate Professor, School of Social Work
Columbia University

Ronald Mincy
Professor, School of Social Work
Columbia University

Kristin Moore
President
Child Trends

Richard Nelson
Professor, School of International and Public Affairs
Columbia University

Helen Neuborne
Deputy Director, Human Development and
Reproductive Health
The Ford Foundation

Wendell Primus
Director of Income Security
Income Security Division
Center on Budget and Policy Priorities
Washington, D.C.

Tony Raden
Associate Director, Institute for Child and Family Policy
Columbia University

Elliot Sclar
Professor, School of Architecture, Planning,
and Preservation
Columbia University

Timothy Smeeding
Professor and Director, Center for Policy Research and
Luxembourg Income Study
Syracuse University

Judith R. Smith
Associate Professor, Graduate School of Social Service
Fordham University

Matthew Stagner
Principal Research Associate, Population Studies
The Urban Institute

Ruby Takanishi
President
Foundation for Child Development

Jane Waldfogel
Associate Professor, School of Social Work
Columbia University

Richard Wertheimer
Senior Research Associate
Child Trends

Rapporteurs

Christina Borbely
Ph.D. Candidate, Department
of Human Development
Teachers College
Columbia University

Margaret Johansson
Ph.D. Candidate, School of
Social Work
Columbia University

David Harris
Ph.D. Candidate, School of
Social Work
Columbia University

Lenna Nepomnyaschy
Ph.D. Candidate, School of
Social Work
Columbia University